LIFE IN EGYPT UNDER ROMAN RULE

American Society of Papyrologists

CLASSICS IN PAPYROLOGY

Volume 1

LIFE IN EGYPT UNDER ROMAN RULE

by

Naphtali Lewis

LIFE IN EGYPT UNDER ROMAN RULE

by
Naphtali Lewis

AMERICAN SOCIETY OF PAPYROLOGISTS
OAKVILLE, CONNECTICUT

LIFE IN EGYPT UNDER ROMAN RULE

by
Naphtali Lewis

Copyright © 1999 by the American Society of Papyrologists

Offset from the Oxford University Press edition of 1986.

Library of Congress Cataloging in Publications Data

Lewis, Naphtali.
    Life in Egypt under Roman rule / by Naphtali Lewis.
       p.   cm. —(Classics in papyrology ; v. 1)
    Originally published: Oxford, England : Clarendon Press, 1983.
    Includes index.
    ISBN 0-7885-0560-2 (pbk. : alk. paper)
     1. Egypt—Civilization—332 B.C.–638 A. D. 2. Romans—Egypt.
I. Title. II. Series.
DT61.L646   1999
932'.02—dc21   99-26772
                           CIP

Printed in the United States of America
on acid-free paper

To

Helen, Judith, John,

Mary Jo, Jerry, Emma, David

. . . and the light of the sun shall be sevenfold
Isaiah 30: 26

CONTENTS*

*The Latin phrases in the chapter titles are quoted from a famous thumbnail sketch of Egypt offered by Tacitus in his *Histories* (Book 1, ch. 11): *provinciam aditu difficilem, annonae fecundam, superstitione et lascivia discordem et mobilem, insciam legum, ignaram magistratuum* — 'a province difficult of access, prolific in grain, contentious and mercurial because of superstition and licence, knowing no restraints of laws, having no experience of magistrates.'

PLATES
(*at end*)

PREFATORY NOTE

Spelling of Names

For personal names this book adheres to the current practice
of transliterating rather than Latinizing the Greek – Lysandros
rather than Lysander, Kosmos not Cosmus – but for some
placenames it seems preferable to use the Latinized forms
introduced by the Roman government: Latin Hermopolis
rather than Greek Hermoupolis, Coptus rather than Koptos.

The capitals of the Arsinoite and Oxyrhynchite nomes,
the two nomes from which most of our extant papyri come
and which therefore figure most prominently in this book,
present a special problem. It has recently been demonstrated
that the official nomenclatures of those metropoleis were
'the city of the Arsinoites' and 'the city of the Oxyrhynchites'
or 'the city of the oxyrhynchoi' (the 'sharp-nosed' Nile fish
venerated there). Though it is now clear that they were never
in antiquity called Arsinoë and Oxyrhynchus, those forms
are so embedded in the century-long literature of papyrology
as to preclude their abandonment now, the more so as they
couple familiarity with the convenience of brevity.

Roman Imperial Titles

The modern convention is to designate each emperor by one
or two distinctive names: Augustus, Caligula, Antoninus Pius,
and so forth. In reality, however, each had a series of personal
names (normally three for a Roman citizen), to which were
added imperial titles upon his accession to the Principate.
The term Augustus was a title, not a name. It was assumed by
Octavian in 27 BC and automatically acquired by all the
emperors after him as an official designation of the office.
In similar fashion, beginning with Claudius all the emperors
took the title of Imperator (whence our English word

'emperor'), at first at the end then regularly as the first word of the imperial nomenclature. With the passage of time the titles grew longer and more pompous, most especially through the addition of epithets celebrating (sometimes wishfully) military victories over foreign foes: Germanicus, Germanicus Maximus, Parthicus Maximus, etc. At times it almost seems as if the less secure the regime, the longer and more vainglorious the titles. Here are some examples.

TIBERIUS (AD 14-37)	Tiberius Caesar Augustus (Imperator sometimes added)
TRAJAN (AD 98-117)	Imperator Caesar Nerva Traianus Augustus Germanicus (additional epithets: Dacicus Parthicus)
COMMODUS (AD 176-92)	Imperator Caesar Marcus Aurelius Commodus Antoninus Augustus Felix Pius Armeniacus Medicus Parthicus Sarmaticus Germanicus Britannicus Maximus
PROBUS (AD 276-82)	Imperator Caesar Marcus Aurelius Probus Pius Felix Augustus Gothicus Maximus Persicus Maximus Germanicus Maximus Medicus Maximus Parthicus Maximus

INTRODUCTION

'History rewards the victors', says an oft-quoted truism. The standard history of Rome and its empire is a familiar story of military successes and governmental decisions. The voice of the subjugated and the governed is rarely heard, and then it is usually filtered to us through the writings of Romans, or supporters of theirs such as Polybius and Josephus. There are two principal exceptions to that rule: the Greeks, widely known and admired today for their continuing literary and philosophical output during their centuries under Roman rule; and the dwellers in the ancient land of the Nile, known today to only a relatively restricted group of specialists. From Egypt under Roman rule comes no great literature to claim general attention, but in recent years many thousands of papyri and ostraca of Roman date have been discovered in the ruins of ancient towns and villages there. Those documents, coming to us just as they were written, unalloyed and uninterpreted by ancient authors, constitute a record such as is available for no other Roman province, bringing us into direct and intimate contact with the people of the province in their private lives and thoughts, their business dealings, their relations with officialdom. Nevertheless, histories of Roman Egypt, while profiting from this unique body of source material, have continued to be cast in the traditional mould, remaining essentially, in purpose and outlook, studies in Roman government. The present book abandons that traditional approach, instead taking its departure and its direction from the source material itself. This book concentrates on the people who wrote and figure in those private and official papers. It looks for answers to the question: What was life like for the inhabitants of Egypt when it was a Roman province?

Such a 'view from below' is a treat that no other part of

the Greek or Roman world can offer us. The surviving works of ancient authors provide the broad base of our knowledge and perception of the world of classical antiquity. Since the Renaissance those Greek and Latin texts have been the focus of half a millennium of cumulatively informed and increasingly trenchant scholarship, with the result that today we can project far beyond the individual authors and their several works: we can usually trace their sources and commitments, evaluate their strengths and shortcomings, discern and explain their attitudes and purposes. To this growing body of knowledge the centuries since the Renaissance have added thousands upon thousands of stones (and some bronze tablets) inscribed in Greek and Latin. Found in all parts of what once was the Roman Empire, and ranging in contents from humble tombstones and brick stamps to imperial and other official pronouncements, they received for a long time only incidental, almost condescending, attention from classical scholars, intent as the latter were upon their mastery of the works of the ancient authors. But intensive work since the early nineteenth century has raised epigraphy, as the study of inscriptions is called, to a major, indeed an indispensable, resource for the study of Greek and Roman history and civilization.

Egypt, however, stands alone amongst the Mediterranean lands in offering us vast resources of information written on papyrus, the writing 'paper' produced in Egypt but used throughout the ancient world. Almost everywhere else papyri in ancient ruins have simply disintegrated in the moist soil. But in Egypt, in ruins covered over and sealed against the elements by dry desert sands, clandestine diggers as well as archaeologists have over the past hundred years uncovered tens of thousands of papyri (and thousands of ostraca, pottery shards bearing written messages) covering a period of some four thousand years, *c.* 3,000 BC – AD 1,000. Small, isolated finds of papyri have been made in a few other places in similarly airtight ruins and burials — documents of Roman and Byzantine date in the Judaean and Negev deserts of Israel, a roll containing a commentary on an Orphic poem in a tomb of the fourth century BC in Macedonia, a quantity of books from a library in Herculaneum, carbonized and petrified under the fall-out from the eruption of Mt Vesuvius in AD 79. In the spring of 1981 came the sensational news of the discovery in Athens of a small papyrus roll in a tomb which the archaeologists date *c.* 450–400 BC. This — its contents not yet determined in its badly damaged and mud-caked state — is now our oldest extant sample of ancient Greek writing. But Egypt still stands quite alone in the sheer numbers as well as the chronological range of the papyri found there.

Beginning in 1770 European travellers and officers would sometimes bring home with them from Egypt handsome specimens of ancient papyri, some of them whole rolls, written in hieroglyphic or Greek scripts. In the late 1870s there began the era of massive finds. The first of these to appear on the antiquities market of Cairo was a treasure trove consisting of many thousands of papyri — written in Greek, Latin, Coptic, Hebrew, Syriac, Persian, and Arabic — that peasants in the Fayyum had come upon when digging for compost in mounds that turned out to be the garbage dumps of ancient villages. Parts of the new find were speedily snatched up for their respective museums by the consuls of England, France, and Germany. But the lion's share of this and other early finds went to Austria, so that by the end of the nineteenth century the collection deposited in the then Imperial, now National, Library in Vienna totalled nearly 100,000 papyri, some seventy per cent of them written in Greek.

The Egypt Exploration Fund (now Society), organized in London in 1882, was the first and has remained the most consistent sponsor of archaeological work in Egypt. Beginning in 1895 and continuing for a dozen winters, excavations of Hellenistic and Roman ruins aimed specifically at the recovery of papyri were conducted for the Fund by two young classical scholars of The Queen's College, Oxford, B. P. Grenfell and A. S. Hunt. They explored a whole series of sites, using criteria and *ad hoc* techniques which they developed themselves, and they were rewarded with spectacular finds from which they shipped thousands of papyri to Oxford.

Far and away the most prolific of the sites that Grenfell Hunt — and others after them — excavated was at Behneseh, some two hundred kilometres upstream from (i.e. south of) Cairo. There, almost from the very start of their first season, they struck an enormously rich deposit in the ruins of the capital of the Oxyrhynchite nome. After three weeks of excavating in the ancient cemetery with disappointing results, they moved on to the ancient town itself, with staggering results. Behind the scholarly sobriety of Grenfell's report to the Fund we can still sense the excitement of those days of discovery:

As we moved northwards over other parts of the site, the flow of papyri soon became a torrent which it was difficult to cope with. . . . We engaged two men to make tin boxes for storing the papyri, but for the next ten weeks they could hardly keep pace with us. . . .

It was not infrequent to find large quantities of papyri together, especially in three mounds, where the mass was so great that these finds probably represent part of the local archives thrown away at different periods. . . . The third and by far the greatest find, that of the Byzantine archives, took place on March 18th and 19th, and was, I suppose, a 'record' in point of quantity. On the first of these two days we came upon a mound which had a thick layer consisting almost entirely of papyrus rolls. There was room for six pairs of men and boys to be working simultaneously at this storehouse, and the difficulty was to find enough baskets in all Behneseh to contain the papyri. At the end of the day's work no less than thirty-six good-sized baskets were brought in from this place, several of them stuffed with fine rolls three to ten feet long, including some of the longest Greek rolls I have ever seen. As the baskets were required for the next day's work, Mr Hunt and I started at 9 p.m. after dinner to stow away the papyri in some empty packing-cases which we fortunately had at hand. The task was only finished at three in the morning, and on the following night we had a repetition of it, for twenty-five more baskets were filled before the place was exhausted.[1]

Along with the papyri there have been found at many sites — but mostly in Upper Egypt, in general the poorer part of the country — large quantities of ostraca, written on with the same ink, made of lampblack, that was used on papyrus. The messages that the ostraca bear are brief — lists, letters, school exercises, and above all tax receipts — but cumulatively they provide valuable supplements to the information gleaned from the papyri. The use of bits of ceramic for such purposes was not dictated by considerations of durability, as the modern reader might think, but by cost. Papyrus, however inexpensive it might be in the land of its manufacture, had to be bought and paid for; potsherds were available from every scrap-heap for the taking, and cost nothing.

Rubbish mounds have been our richest source of ancient papyri because they are the repository of every kind of discarded 'paper', from scraps of private notations to official documents and books. In smaller numbers papyri have also been found in collapsed buildings.

The discovery of papyri in cemeteries is principally due to a burial custom that enjoyed a vogue for some centuries, especially in the Arsinoite nome. Mummies, of the nome's sacred crocodiles as well as of humans, were wrapped in or covered with a cartonnage made of papyrus in place of the traditional linen. Sometimes only a single thickness of papyrus was used for that purpose. but usually several layers were stuck together for greater strength, and the whole packet was plastered over to provide stiffening and also a surface for painted decoration. In recent years chemical processes have been developed for separating the individual layers without damaging the writing. The texts thus released show that not only waste paper but even books in good condition were cut up for cartonnage — perhaps as a funeral gift? — and that the practice of using papyrus for that purpose, quite common all through Ptolemaic times, was apparently discontinued not long after the advent of Roman rule. We have no idea why.

As a result of excavations by archaeological expeditions from a number of countries, but more often as a result of purchases made in the antiquities markets, collections of papyri and ostraca, large and small, are now to be found in many museums and universities (and in some private libraries) in Europe and the United States, as well as in Egypt itself. As Grenfell reported, the papyri are found in all sizes, from exiguous fragments to whole rolls; one of the latter, a tax register of the village of Karanis now in the library of the University of Michigan, contains over 6,000 lines of writing. A few of the papyri of the period to which this book is devoted are written in Latin, mainly records of the Roman army of occupation. A few are in the Egyptian language, in its late form of writing that we call Demotic. All the rest of Roman date are written in Greek, which became the lingua franca of the eastern Mediterranean with its conquest by Alexander the Great. After Alexander's death, and that of his young son and presumed successor, Greek-speaking dynasties established by his leading generals ruled those lands, the Ptolemies in Egypt, the Seleucids in Syria. The Romans, impressed by the advanced civilization of those regions, as they annexed them one after the other, saw no need to disturb existing local customs and practices — a policy (wise, tolerant, indifferent, or self-interested, according to one's point of view) that has often been cited as one of the main reasons why Roman rule lasted as long as it did.

As the papyri and ostraca came to light in such great quantities they presented the classical scholars of the day with an exhilarating challenge. Not only did the finds take the history of Greek palaeography back a thousand years before the previously known medieval manuscripts, but the handwritings that now came to light took every imaginable form, from elegant book hands to the cursives of skilled scribes, from the awkward efforts of the semi-literate to totally incomprehensible scrawls. The dual task of deciphering these cursives and of interpreting their contents, replete with the phonetic misspellings and erratic grammar of the popular speech of the uneducated, gave rise to a new branch of classical studies. In the very years when they were excavating, Grenfell and Hunt began publishing, at an almost febrile pace yet with a consummate skill that few have matched since, hundreds of texts from their finds, texts both literary and documentary. Together with F. G. Kenyon at the British Museum and U. Wilcken and his associates in Berlin they were the pioneers in creating within the field of Classics the new discipline of papyrology. At the time of writing (October 1981) 3,430 papyrus rolls and pieces have been published in forty-eight volumes of *The Oxyrhynchus Papyri*. That is the single most extensive series, and there are many more volumes still to come. Altogether, from all collections, some 25,000 papyri of Roman date have now been published, and there are probably twice that number still to be published.

Writings of a private nature — letters, memoranda, jottings —

were rarely dated. How, then, can we tell when an undated papyrus belongs to the Roman period? If we are lucky, the papyrus will have been found with, or will turn out to belong with, others that do bear dates. Otherwise we have only the style of the handwriting to fall back upon. Fortunately, the thousands of dated papyri constitute a repertory which enables us to follow the changing fashions in Greek cursive writing from the fourth century BC to the eighth century AD. That is not to say, however, that we can establish a hard-and-fast chronology based on absolute sets of characteristics. Within any contemporary matrix every handwriting shows individual variations — archaistic traits, for example, in the writing of an elderly person, or clumsy lettering in the case of an unskilled writer or an illiterate who had painfully mastered the ability to trace the letters of his name. Constantly aware of such personal variables, the papyrologist must usually be content, when a papyrus or ostracon bears no date, to place the document within the century to whose dominant writing patterns the hand most closely conforms; where the handwriting traits are very distinctive, the papyrologist may feel confident enough to reduce the range of his estimate to half a century, but only in rare instances will he or she be ready to insist upon a span of less than a few decades.

On the other hand, documents of an official or contractual nature were normally dated, though the date may be lost to us if the papyrus has not survived complete, or it may have been omitted if the papyrus contains a draft or a copy. The practice in dating was to give the regnal year of the then Roman emperor(s), followed by the month and day. The emperor's first year was reckoned from the day of his accession — which for practical purposes meant the day his accession became known in Egypt, and that, as actual instances show, could be from one to four months after the event — to the end of the then current year in the Egyptian calendar. His second and all subsequent regnal years began on the Egyptian New Year's Day, the first day of the month Thoth, which corresponded to 29 August in the Roman calendar. Where Egyptian dates occur in this book their equivalents in our calendar are given instead or in addition.

To sum up: the Greek (and Latin) papyri and ostraca have made and continue to make an unprecedented contribution to our knowledge of ancient civilization. To the works of classical literature known since the Renaissance they have added scores of hitherto lost books, only a few of them complete, to be sure, the rest in large and small fragments. They also provide us with fragments of known works that are up to a thousand years earlier than the extant medieval manuscripts. The vast bulk of the papyri, however, is non-literary, or documentary. A few of them, like inscriptions, preserve public records — edicts, legislation, and official records of all kinds. The rest contain the writings of everyday life, such as are still today committed to paper by ordinary people: accounts, contracts, letters, notations, memoranda, exercises, scribblings. These give us a close-up view of the 'silent majority', the men, women, and children in the middle and bottom strata of society in their daily lives. In works of literature we see the subject through the author's eyes, in the guise in which he presents it or in the interpretation he puts upon it. In inscriptions we read what a government or an individual wanted preserved for the future, a monument erected with an eye to posterity as well as to the present. Only with a mundane papyrus — its message being preserved just as it was written in a particular occasion or circumstance — do we experience what Virgina Woolf so aptly called a 'moment of being'. Only in such writing do we seize the moment and the matter *sur le vif*, making direct contact with the situation and with the people involved. We meet them not as characters in a book or a play; we meet them on their own terms, face to face, 'warts and all'.

The chapters that follow are focused on a period of just over three hundred years, 30 BC – AD 285, from Octavian's conquest of Egypt to the end of the Principate that he founded after his elevation to the dignity of Augustus. The period after 285, which we call the Dominate, was also one of rule by Roman emperors, but one whose institutions were changing rapidly in the direction of Byzantinism, and that is another story.

1

THE COMING OF THE ROMANS

The Ptolemaic Dynasty

It dawned like any other day of the hot Egyptian summer, that mid-August day of 30 BC. Eluding the Roman watch set over their queen, faithful servants smuggled in to her the instrument of her suicide. It was an asp, the poisonous cobra depicted as the uraeus of the Egyptian royal head-dress; or, if we are to believe the Roman poets Virgil, Horace, and Propertius, it was a pair of asps. It was the royal left arm that received the fatal bite; not so, others insisted, it was the bared left breast. Though many such details are disputed, the essential fact remains clear: the self-inflicted venom took the life of the seventh Cleopatra, surnamed Thea Philopator ('father-loving goddess'), the last ruler in the line of the Ptolemies, that dynasty of Macedonian origin that had reigned in Egypt for most of the three hundred years since its conquest by Alexander the Great. The new conqueror, Octavian Caesar, who had intended the queen for the prize exhibit of his triumphal procession in Rome, gazed briefly at the corpse that mocked his triumph, swallowed the gall of his frustration, and set about the business of government. Before the month was out he formally 'added Egypt to the empire of the Roman people'. With that carefully bland statement — no more than five words (*Aegyptum imperio populi Romani adieci*) in the political testament he drew up toward the end of his life — Octavian-renamed-Augustus designedly glosses over the inconvenient fact of his civil war against Antony that led to the Roman take-over of Egypt. That laconic remark also gives us no hint of the fact that Egypto-Roman relations had a fairly long prior history.[1]

In the dismemberment of the empire of Alexander the Great, it was the general named Ptolemaios — or Ptolemy, as we say in English — who succeeded in establishing himself as King of Egypt and some peripheral territories. Diplomatic relations between Egypt and Rome were initiated by his successor in or about 273 BC. Two years before King Pyrrhus of Epirus — he of the 'Pyrrhic victory' — had been repulsed by the Romans and forced to abandon his invasion of Italy. It was that news, presumably, which decided Ptolemy II, surnamed Philadelphus ('lover of his sister', whom he married), to send an embassy to Rome to exchange assurances of friendship. The other Hellenistic monarchs, it seems, were content to ignore the events taking place in the western Mediterranean. While Philadelphus can hardly have foreseen that Rome would in three generations come to dominate the entire Mediterranean world, his move was a shrewd one that was to pay handsome dividends to later Ptolemies. As Roman power spread eastward in the second century BC, it came into conflict with one Hellenistic kingdom then another; but Egypt, Rome's friend of long standing, was not only left on the sidelines of those hostilities, but was given protection by Rome on occasions when the need arose. Protection evolved almost imperceptibly into protectorate. Long before the last Cleopatra ascended the throne of her ancestors, Egypt, though nominally still independent, had become in reality a client-state of all-powerful Rome.

Various bits of surviving evidence enable us to trace the stages in Egypt's transition from proud Hellenistic kingdom to Roman vassal. In 210 BC, when Italian agriculture had been ravaged by almost a decade of Hannibal's depredations, the Romans were able to obtain a supply of grain from Egypt. Five years later Ptolemy V, surnamed Epiphanes ('[god] manifest'), ascended the throne, a boy-king of five. Intrigues and internal discord erupted, including bloody riots in the streets of Alexandria. To the Seleucid monarch of Syria, Antiochus III, it seemed a heaven-sent opportunity to dismember the Ptolemaic Empire. He seized Phoenicia, and his army stood at the gateway to Egypt when Rome, now quit of the Hannibalic war, intervened, ordering Antiochus 'to keep out of the kingdom of our ward, who was entrusted to our care in his father's last requests'.[2] The wily Antiochus, bowing to the ultimatum, retained his conquests outside Egypt proper, and sealed the status quo by the marriage of his daughter to Ptolemy.

A generation later, when the throne of the Ptolemies was once again occupied by a youth (Ptolemy VI Philometor ['mother-venerating']) and Rome was preoccupied by its war with Perseus of Macedon, Antiochus IV invaded Egypt, took the young Ptolemy prisoner, and proclaimed himself king of the land of the Nile. In the summer of 168 BC he was encamped with his army near Alexandria when the news arrived that the Romans had crushed Perseus at Pydna. Gaius Popillius Laenas arrived on the scene, armed with a decree of the Roman senate. There followed a celebrated drama. As the Greek historian Polybius, a contemporary, tells it:

[Laenas handed Antiochus] the senate's decree ordering him to end his war against Ptolemy at once and withdraw his army into Syria within a stated time. The King read it and said he wanted to consult his friends about this new development. Whereupon Popillius did something peremptory and exceedingly arrogant, to all appearances. He was carrying a stick cut from a vine. With it he drew a circle around Antiochus and bade him give his reply to the communication right in that circle. The king was taken aback at this high-handed action, but after hesitating a little he said he would do everything required of him by the Romans.[3]

We have come to the watershed in the political history of the Hellenistic world. To realize this does not require the wisdom or clarity of hindsight; it was no secret to perceptive contemporaries. The historian Polybius states it in so many words in the opening chapter of his monumental work. Henceforth the entire Mediterranean Sea was a Roman lake and those who lived on and around it looked to Rome as the arbiter of their fortunes.

The expulsion of Antiochus from Egypt was followed by a dynastic dispute between Ptolemy VI and his younger brother. The Roman senate settled the matter by leaving the older brother on the throne of Egypt but detaching Cyrenaica (roughly the territory of present-day Libya) as a separate kingdom for the younger brother. A few years later the latter, asserting that his brother aimed to regain Cyrenaica by having

him assassinated, cleverly foiled the plot — if indeed there
was a plot — by drawing up and publicizing a will in which
he left his kingdom to Rome. The will is preserved in an
inscription found at Cyrene. It was never executed, because
this Ptolemy survived his brother and lived to reign in Egypt —
as Ptolemy VIII, surnamed Euergetes ('benefactor') II but
nicknamed Physkon ('potbelly') — for a total of fifty-four
years, by far the longest reign of the dynasty.

By this time the commercial opportunities afforded by
Alexandria had led numbers of Roman merchants and
shippers to settle there. Inspection tours and visits to Egypt
by Roman officials became more frequent. A papyrus of 112
BC, found in the ruins of a village about a hundred kilometres from the Sphinx and the great pyramids, contains the
following instructions from a high official at Alexandria:

Lucius Memmius, a Roman senator, who enjoys a position of great
dignity and honour, is making the voyage from Alexandria to the
Arsinoite nome to see the sights. Let him be received with special
magnificence, and see to it that the guest-houses are made ready at
the proper places and that the landing-stages leading to them are in
working order, also that the welcoming gifts listed below are presented
to him at each landing-place, that the furnishings of each guest-house
are ready for him, as well as the titbits for Petesouchos [the crocodile
god] and the [live] crocodiles, and the necessaries for viewing the
labyrinth, and the offerings for the sacrifices. And in general take the
greatest pains for the visitor's complete satisfaction, and show the
utmost zeal . . . [The rest is lost.] [4]

Clearly, Roman interest in Egypt, commercial as well as
political, has been growing. But now Rome was caught up
in a continuing crisis of domestic strife and foreign wars,
and for the next thirty years Egypt played out its dynastic
intrigues and palace revolutions free from Roman intervention.
The two political orbits, Roman and Egyptian, met again in
the decade of the 80s BC, when Sulla was campaigning in the
East, and from then on Egypt fell increasingly under direct
Roman control. In 80 BC, when Ptolemy IX Soter II died
without legitimate male issue, it was Sulla who filled the
hiatus by placing on the throne a Ptolemaic prince who
had become his protégé. Henceforth Egypt existed under
a permanent shadow of potential Roman intervention, a

plaything of Roman politics. In 58 BC Ptolemy XI, nicknamed Auletes for his skill as a flautist, fled for safety to Rome, where he obtained the support of Pompey, who recommended him to his friend Gabinius, then the Roman governor of Syria. Gabinius invaded Egypt and restored Auletes to the throne (54 BC). Unable — or so he claimed — to pay Gabinius the enormous reward (10,000 talents of silver) that he had promised, or to pay back the loans he had taken from other Romans, Auletes in effect offered his whole kingdom as security for his debts, appointing one of his Roman creditors, Gaius Rabirius Postumus, to be his finance minister. But who got what out of the accommodation is unclear. In the end, as we know from Cicero's speeches defending both men, Gabinius back in Rome was convicted of bribery and forced into exile, while Rabirius was acquitted of the same charge.

Ptolemy Auletes died in 51 BC. His will named as his joint successors his eldest daughter, Cleopatra, then eighteen, and his eldest son, Ptolemy, then a lad of nine or ten;and Rome was named their guardian. Two years later not only Pompey and Caesar were at war, but the partisans of the royal siblings as well. The following year, 48 BC, Pompey was dead and Caesar, who had pursued him thither, was in Egypt. Young Ptolemy XII died when his troops were routed by Caesar's, with whose approval the next oldest brother, a mere boy, was then proclaimed Cleopatra's consort, Ptolemy XIII. There followed two months of celebration and relaxation, during which the royal barge conveyed Caesar and Cleopatra up the Nile in amatory dalliance amidst the touristic wonders of Egypt.

When Caesar left Egypt Cleopatra was carrying his child. In 46 BC she arrived in Rome with her boy-husband and her infant son, whose dynastic name was Ptolemy, but whom she called — and we still call — Caesarion, 'son of Caesar'. The royal party was installed in Caesar's estate on the Janiculan Hill across the Tiber from the centre of Rome — to the mingled indignation and titillation of society. A month after Caesar's assassination Cleopatra deemed it wise to leave Rome and return with her family and retinue to Egypt.

The liaison of Antony and Cleopatra was one of a dozen years' duration, 42-30 BC. Its romantic element, immortalized in song and story, needs no retelling here. What is not so widely known is that Cleopatra bore Antony twin sons and a daughter, and that their union was eventually solemnized by a formal marriage. Whatever the part to be assigned to passion, there was underlying political shrewdness in Antony's choice. Octavian and he both knew that a show-down between them for sole control of Rome and its empire was inevitable, and in choosing 'Egypt and the resources of the East [together with] an Egyptian spouse', Antony obtained the command of the half of the Roman world that was by far the richer in men and treasure.[5]

Some ten years before the show-down occurred Virgil had sung in his tenth Eclogue that 'love conquers all'. But Cupid's arrows proved to be a poor match for the armed forces of Caesar Octavian. In September 31 BC, largely as a result of their own strategic miscalculation, Antony and Cleopatra were decisively defeated in a naval battle off Actium in western Greece. They fled back to Egypt, where, pursued by Octavian, they took their own lives — first he, later she — rather than fall into the conqueror's hands. The victor spared their three children; in fact, he sent them to Rome, where his own sister Octavia, once Antony's wife, saw to their upbringing. Caesarion, however, he had put to death: as an Alexandrian philosopher had reminded him (if he needed reminding), there was political danger to him in a multiplicity of Caesars.

Thus, in 30 BC Egypt was left with a Roman conqueror and no dynastic claimant to the throne of the Ptolemies. Octavian made what must have seemed the obvious decision: to install a Roman governor and administrative staff, together with a Roman army of occupation to assure public tranquility.

Roman Egypt

In 27 BC Rome's ruler went through a carefully planned metamorphosis, shedding the persona of Octavian and emerging in that of Augustus, the first of the line that we call Roman emperors, although the designation that Augustus chose for himself and his successors in office was *princeps,* 'first citizen'. Augustus ruled for forty-one years, during which he enacted a broad range of institutional and social reforms in Roman society, a reorganization notable for its marked atavistic quality. The extent to which he altered the way things were done in Egypt is still debated among scholars, but a consensus appears to be emerging along the following lines.

For the peasant mass of the population life in their villages continued essentially unchanged, except that the burden of taxation was felt to be heavier — the Romans were much more efficient in the work of collection than the weak governments of the last Ptolemies had been. Otherwise, life in the villages continued in its age-old ways, as the Nile continued to produce its annual fertilizing flood, in some years too high, in others too low, but sometimes just right for a fine or even a bumper crop. To the extent that an awareness of their far-off ruler penetrated the pattern of their daily lives, they conceived of him and his line, like the Ptolemaic and still earlier the Persian kings before them, as a new dynasty of foreign Pharaohs. Temples continued to be built and decorated in the native Egyptian style all through the three centuries of the Principate. On their walls the Roman emperors appear in the traditional settings, attitudes, and trappings of Egyptian royalty — the Pharaonic garb and crown, the hieroglyphic cartouche enclosing the ruler's name, the adjacent hieroglyphic inscriptions repeating for him the standard titles and honorifics of the Pharaohs, such as 'son of Ra', 'beloved of Ptah and Isis', and so on.

It was in the administrative organization and practices, local as well as central, that Egypt acquired, beginning with Augustus, the stamp of a Roman province. As its chief function in the grand design of the empire, Egypt was assigned the duty of providing one-third of the annual supply of grain needed to feed the city of Rome. To assure against disruption of that lifeline Augustus consolidated the province as something like a pocket borough of the emperor. Unlike other provinces, which were governed by Romans who had risen to the distinguished rank of proconsul, Egypt was placed under a modestly titled prefect, 'chargé d'affaires', appointed by the emperor as his personal representative. Moreover, by classifying the post as a prefecture Augustus placed it among those that would always be filled by a member of the equestrian order, the class of his own origin, the class that had from the start of his career formed the solid backbone and bulwark of his support. He also provided that no Roman of senatorial rank, or even equestrians if they were prominent public figures, might so much as enter the province without the express permission of the emperor. To be outranked repeatedly by visiting dignitaries from Rome could have diminished the prefect in the eyes of those he had been sent to rule, and Augustus may well have been concerned to preclude that embarrassment. But his prime motivation in placing Egypt off limits to men of importance was to exclude potential leaders of disaffection, to obviate the possibility that Egypt might again serve as a base for political opposition with military backing, as it had done for Antony. In unrivalled splendour the prefect was, to the people of Egypt, an untrammelled viceroy acting for their Pharaoh residing in distant Rome.

Augustus retained the pre-existing division of the country into some thirty administrative districts, or 'nomes', each governed by a strategos. But within that unchanged framework he effected a radical change in the power structure. Under the Ptolemies the strategoi had military as well as civil authority; Augustus reduced them to purely civil officials. Henceforth the only military officers would be those of the Roman armed forces. Those military effectives were distributed strategically about the province, not in the Ptolemaic pattern of soldier-farmers living with their families on lands allotted to them by the king, but in the Roman system of fortified camps and lesser outposts. One legion was stationed at Alexandria, a second at Babylon, which was across the river and a little downstream from Memphis. Small detachments were dispatched in rotation to garrison duties in various key places, such as frontiers, mines and quarries, important road junctions, and depots of the grain supply.

The civil government, too, as instituted by Augustus and elaborated by his successors, was distinctively Roman, but its personnel, except in the top posts, was drawn from the local population and conducted its business in Greek, not Latin. In Alexandria the governor's staff included some officers and clerks who were bilingual, and they would produce from the Latin texts of communications from the emperor or the prefect Greek versions for dissemination in the province. In local administration some Ptolemaic titles were retained, but where that was done the responsibilities of the office, as in the case of the strategoi, were usually altered. For the rest, new offices and new titles were created as needed, and new regulations are in evidence governing important aspects of economy, society, and religion.

So much for the outline. To fill in the details we turn our attention now to the people of the Roman province of Egypt and the conditions of their lives.

CLASSES AND MASSES
or
KNOWING YOUR PLACE

Writing in Rome *c.* AD 100 the younger Pliny, gentleman, scholar, millionaire, distinguished public servant, addresses Emperor Trajan:

Thank you, Sire, for granting Roman citizenship so promptly to my chiropractor, Harpocras. But I am reminded by persons more learned in the law than I that, as the man is an Egyptian, I should have obtained Alexandrian citizenship for him first. I pray you, therefore, also to bestow Alexandrian citizenship upon him, so that I may enjoy your grant in conformity with the law.

To which the emperor replies:

Following the established practice of the emperors, my policy is not to grant Alexandrian citizenship lightly. But since you have already obtained Roman citizenship for your chiropractor Harpocras, I cannot deny your supplemental request. You must let me know what nome he is from, so I can write my friend Pompeius Planta, the prefect of Egypt.[1]

The sociopolitical structure of Roman Egypt is neatly summed up in that exchange of letters. The diagram of that structure takes the form of a pyramid. The tip, flaunting the height of privilege, comprises the small number of Roman citizens residing in the province; below them is a larger segment of lesser privilege, the urban Greeks and — till their fall from favour — the Jews; and those two upper strata repose upon the broad and deep base embracing the rest of the population, peasants, artisans, landowners, merchants, the rich few and the many poor, townspeople whose status bestowed certain benefits, and villagers enjoying no benefits at all, in short the great mass that the Roman government lumped disdainfully and indiscriminately together under the appellation of 'Egyptians'. The barrier against advancement from a lower status to a higher one was impenetrable except by special dispensation of the emperor. Wealthy and prominent Alexandrians were often rewarded with Roman citizenship — there was, after all, an underlying affinity between citizens of the two world capitals, and wealthy provincials everywhere in the empire were generally pro-Roman anyway. But rulers whose aim was to preserve social stability would obviously have no motivation for encouraging the advancement of Egyptians from their assigned place in the scheme of things. In AD 212 the emperor, with a stroke of his pen, made Roman citizens of practically everyone living within the boundaries of the empire. Before that, however, an Egyptian was only exceptionally admitted to Alexandrian or Roman citizenship.

Romans

The governor of the province, who bore the title of *praefectus Aegypti*, was sent out from Rome as the emperor's personal representative. He served, naturally, at the emperor's pleasure, usually for a term of one to three years, rarely for more than four or five. He and a few adjuvant Roman officials lived and worked in Alexandria. Once each year, accompanied by one or more of those Roman associates, he left Alexandria for a period of four or five months, travelling to two Egyptian towns — one in the Delta, the other in the up-country — where he held assizes, received petitions from grievants, and scrutinized the accounts and performance of the local administrators. To the vast majority of he province's population he and the dignitaries of his entourage remained distant and unseen symbols of government.

The seen symbols, visible everywhere to the population, were the soldiers who garrisoned the province. During most of the period of Roman rule the army of occupation consisted of two legions of Roman citizens, plus various auxiliary units of provincials (plus a few Romans) under Roman officers, the whole constituting a military establishment of some seventeen or eighteen thousand men. The auxiliary units included infantry, cavalry, and a naval squadron based at Alexandria for sea- and river-patrol. In the papyri we encounter personnel from a fair number of the units stationed at strategic places in the up-country, sometimes in their garrison posts, at other times dispatched, singly or in groups, on special details. Typical is the auxiliary cohort that was first stationed across the river from Apollinopolis, in Upper Egypt, in AD 131. Twenty-five years later we see it in the same camp, with a total strength of 505 men, comprising six centurions, three decurions, 363 infantry, 114 cavalry, and a camel corps of nineteen.[2]

Only Roman citizens were enrolled in legions, their term of service twenty-five years. Auxiliary troopes were rewarded with Roman citizenship upon honourable discharge after twenty-six years' service. However, all routes to privileged status, including this military route, long remained barred to the mass of the population, the native Egyptians. Till late in the second century recruits for the auxiliary units were drawn exclusively from the gentry of the nome capitals (Chapter 3), a class which traced its descent from the Greeks who had settled in Egypt under the Ptolemies.

At the opposite social pole from the common soldiery we find a certain number of moneyed Romans sojourning — as many Europeans have done in modern times — in Egypt's mild winter to alleviate a variety of ailments, real or imagined.

There was, finally, an increasing number of Roman citizens who made their homes permanently in Egypt. A few belonged to Alexandrian families that had received Roman citizenship, but most were veterans of the armed forces. For the first century and a half of Roman rule the emperors made it their policy to assign provincial recruits to military units stationed in other provinces or areas. During those decades, therefore, the veterans who settled in Egypt would be men of foreign origin. Stationed in Egypt for most of their adult lives, they came to feel at home there, and many, even though it was the third century before soldiers were allowed to marry, acquired during their years of service 'common-law' wives and children, whose status was legitimized upon the soldier's honourable discharge. It was Emperor Hadrian (AD 117–38) who began the shift toward local recruitment of soldiers, and from the middle of the second century veterans settling in Egypt tended more and more to be men from the country towns making their way through enlistment and military service into the world of Roman privilege.

Unless he had been unusually spendthrift or improvident, a soldier at discharge was fairly well-to-do and ready to settle down as a man of substance. Not only did he receive a substantial discharge bonus (12,000 drachmas for a legionary, something less for an auxiliary), but during his quarter-century of service some part of his stipend had, it seems, been put aside in enforced savings, and in those years of garrison duty, policing, and related activities, a man with idle cash could find many an opportunity for quick and easy profits as well as for long-term investments. These included buying and selling slaves, acquiring interests in various businesses, and above all making loans, in which the legal interest rate of one per cent per month was often quietly exceeded with impunity. One soldier is on record as purchasing a loom for 13,000 drachmas in spot cash, a tidy sum even in a time of incipient inflation. Another, in this instance a centurion, owned a small river-boat of 500 artabas burthen (about twelve and a half tons) and hired a skipper to operate it for him. Or take the last will and testament of a centurion in a cavalry unit, who, in itemizing his possessions, lists a variety of military and personal effects, plus cash amounting to eight gold coins and 199½ talents of silver (= over a million drachmas, but in the inflation of his time drachmas were counted in units of a thousand and ten thousand); a little of his money was kept in his strong-box, but by far the greater part of it was out in fifteen different loans.

In planning for his life in retirement the veteran's first concern was to be sure his papers were in order. For example, a papyrus dated at Caesarea in Judea on 22 January AD 150 but found in Egypt where it had obviously been taken by one of the interested parties, certifies that the twenty-two named veterans had been honourably discharged from a legion, not an auxiliary unit.

A papyrus in Oslo, published only last year, has acquainted us with another kind of document produced for the benefit of veterans. Written on 10 December AD 149, it is a letter from a Roman official instructing a nome secretary to provide a soldier who has completed his period of service with a certificate attesting his exemption from the payment of poll tax.[3]

Papers and fortune in hand, the veteran's next step was to find a desirable property, preferably one that would serve as both residence and investment. Extant records show how the veterans tended to concentrate in the larger and more prosperous villages. In Philadelphia in the Arsinoite nome they may by the early third century have constituted as much as a fifth of the number of property-owners. In sharp contrast is the village of Soknopaiou Nesos, some fifty kilometres to the west (and slightly north) in the same nome. Located in the outback of the nome, on the edge of the desert, at the outer limit of the irrigation system, it had no prime land to speak of, and not a single Roman property-owner has yet turned up in the documents from or relating to that village.[4]

As we might expect, many a soldier began to search for his new home in advance of discharge, in the last year or two of active service. We see this vividly in a letter of AD 136, in which a soldier expecting his discharge after one more year of service writes to his brother, who is already discharged and back in their native village of Karanis, in the Arsinoite nome:

Receive with my recommendation the bearer of this letter, Terentianus, an honourably discharged soldier, and acquaint him with our villagers' ways, so he isn't insulted. Since he is a man of means and desirous of residing there, I have urged upon him that he rent my house for this year and next for sixty drachmas, and that he take a lease of my field for sixty drachmas, and I'd like you to use the one hundred and twenty drachmas to buy for me from our friend the linen-merchant by the temple in the city . . . [A few irrelevant details follow.][5]

We know nothing of Terentianus' life thereafter, except that he must have settled in Karanis, where the University of Michigan expedition which excavated the site between 1924 and 1934 found a packet of his letters in one of the houses.

We learn from those letters that Terentianus was himself the son of a veteran, and that he had served in the fleet stationed at Alexandria.

Reading between the lines of the letter just quoted we sense that the native population did not always welcome an incoming veteran with open arms, nor regard his presence amongst them as an unmitigated blessing. Much would depend on the kind of person he was, and the writer of the letter was obviously concerned to assure that, with his brother's help, Terentianus would not begin by putting a foot wrong. The peasantry's suspicion of soldiery, whether active or retired, was understandable. Generally when military units or officers appeared in the villages it was to demand something — billets, food, taxes, and so forth; and while such demands were usually authorized, the man under arms was often seen to line his own pockets as well, and the intimidated villagers were powerless to stop such extortions (see Chapter 8). In retirement a veteran might decide to live as a good neighbour, and might even become a local benefactor. But if not, he was apt to be perceived as a burden upon the community: for example, his exemption from many of the taxes and services imposed upon the non-Romans could not but be resented, not only for the privileged status it proclaimed but even more because it would increase proportionately the burdens imposed upon his unprivileged neighbours. Experience had shown, moreover, that these newcomers often insisted on exercising their privileges to the last iota, and were openly contemptuous of the Egyptians and Greco-Egyptians among whom they lived. For many veterans, of course, this was a way of putting as great an emotional and social distance as possible between themselves and their own humble origins. A papyrus of AD 162 contains a petition from a veteran named Gaius Julius Niger. The substance of the complaint is lost in the mutilated top of the papyrus, but in the well-preserved portion we find Niger saying, 'Therefore, as the injuries done me are manifest, and as I am a Roman man suffering such indignities at the hands of an Egyptian, I ask . . .' Equally revealing is the following episode of a few years earlier.

The undersigned swear by the fortune of the Emperor Caesar Titus Aelius Hadrianus Antoninus Pius that they offer the following testimony in good faith. We were in the village of Philadelphia in the Arsinoite nome, Herakleides division, at the temple of the Caesars, and that is how we happened to behold Gaius Maevius Apelles, veteran of the Aprian division, being flogged with rods and scourges by two guards on orders of the strategos Hierax. Therefore in good faith we depose that we beheld him being flogged in the village of Philadelphia. [Date, 11 February AD 153. Signatures of seven witnesses, all Romans.] .

This case was all the more shocking to Roman sensibilities in the light of the proud tradition that after the ouster of the kings the very first law passed by the Roman Republic provided that 'no magistrate might execute or (even) scourge a Roman citizen who exercised his right of appeal'. And here was a mere provincial civil officer violating the person and rights of a Roman citizen in a manner forbidden even to Roman magistrates! What was this world coming to?[6]

Many veterans were powerful figures in their adopted communities by virtue not only of their privileged status but also of their wealth. They were already rich by village standards when they arrived on the scene. They proceeded to acquire lands, and they prospered — many of them — in agriculture and related enterprises. We have details of several such local tycoons. One large group of papyri relates to a veteran named Lucius Bellenus Gemellus, who after his discharge settled, about AD 80, in the Arsinoite nome. When he died some thirty years later, at the ripe age of seventy-seven or more, he was the possessor of landed estates near the villages of Euhemeria, Dionysias, and at least three others. He had agents to help operate the properties, the most remote of which were fifteen or more kilometres apart, but his personal supervision extended to the most minute details. On one of his farms he employed as many as twenty-seven labourers at harvest time. He also owned an oil-press. He remembered to send presents to the nome strategoi when the festival of Isis came around, ordered ten chickens to be served at the celebration of the Saturnalia, and was rich enough to sacrifice a calf at another holiday. All in all, with his daughter and three sons, a family that was a pillar of local society.

Another example is the Gaius Julius Niger mentioned above.

In AD 154, upon his discharge from the cavalry at the age of forty-seven, he settled in Karanis, buying a house with two courtyards for 800 silver drachmas — a price which, when compared with others known from the same period, bespeaks a domicile of some size and substance. There he lived to be eighty-one, surviving the plague that ravaged a large part of the Roman Empire, including Egypt, in the 170s. During his years at Karanis he acquired a considerable amount of additional property, including farmland in several villages. At his death his estate passed to his two sons, and upon their death to the widow and children of one of them (the other son apparently had no wife or offspring).

Urban Greeks and Jews

The Egypt that Octavian annexed included within its borders three Greek cities (*poleis*), which enjoyed local autonomy and various other privileges. In order of creation the cities were Naukratis, in the Nile Delta, organized by a Pharaoh of the sixth century BC in recognition of services rendered by Greek merchants and mercenaries; Alexandria, the great port city established in 331 BC by Alexander the Great; and a generation later, in Upper Egypt, some 120 kilometres northwest of the Pharaonic capital of Thebes, Ptolemais, founded by and named for the first ruler of the new Hellenistic dynasty. In AD 130 Emperor Hadrian built in Middle Egypt a fourth city, Antinoopolis, to perpetuate the memory of the handsome youth Antinous, the emperor's constant companion, who had drowned at that spot in the course of their royal progress on the Nile. The new city, as constituted by Hadrian, had the traditional governmental organs of a Greek polis plus some of the advantages of a Roman municipality, and its citizens were granted an array of privileges in keeping with their enviable status. Some of the original colonists of Antinoopolis came from Ptolemais, whether responding to the inducement of the privileges offered or simply selected for transfer we do not know.

Queen city of the eastern Mediterranean, cultural capital of the Hellenistic world, crossroads of commerce between the Graeco-Roman world and the lands to the east and south, a city frequented by Arabians, Ethiops, Indians, and a host of other peoples, exotic and familiar, Alexandria figures importantly in Greek and Latin literature. Of contemporary historical records, however, only some inscriptions have survived. Papyri have rotted away in the damp soil of the Delta (though a few dozen have been found there, preserved by accidental carbonization), and except for a few relics, monuments of more durable material have disappeared in the centuries of continuous inhabitation of the site. Of its topography we know about the Pharos, its lighthouse that ranked as one of the Seven Wonders of the World, and about some of the major landmarks. We know something about its two harbours, and also that its main thoroughfare was thrity metres wide and the side streets six to seven metres wide and paved with cobblestones. According to Diodorus of Sicily, Alexandria in the time of Augustus had 300,000 free inhabitants, which presumably indicates a total population in the neighbourhood of half a million.

Information about Naukratis and Ptolemais under the Principate is slight. About Antinoopolis, on the other hand, the papyri published in the past hundred years have brought us a considerable body of data, especially about its political structure and about its citizens' privileges. Although some variations are evident, the four cities appear to conform essentially to the same organizational pattern.

One of the most prominent elements common to the four cities was the enrolment of the citizenry in tribes and demes — a pround constitutional link with the city-states of classical Greece. Another characteristic feature, the gymnasium, was jealously preserved in its full institutional panoply as a visible symbol of polis tradition. Following the classical mode, the citizens of the Egyptian poleis took turns serving as gymnasiarchs (who supplied oil for lighting and for massage) and kosmetai (who supervised the rituals prescribed for the ephebes, as the young men continued to be called). Popular sports, however, were increasingly centred in the Roman amphitheatres which now sprang up all over the eastern Mediterranean. Wrestling, boxing, racing, and the other contests of the traditional Greek games were increasingly left to professional athletes, and the ordinary citizen became less and less a participant in sports and more and more, in the Roman manner, a spectator.

A traditional organ of self-government in the polis was the council (*boule*), elected by the citizens from amongst their own number. For more than two centuries of Roman rule Alexandria suffered the indignity of not being allowed to have a boule – a policy, we are told, instituted by Octavian as punishment for the hostility that the Greeks of that city had manifested first to Caesar and subsequently to himself. There is a possible indication in one papyrus that Naukratis, like Ptolemais,[7] was allowed to keep the boule that it had. Antinoopolis, we know, was granted that instrument of local autonomy in its foundation charter. A boule was finally granted Alexandria in AD 200, when Emperor Septimius Severus instituted such councils in all the nome capitals. But the Alexandrians could then hardly rejoice at seeing their proud city placed on a par with country towns.

On the economic side the privileges enjoyed by the citizens of the four cities were considerable. The commercial opportunities offered by Alexandria were, to be sure, available also to non-citizens. But only the citizens were, like the Romans, exempt from the payment of the poll tax, which was for the provincial population at large both a financial burden and a symbol of subjection. In addition, in the first century of Roman rule no Egyptians but only urban Greeks, it appears, were allowed to purchase certain public lands when they were put up for sale. And what is clear beyond any doubt is that throughout the period of Roman rule many citizens of Alexandria and Antinoopolis (and presumably, therefore, of Naukratis and Ptolemais as well) owned parcels of farmland, and in some instances extensive estates, in various parts of Egypt, often hundreds of kilometres removed from the cities in which they lived. Their lands within Alexandrian territory were exempt from taxation, and wherever they owned property they and their families were exempt from the peformance of liturgies, those compulsory services of various kinds, costly in time and money, to which local residents were obligated (ch. 8).

Last, but far from least, citizens of the poleis were eligible to serve in Roman legions. Thereby they would become

Roman citizens immediately upon enlistment, while other inhabitants of Egypt could, as we saw above, enrol only in auxiliary units, through which they would attain Roman citizenship only after more than a quarter-century of military service.

Residence in a polis did not, of course, automatically make one a citizen. Entrepreneurs, domestic and foreign, pursued the business opportunities that the cities afforded, and the city populations were also swelled by the slaves, menials, and Egyptians of every stripe who catered to the citizens' needs. Another large group in the urban population, most notably in Alexandria, was that of the Jews, whom we turn to consider next.

After the Biblical exodus Jews are again in evidence in Egypt at least from the middle of the sixth century BC. For the fifth and fourth centuries a hundred or so papyri and scores of ostraca, written in Aramaic, have acquainted us with a Jewish settlement at the First Cataract of the Nile, guarding Egypt's southern frontier for its then Persian rulers. In those Aramaic documents we read of marriage and divorce, of keeping and freeing slaves (some with Egyptian but others with Semitic names), of supplying the garrison with foodstuffs. We encounter details of private life, complaints and lawsuits over a variety of issues, conveyances of houses and lands by gift or sale, loans in money (at an annual interest of sixty per cent) and in kind (in one instance repayable twofold in twenty days). We learn, without surprise, that they had their temple of Yahweh on the island of Elephantine, that it was rebuilt after being damaged or destroyed (we know not how or why); we also learn, with some surprise, that other gods were worshipped there as well — early foreshadowings, it would seem, of the syncretistic tendencies so prominent later, in Hellenistic and Roman times (ch. 5).

Thereafter Jewish communities spread in Egypt and flourished. The Ptolemies allowed them to live according to the dictates of their religion, but while continuing their traditional practices the Jews were not impervious, especially in urban centres like Alexandria, to the attractions and influences of Greek culture. Once regarded with scepticism by modern scholars, the ancient tradition that the Septuagint, the Greek translation of the Old Testament, was produced in Alexandria in the third century BC is now generally accepted. In the first decades of the first century AD Philo, a wealthy Jew of Alexandria steeped in Greek philosophy, produced voluminous works in Greek, works that we still read today, in which he explains the books of his Bible to non-Jewish readers in terms and concepts belonging to the Hellenic tradition.

In one of his writings Philo states that in his time a million Jews lived in Alexandria. That figure is undoubtedly an exaggeration, perhaps a rhetorical one; the entire population of the city seems to have been about half that number (p. 26). The city was divided into five districts, one of which was totally Jewish. In return for their support Augustus confirmed the privileges that the Jews had enjoyed under the Ptolemies, which included having their own council of elders — and that at the very time when the Greek citizens were denied a boule. Small wonder that in such circumstances the Jews felt themselves to be full-fledged Alexandrians, entitled to parity with the Greeks, which would include, for example, admission to the gymnasia, the quintessential hallmark of a Hellenic body politic; or that the Alexandrians reacted with resentment and almost paranoid hostility, an animosity which eventually, in AD 38, erupted into a major pogrom. The aftermath of that bloody affray saw rival delegations of Greeks and Jews appealing to Emperor Caligula in Rome. Within months of his accession in 41 the new emperor, Claudius, was visited by similar embassies, to which he responded in a now famous ruling (preserved on a papyrus acquired by the British Museum in 1921), in effect ordering both sides to preserve the status quo in peace. In a private letter written a few months earlier that same year an otherwise unknown Alexandrian remarks *en passant*, in the course of a series of instructions about business matters, 'Like everyone else, you too beware of the Jews'.[8]

The privileges of the Jews were sharply curtailed following the Jewish revolts of the first and second centuries. In the first revolt, even when refugees from Judaea sought to rouse resistance elsewhere after the fall of Jerusalem and the destruction of the Temple in AD 70, the Jews of Egypt remained loyal to Rome. Even so, their chief temple in Egypt, at Leontopolis near Memphis, was stripped of its treasures and demolished; there was fear in high places, apparently, that it might replace the razed temple of Jerusalem as a centre of Jewish disaffection. And there was instituted as reparations a 'tax on Jews': the half-shekel (= two drachmas) per adult male that the Jews had contributed each year for the upkeep of the Temple was quadrupled, imposed on every member of a Jewish household (including slaves) from the age of three, and devoted to the Romans' chief god, Jupiter Capitolinus, whose temple in Jerusalem had been burnt down by the Jews in the course of the revolt. The punitive, rather than compensatory, intent and nature of the 'tax on Jews' are revealed by the fact that it continued to be collected well into the second century, long after its ostensible purpose, the rebuilding of Jupiter's temple, had been accomplished and paid for. However, the Jews' privilege of living 'according to their ancestral laws' was not impaired.

In contrast to the first revolt, which occurred in Judaea and only afterwards had repercussions for Egyptian Jews, the second uprising of the Jews against Rome was centred in Egypt. Its roots are doubtless to be found in the continuing hostility, tensions, and clashes between Greeks and Jews in Alexandria, and the immediate precipitant may well have been the opportunity seemingly presented by the withdrawal of military units from Egypt for Trajan's war against Parthia. The revolt erupted in AD 115 in Egypt and Cyrene and quickly struck responsive sparks in Cyprus, Judaea, and Mesopotamia. It was rapidly put down in Alexandria itself, but elsewhere it was not finally suppressed till shortly after the accession of Emperor Hadrian in 117. For almost three years the up-country of Egypt, from the Delta to the Thebaid, was wracked by guerrilla warfare. Some two dozen papyri, from several sites, attest to the ferocity of the struggle, the numbers of people killed or driven from their homes, and the extensive devastation of farmland and buildings wrought in 'the Jewish disturbance'. Inscriptions found in Cyrene tell of roads ripped up, public buildings burnt. A particularly interesting letter, written on 28 November 117, contains a request from a nome strategos to the prefect of Egypt for sixty days' leave to put my affairs in order . . . . For, not only have my affairs been completely neglected owing to my long absence, but also on account of the onslaught of the impious Jews practically everything I possess in the villages of the Hermopolite nome and my interests in the nome metropolis require restoration by me. If you accede to my request, after straightening out my affairs as best I can I will be able to turn to the duties of my office in better spirits.

Nearly a hundred years later the town of Oxyrhynchus still commemorated

the goodwill, faithfulness, and friendship to the Romans which [our] people exhibited, fighting side by side with them in the war against the Jews, and even now still celebrating each year the day of victory.[9]

In AD 117 Jewish resistance in Egypt was broken forever. Seventeen years later there raged in nearby Judaea, the national homeland, the last (as it turned out) and fiercest of the Jewish attempts to shake off the Roman yoke. That was the revolt led by the charismatic 'Son of the Star', Bar Kochba. But even the Messianic overtones of that movement fanned no fires of revolt against the power of Rome amongst the quiescent remnant of Egyptian Jewry.

Egyptians

If you were an inhabitant of Egypt but not a Roman, a citizen of one of the four poleis, or a Jew, to the Roman government you were an Egyptian. No matter that you were descended from six or seven generations of military reservists, that class of hereditary privilege settled on the land under the Ptolemies. That privileged status was now gone, and with it those ethnic designations by which you used proudly to proclaim your family's origin in the Greek or Macedonian homeland — Coan, Cretan, Thessalian, and so forth. In the government records you were all now Egyptians, nothing more. In another context (but doubtless with contemporary overtones) the historian Livy, who wrote in the time of Augustus, remarks that 'the Macedonians had degenerated to the level of Egyptians'.[10]

When heterogeneous populations are lumped together in a single political or judicial category, they are usually quick to create their own social gradations within the total group. In recent history such distinctions have often been based on skin pigmentation, as in India and in the Caribbean area. For the mass of Egyptians under Roman rule the touchstone of status was Hellenism. Intermarriage between indigenous Egyptians and descendants of Greek settlers had become fairly common, especially in the country districts, and children of such marriages were given names from both family backgrounds. (Examples occur throughout this book.) But once an individual was registered under an Egyptian name, to change it to a Greek one required permission from the appropriate Roman authority. The following such request was submitted on 27 August AD 194:

To his · Excellency Claudius Apollonios, administrator of the Privy Purse, from Eudaimon son of Psois and Tiathres, of the village of — in the Nesyt nome. I desire my lord, from now on to have my designation changed and style myself Eudaimon son of Heron and Didyme instead of son of Psois and Tiathres, as no public or private interest will thereby be injured but I will be benefited. Farewell. I, Eudaimon, have submitted [this. Date.]
[Subscript] As no public or private interest is injured, I allow it.[11]

All matters of status and inter-class relationships came under the jurisdiction of the emperor's Privy Purse, the administrator of which — a Roman appointed by the emperor, of course — saw to the enforcement of the numerous rules and restrictions, and collected the fines for infractions. A papyrus roll in East Berlin's Egyptian Museum, published soon after the First World War, contains over a hundred of the rules. A perusal of the stringent regulations leaves no doubt that a prime objective set by Augustus and maintained by his successors for two hundred years was to impede social mobility and keep the several population strata as discrete and immutable as possible: *divide et impera*. A small selection from the lengthy document will suffice to make the point.

Copy of the code of regulations which the deified Augustus established for the administration of the Privy Purse, and of additions made to it from time to time by either the emperors or the senate or the several prefects or the administrator in charge of the Privy Purse.

8. If to a Roman will is added a clause saying, 'Whatever bequests I make in Greek codicils shall be valid', it is without force, since a Roman is not permitted to write a will in Greek.

18.. Inheritances left in trust by Greeks to Romans or by Romans to Greeks were confiscated by the deified Vespasian; nevertheless those disclosing such trusts have been given half.

38. Those born of an urban Greek mother and an Egyptian remain Egyptians but inherit from both parents.

39. If a Roman man or woman is joined in marriage with an urban Greek or an Egyptian, their children follow the inferior status.

42. Those who style themselves improperly are punished with confiscation of a fourth [of their estate], and those who knowingly concur therein are also punished with confiscation of a fourth.

43. If Egyptians after a father's death record their father as a Roman, a fourth is confiscated.

44. If an Egyptian registers a son as an ephebe [of a polis], a sixth is confiscated.

45. If an urban Greek marries an Egyptian woman and dies childless, the fisc appropriates his possessions; if he has children, it confiscates two-thirds. But if he has begotten children of an urban Greek woman and has three or more children, his possessions go to them; if two children, a fourth or a fifth [to each]; if one child, a half.

49. Freedmen of Alexandrians may not marry Egyptian women.

51. The son of a Syrian man and an urban Greek woman married an Egyptian woman, and was sentenced to a stated fine.

53. Egyptians who, when married to discharged soldiers, style themselves Romans are subject to the provision on violation of status.

56. Soldiers who style themselves Romans without having received a legal discharge are fined a fourth of their property.[12]

Historians have differed widely in interpreting the political career of Octavian-Augustus, but even his most ardent admirer in this century has agreed that the code of regulations of the Privy Purse may be 'aptly called an instrument of fiscal oppression'. The lot of the humble and the poor was not enviable anywhere in the Roman Empire — is it ever? — but the population of Egypt appears to have been singled out for exceptionally harsh treatment. Roman policy toward Egyptians conveys to us a quality of repression suggestive of vindictiveness. Trying to understand how or why Augustus set that course involves some speculation, to be sure, but not without some discernible clues. For one thing, from early in the second century BC, proceeding *pari passu* with the Romans' overseas conquests and their resultant absorption of foreign (mainly Greek) influences, a strong vein of xenophobia had imbued Rome's political and cultural life. Cato the Elder — he of 'Carthage must be destroyed' fame — is usually cited as the prime mover of the anti-foreigner policy, in which the oriental cultures were objects of particular disdain. By the time Octavian appeared upon the scene, a hundred years later, the Roman stereotype of Egypt was that of a land grown dissolute in fabulous wealth, a land ruled by fat and gluttonous kings who capped their debauched existence with incestuous brother–sister marriages. Against this background Antony's liaison with Cleopatra — Caesar's was conveniently overlooked — handed Octavian a ready-made propaganda weapon, which he proceeded to use with consummate skill. To an Italy weary of a century of recurrent civil wars Octavian's rallying-cry was not for more civil war (against Antony) but for a crusade against 'a foreign danger that menaced everything that was Roman . . . The propaganda of Octavianus magnified Cleopatra beyond all measure and decency.' And when Antony defiantly divorced his Roman wife — Octavia, the sister of Octavian — the vituperation and the rumours knew no bounds. Even Horace, normally the poet of the light and frivolous vein, joined the frenzy, singing of 'the mad queen, the deadly monster, leading gangs foul with unnatural vice to try to destroy the Capitoline and the Roman Empire.' Whatever other considerations may have entered into Augustus' organization of Roman rule in Egypt, the repressive provisions of the Privy Purse regulations, amounting to a veritable ancient apartheid, are totally in accord with inveterate Roman attitudes, climaxed in his own military and propaganda campaigns against Cleopatra.[13]

In AD 212 Emperor Caracalla issued his famous edict granting Roman citizenship to all the inhabitants of the Roman Empire (only 'the capitulated', whose identification remains a matter of scholarly dispute, were excluded). The motivations of Caracalla's action can only be guessed at. But one thing the papyri have made clear: the change, at least initially, was largely psychological and cosmetic. The social structure of Egypt, the class relationships, the restrictions, show no essential modifications. For the Egyptians in their towns and villages it was a case of *plus ça change, plus ça reste la même chose.*

THE COUNTRY TOWNS
or
MEET THE MINOR GENTRY

The Metropolis

The Egypt that Octavian annexed was divided into some thirty administrative districts called *nomoi*, a Greek word that we Anglicize as 'nomes'. As already mentioned, Augustus and his successors retained those divisions, but stripped the strategoi, as the nome governors were called, of all military authority. The strategoi were appointed by the prefect of Egypt and and served at his pleasure. Each strategos had a chief assistant, who automatically filled in whenever the office of strategos was temporarily vacant; his title of royal secretary was also continued from Ptolemaic times.

Each nome had a capital, the metropolis, where its administration was centred. That the capitals varied with their nomes in size and population is not only a safe assumption, but is also reflected in archaeological findings as well as in papyrus documents. Population statistics, however, are neither available nor calculable. As revealed by excavations the perimeter of Memphis was an almost pear-shaped ellipse of about five kilometres in length, enclosing an area of about a square kilometre; that of Hermopolis, squarish, enclosed an area half as large again. But it does not necessarily follow that the population of Hermopolis was one and a half times that of Memphis. There are too many unknowns and uncontrollable variables for us to trust such straight-line projections: What were the respective areas given over to public buildings, for example, or to religious precincts? At Oxyrhynchus the visible remains of the theatre indicate that it could have seated between eight and twelve thousand persons. But even assuming those upper and lower limits to be reasonably accurate, any attempt to calculate the total population from them is frustrated by a swarm of unanswerable questions. The chief difficulty is that we have no way of knowing what portion of the total population the theatre was intended to hold. Was it all the adult males? Or, since we know that Greek plays were presented there, was it built to hold only the Greek-speaking metropolities? The answers to these and similar questions are beyond reach.

From one metropolis there comes the following survey, drawn up in AD 116.

From Hierakion, city clerk. Security arrangement for the avenues and
  streets of the city.
— from Women's-Bath Street to the house of Phanaïs son of Sisoïs in
  the alleyway of Onnophris the oil merchant, 123 houses:
    Antaios son of Heliodoros, chairman; Paaretos son of —•——— and
    Hergeus jun. son of Thotsytmis, honourable members.
— from the temple of Serapis to the house of Orsenouphis son of
  Petosiris and the house of Chairas the painter, 129 houses:
    Pachomos son of Hierakion, chairman; Phmoulilous son of Seias
    and Pangorsauïs son of Psachis, honourable members.
— from the approach to the temple of Apollo and Aphrodite, gods
  most great, to the assembly place of the processions, 132 houses:
    Antaios son of Psentarpsais, chairman; Hasies son of Kolloutech-
    mis sen. and Peteimouthes son of Miysis, honourable members.

[After ten such entries]   Total = 1,273 houses.[1]

If the above was a complete survey of the town, as from the caption of the document it appears to be, then this was one of the smaller nome capitals. For Hermopolis, in contrast, a total of some 7,000 houses has been projected from a demonstrable partial count of over 4,000. In fact, we know quite a bit about the layout of Hermopolis as a result of its excavation in the ten years immediately preceding the Second World War. The whole town was surrounded by a brick wall. In the northern half, a sacred precinct, the walls were inordinately thick and perhaps as high as twenty-five metres — truly a temple-fortress. In the centre of the precinct, its façade fifty metres wide, its depth more than a hundred metres, stood the temple of the god whose name the metropolis bore, Hermes, the Hellenized form of the Egyptian

Thoth; inside it was a temple to Augustus. In addition to the temple personnel the large sacred precinct may have housed also the local garrison, and even some local families not connected with the cults. The principal thoroughfare of the metropolis, skirting the southern edge of the precinct, ran from the Moon Gate on the west to the Sun Gate on the east, and continued on to the town's river port, across from which lay Antinoopolis. This broad avenue, whose name Emperor Hadrian changed (at least on its eastern half) from Sarapis Street to commemorate the dead Antinous, was crossed at right angles by the southward prolongation of the mall approach to the Hermes temple. The intersection of those two main avenues was the hub of the town's activities. In its vicinity were the central market-place, the monumental public buildings, and the temples to Antinous, Hadrian, Sarapis-Nile, Aphrodite, Fortune, Athena. The southern half of the town was the chief residential area, in which the excavation also uncovered two public baths, a gymnasium (with its own bath, a gift from Emperor Hadrian), and several houses sumptuous enough to boast their own private baths. Amongst its other amenities Hermopolis had a large park and a lake.[2]

The two metropoleis that we know best are Arsinoë and Oxyrhynchus. In the thousands of papyri found at the site of the latter and in the villages near the former we find such information as the names of the different sections of the town, and of numerous streets. At Oxyrhynchus we can also identify, and in many instances even locate, a gymnasium, public baths, a theatre, a bank at the great Sarapis shrine, some twenty other temples, and, by the end of the third century, two churches. From a papyrus roll in the British Library, which contains an account of receipts and expenditures drawn up in AD 113 by the commissioners of water supply, we learn that Arsinoë had running water, at least in some parts. There were two reservoirs, into which the water was pumped from an arm of the Nile by a score or more of Archimedean screws and other machines (ch. 6); the machinery was operated by crews of from six to more than twenty men working day and night shifts. Among the customers supplied, at fees of one and a half to more than forty drachmas a day, were public baths, a beer shop in the close of the Sarapis temple, and the synagogue and prayer-house of the Theban Jews (which seems to imply that there was at least one other synagogue in town). Whether private homes also received town water is not clear.[3]

The Gentry and their Elite

But most of all it is the people who lived in the metropoleis that we encounter in the papyri. As we saw in Chapter 2, all the townspeople, including those who claimed to be of purely Greek descent, were relegated by the Roman government to the status of Egyptians. Nevertheless the metropolites — as the local gentry were styled — persisted in flaunting their ties, real or imagined, to Hellenism. They modelled their lives and their physical surroundings as much as possible on those of the four Greek cities of Egypt, especially Alexandria. They laid out their streets on the grid plan, erected opulent public buildings, and mounted Greek games and festivals of Greek gods on a scale that often exceeded what fiscal prudence would dictate. By the end of the second century many of the metropoleis were experiencing difficulty in meeting all of their current expenses. Various expedients were tried, but curtailment of conspicuous display appears to have been regarded as unthinkable, except as a very last resort. At Oxyrhynchus in AD 200 a public-spirited bene-factor established a trust fund 'the interest of which is to go for staging our annual ephebic contests in the same style as those currently staged at Antinoopolis.' In fact, these ritual manifestations of Hellenism were kept going all through the politically and economically troubled decades of the mid-third century, and far from reducing such outlays the metorpolites kept adding new, and frequently expensive, ones. At Oxyrhynchus, for example, they instituted an honorific category of two hundred metropolites privileged to be maintained at public expense, designating them a 'Council of Elders', a lofty title reminiscent of classical Greece. Also at Oxyrhynchus and in some other nome capitals — whether in all we cannot say — they introduced a free distribution of grain to sizeable number of their members.

The cachet of this last must have been specially dear to their hearts, as it was an institution characteristic not only of Alexandria and Antinoopolis, but of Rome as well.[4]

Not surprisingly, the metropolites reinforced their affectations of Greek urbanism with an urbane disdain of everything rustic and Egyptian. An Oxyrhynchite, about to revisit friends and family after living away for a year, writes, 'Perhaps you expect me to be some kind of barbarian, or some uncivilized Egyptian.' He writes to reassure them that no such transformation has taken place.[5]

Even though the extant documents relating to the nome capitals number many hundreds, we are still unable to define with complete assurance the boundaries of the class designated by the alternative terms 'metropolites' and 'those of the metropolis'. The class comprised, presumably, the descendants of the Greek settlers attracted to Egypt by the Ptolemies. But were such families the totality of the metropolite class, or only its nucleus? We do not really know. Were the descendants of intermarriages with Egyptians or others included or excluded? Did having one's domicile of record in a metropolis *ipso facto* confer metropolite status? Those two questions can confidently be answered in the negative, because the documents make it abundantly clear that only those would be enrolled as metropolites who could demonstrate that both their parents belonged to that class. (In this respect, too, the metropolites could pride themselves on perpetuating a practice of the classical Greek city-state, most notably Athens in its Periclean heyday.) Consequently, Egyptians residing in a metropolis and offspring of mixed marriages were disqualified from acquiring metropolite status.

Were the metropolites themselves a single, undifferentiated class? Probably not. A group called in Arsinoë 'the 6,475 colonists', in Hermopolis and Oxyrhynchus 'those of the gymnasium', was in all likelihood an élite corps within — rather than a class apart from — the metropolite class.

The origin and significance of the designation 'the 6,475 colonists of Arsinoë' are problems for which we have, as yet, no demonstrable solutions. On the face of it the expression sounds like a *numerus clausus*, which the corporate entity was not allowed to exceed. But if that were the case, what would happen when (or if) that figure was exceeded by population increase? What of the children of that élite class? Would they be expected to remain non-members till a place 'was vacated by death? And by what mechanism would such a vacancy be filled? By priority of age? By a lottery? All such restrictions would contravene the children's. right to be enrolled in their parents' class in their own right at the age of fourteen. In that light the likely — though as yet unprovable — explanation would appear to be that 6,475 represents the number of the élite corps when it was constituted, and subsequent generations proudly retained that exclusive title, quite untroubled by any thought that it was, strictly speaking, anachronistic.

Between the ages of fourteen and sixty (the latter an age that relatively few attained in antiquity), all male residents of Roman Egypt except Romans, urban Greeks, and Jews — all, in other words, who came under the government's sweeping classification of 'Egyptians' — were required to pay an annual poll tax, but metropolites were taxed at a reduced rate both for themselves and for their slaves. We know that metropolites paid eight drachmas a year in Herakleopolis and Hermopolis, twelve in Oxyrhynchus, and twenty in Arsinoë. This variation in the rate probably reflects the relative levels of affluence in those places: as the Arsinoite nome was especially fertile and productive (see ch. 6), its per capita income was proportionately higher.

When a metropolite boy approached his fourteenth birthday his parents submitted a formal application for his epikrisis ('verification' of status) with a view to his enrolment in the registry of their class. For metropolitan status the application stated, at a minimum, the year of enrolment of the boy's father and of his mother's father. For the élite status it apparently sufficed in Arsinoë to prove that the applicant's father and mother both belonged to the class of 'the 6,475 colonists'. In Oxyrhynchus and Hermopolis, in contrast, it was customary to demonstrate membership in the gymnasial élite by every male ancestor, maternal as well as paternal, all the way back either to the initial list, which was established in AD 4-5, or to a specific grant by competent authority at some time between then and 72-3, when the books were apparently closed to new admissions. In the following application, submitted in Oxyrhynchus on 28 August AD 260, the boy's ancestry in the status 'of the gymnasium' is proudly traced back seven generations.

According to the regulations on epikrisis, to see if those approaching admission are of the status of the gymnasium, my son [name lost], who is fourteen years old in the current 7th year [of the emperors Valerian and Gallienus], without distinguishing mark, a runner-in-training, was registered in the —— district. Wherefore, in support of his epikrisis I declare that my grandfather's great-grandfather, Dionysios son of Philon, was enrolled in the Metroön district in the epikris of gymnasial status that took place in the 5th year of the deified Vespasian [AD 72-3], pursuant to the proofs he offered that his grandfather, Dionysios son of Philon, was in the list of the 34th year of the deified Augustus [AD 4-5]; that my father's great-grandfather [names lost] was enrolled in the Cretic district in the epikrisis of the —— year of the deified Domitian [AD 81-96]; that my great-grandfather Cornelius was enrolled in the Metroön district in the epikrisis of candidates in the 17th year of the deified Trajan [AD 113-4]; that my grandfather was enrolled in the same district in the epikrisis of the —— year of the deified Antoninus [AD 137-61]; that my father Sarapion was enrolled in the Anamphodarchs' district in the epikrisis of candidates in the 6th year of the deified Marcus Aurelius and Lucius Verus [AD 165-6]; that I myself was enrolled in the Cretic district . . .; further, that on my son's mother's side her grandfather's great-grandfather, Apollonios son of Apollonios, was registered in the —— district in the epikrisis of the said 5th year of the deified Vespasian; [there follow, with the year of enrolment of each, the maternal great-great-grandfather, great-grandfather, grandfather, and father].

I swear by the fortune of our emperors [names] that the above-written is true; that [name lost] is my natural son by [mother's name lost], neither adopted nor suppositious, and that I have not made use of others' credentials or of homonymy — or may I be liable to the consequences of this oath. [Date. Signatures of three witnesses.] [6]

A recent volume of *The Oxyrhynchus Papyri* contains the remnant of a file of such applications. The thirteen extant ones were given the file numbers 109-21, and they all date from AD 149. If, as seems probable (though we cannot be certain), numbers 1-108 also dated from the same year, the presentation of over a hundred eligibles in a single year would imply that the gymnasial elite of Oxyrhynchus was a considerably larger class than has hitherto been supposed.[7]

It surely comes as no great surprise to learn that the metropolites and their élite group were markedly endogamous. As we have just observed, marriage with outsiders would automatically exclude the children from the privileged status. What does surprise most modern readers is the discovery that such marriages occurred not only within the class as a whole but not infrequently within families, including marriages of full brothers and sisters. Examples abound everywhere in the papyri — in census records, contracts of marriage and divorce, private letters, and all sorts of other documents — and two should suffice here for illustrative purposes. A document of *c*. AD 165 shows brother–sister unions in three successive generations of a family of gymnasial status; another, of 189, acquaints us with a family that had seven such marriages in four generations. We even have an invitation to such a wedding:

Herais invites you to the marriage of her children, at home, tomorrow, the 5th, starting at the ninth hour [3 p.m.].[8]

The custom of sibling unions began, presumably, in prehistoric times. Its earliest demonstrable occurrences were in the royal houses of oriental monarchies. It was practised by some of the Pharaohs, and by their successors, the Ptolemies. In the centuries of Roman rule the practice spread all the way down the social scale to the Egyptian peasantry. But the metropolites, in their aggressive class consciousness, must have found it easy to ignore the native Egyptian stamp of the practice and to celebrate their own brother–sister unions as the continuation of a tradition stemming from Hellenistic royalty.

When instances of brother–sister marriages first began to appear in the papyri, they were greeted with great scepticism in some quarters, where doubt was expressed that any society would really have countenanced such common violation of the incest taboo, which many anthropologists still regard as a 'universal' of human society. May not, one argument ran, calling a wife 'my sister' have been the counterpart of the age-old Near Eastern custom of calling a friend 'my brother'? Such arguments are ingenious, but they collapse completely in the face of the cumulative evidence of scores of papyri, official as well as private documents, in which the wife is unequivocally identified as the husband's 'sister born of the same father and the same mother'. The prevalence of sibling unions is also noted in the history of Diodorus of Sicily. The Roman government even took official cognizance of the custom: no. 23 of the previously cited rules of the Privy Purse reads, 'Romans are not permitted to marry their sisters or their aunts, but marriage with brother's daughters has been allowed.' This ban on sibling unions had particular relevance for, and may even have been evoked by, the situation of Egyptian men who attained Roman citizenship through military service. Brother–sister marriage was finally forbidden to all everywhere in the Roman Empire by an imperial edict of AD 295.[9]

The marriage of siblings also had an economic advantage. It kept their two shares of their patrimony together, and in that way many an estate was saved from excessive fragmentation. It is apparent from documents of all kinds that most metropolite families were, at the very least, well-to-do. Practically every metropolite family owned at least one house-property in town and at least one farm in the countryside. They also prospered in various business enterprises, and some amongst them were the possessors of extensive properties and huge fortunes. In one village the estate of a metropolite accounted for some fifteen per cent of the village's total land tax. In a list of plantings from another village, the local farmers are recorded as sowing anywhere from one to a dozen artabas of wheat, while on the lands of several absentee landowners — one of them a Roman citizen, the others metropolites — the plantings amount to twenty-one, thirty-four and, in the case of a group of brothers, 134 artabas. Still another metropolite, we find, owned eighteen farms with a total area of well over a hundred arouras; the size of his operation can be gauged from an account showing that monthly expenditures for purchases and the hire of workmen could run to more than 2,300 drachmas and monthly income to more than 2,700.[10]

Amongst the many other business ventures in which metropolites engaged, moneylending was especially prominent. Out of a plethora of examples we may note a loan of 1,500 drachmas, or another of 6,500; at the legal interest of one per cent per month such principals produced amounts of interest not to be sneezed at — certainly preferable to letting the cash lie about idly. Particularly interesting is a document of AD 186 according to which one member of the gymnasial élite lent another the impressive sum of two talents, i.e. 12,000 drachmas, a sum that could then have bought two smallish river-boats, or five or six slaves; and as the interest on that loan was at only two-thirds the usual rate, we are probably justified in regarding the loan as an accommodation between friends. Another document tells us of a metropolite who was able to obtain from a municipal fund — the very fund that had been established twenty-five years earlier to finance the annual ephebic games — a loan of 12 talents 1,700 drachmas, in other words, 73,700 drachmas; as his credit was good for that huge sum, his tangible assets must obviously have amounted to considerably more than that. Still another business document tells us of one of the gymnasial class who owned a factory employing thirty-six weavers.[11]

In addition to providing for their necessities and creature comforts, the metropolites were able to use their wealth in ways that combined conspicuous consumption with social prestige. Throughout the Roman Empire the favourite form of local philanthropy was to give or embellish a public building or facility — baths, stoas, market-places, and so forth. Inscribed pedestals of statues erected to such donors — the statues themselves in most instances long since vanished — have been found in great numbers all over the Mediterranean world. Many a gift of that kind commemorated its donor's incumbency in a public office. Before the third century the metropoleis of Egypt were not accorded any elements of true self-rule, not even to the limited extent enjoyed by the Jewish communities. The metropolites were, however, accorded the privilege of choosing officers to discharge certain communal functions. They were even allowed to dignify those officers with the title of 'magistrates', and modern writers have tended to use that term as if those communal offices did indeed exercise a governmental authority. It deserves therefore to be emphasized here that until AD 200, when Emperor Septimius Severus did grant the metropoleis certain administrative institutions and responsibilities (to be discussed below), those metropolitan 'magistracies' were not organs of government but rather committees overseeing certain activities in the social and economic life of the community. They were no more true 'magistracies' than the metropoleis were true 'cities', but the metropolites enjoyed the ego-inflation that they derived from both those borrowed terms. In the first and second centuries the strategos and his apparatus exercised the governmental authority over the entire nome, including its capital, the metropolis.

Within the metropolite class those offices created an enclave of enhanced prestige. First, there were the prescribed largesses. The designee to such an office paid an entrance fee on taking up his title and duties, and he defrayed the expenses of the office, in whole or in part, out of his own pocket. Then, too, the whole institution was endued with ceremony and flattering grandiloquence: the offices themselves, for example, bore traditional titles going all the way back to fifth-century Athens, and the initiation ceremony, at which a garland was placed upon the head of the new incumbent, was called a coronation. An invitation to one such celebration was found at Oxyrhynchus:

Eudaimon invites you to dinner in the gymnasium on the occasion of the coronation of his son Nilos, on the first of the month, beginning at the eighth hour [2 p.m.].[12]

After holding one of those offices a man retained for the rest of his life the honorific designation of 'sometime gymnasiarch', 'sometime kosmetes', etc., a custom that we still observe with regard to holders of high public office.

The metropolitan offices were six in number. Five continued their titles from Ptolemaic times, but with duties accommodated where necessary to the conditions of the Roman regime; a sixth, the eutheniarchy, was introduced in the first or second century. The six offices, with their principal duties and distinctions, were:

Gymnasiarch ('gymnasium governor'). He was not so much an administrator as a supplier. He was responsible for the day-to-day operation of the gymnasium, assuring in particular the basic supplies, namely, fuel for the provision of hot water, and oil for anointing and lighting. His insignia of office were a purple headband and distinctive white shoes. On ceremonial occasions he was accompanied by an honour guard of four ephebes.

Kosmetes ('order master'). He supervised the procedures and routines laid down for the training of the young men of the gymnasial élite, that is the ephebes. On ceremonial occasions he was accorded an honour guard of two ephebes.

Exegetes ('director'). He presided over the group of magistrates of the year, a group which by the end of the second century, if not sooner, appears to have been organized into something resembling a corporate entity. His other duties, if any, remain obscure.[13] His honour guard consisted of two ephebes.

Eutheniarch ('food-supply governor'). His function was defined as 'providing food for the city'. In practical terms this meant that he saw to it that the milling of the town's grain and the baking of its bread proceeded with as few hitches as possible. As he had no police powers, however, his principal instrumentalities for preventing strikes and other stoppages were a persuasive tongue and a fat wallet. He was probably also expected, even if not officially required, to contribute out of his own pocket to alleviate shortages of supplies. He also rated an honour guard of two ephebes.

Agoranomos ('market regulator'). Beyond what the title implies we have few details about the duties of this office. In a document of the mid-third century we see an agoranomos leasing out market stalls as agent for the town council. He rated an honour guard of one.

Archiereus ('chief priest'). Despite his lofty title suggestive of high office, he was not the chief of an order of priests. His main function was to carry out the ceremonies prescribed for the cult of the emperors and members of the imperial families. He also rated an honour guard of one.

The above list is arranged in what appears to have been the order of importance or prestige attached to the several offices.

Each year one or (usually) more of each title were elected for a term of one year, a practice which obviously spread the expenses as well as the éclat over a large number of participants. Some volunteered to serve for longer terms, especially in the gymnasiarchy. What remains unclear, however, is precisely who were eligible for election. It may be conjectured from collateral evidence that the offices, or at least the most prestigious ones, were originally reserved for members of the metropolitan élite but were thrown open to all metropolites when, with the passage of time and the impairment of many fortunes, it became increasingly difficult to find enough candidates in the élite group.

There is now abundant evidence showing that, beginning in the latter half of the second century and increasingly thereafter, the matter of the expenses of these offices loomed ever larger as the economy of Egypt (and of the empire as a whole) showed unmistakable signs of slowing down, and the prosperity of many metropolites began to falter. The honorific offices, once so eagerly sought, began to be avoided on one pretext or another, and office-holders had sometimes to be coerced into serving. Various expedients were tried to accommodate the demand for magistrates to the realities of the times. For example, the number of incumbents was increased, so that each would enjoy the honour of the office for the entire year but would be responsible for the expenses of only a single month, or even of a lesser period. In another development, nominees began to bargain over which offices they were prepared to accept. After pleading impoverishment because of previously held offices and asking to be excused this time, a nominee might then offer to compromise by accepting a less expensive office than the one to which he was being named.

In AD 200 the administrative structure of the metropoleis of Egypt underwent an essential change when Septimius Severus ordered the creation of a boule, or town council, in each nome capital. Broadly speaking, this was a step in the direction of upgrading the metropoleis to the status of Roman *municipia*. (The final step was not taken till the fourth century.) For the metropolites, however, this elevation, greeted initially with huzzas, proved before long to be a mixed blessing.

Severus' basic attitudes and policies as emperor, which radically modified and in some respects even reversed those of his predecessors, are usually attributed by historians to the conditioning of his North African upbringing. Whatever the aetiology, there is no doubt that his Principate marked the beginning of an era in which imperial policy displayed far-reaching egalitarian tendencies, advancing the provinces' status toward that previously enjoyed by Italy alone, and benefiting the poor and the humble *vis-à-vis* their 'betters'. The institution of the metropolitan boule is a case in point. It meant, to be sure, an access of honour and prestige both for the metropolis itself and for the metropolites who became councilmen. In the new council and in the traditional magistracies, which were retained, they now exercised responsibility for the day-to-day functioning of their town. The metropolitan boule had, however, no legislative authority. It was a purely administrative body, whose principal duties were to manage and supervise the finances, the public works and the public buildings of the metropolis, and the collection of the state taxes in the whole nome.

By the same token these greater responsibilities entailed greater demands upon the purses of the councilmen and magistrates, and as the third century wore on their shrinking affluence finally impelled them to abandon their exclusiveness and look for outside help. A papyrus in the British Library reveals how in the middle of the century the magistrates of Arsinoë tried, unsuccessfully, to ease the burden of the metropolites by calling upon men of sufficient means in the villages of the nome to fill some of the metropolitan posts. The villagers, hitherto the objects of the metropolites' scorn, naturally resisted this raid on their pocket-books. Involving as it did an interpretation of governmental policy, the dispute came before the prefect of Egypt. At one point in the hearing a counsel for the villagers says, 'I will read the law of the Emperor Severus to the effect that villagers must not be drafted for the metropolitan services. . . . And after Severus all the prefects of Egypt have ruled accordingly.' To which one of the opposing counsel replies, addressing the prefect, 'Laws are indeed to be esteemed and reverenced, but in judging this case you must take into consideration how [previous] prefects have been influenced by the needs of the towns. . . . You are sitting in judgement on the metropolites of Arsinoë, formerly a numerous and flourishing body of men, but now they are plunged completely into ruin if they hold a metropolitan magistracy for so much as two days.' A little further along the prefect asks another lawyer for the towns, 'What do you say to the law of Severus and the decisions of the prefects?' He answers ' 'Severus promulgated his law in Egypt when the towns were still prosperous.' Whereupon the prefect observes, 'The argument of prosperity, or of change from prosperity, is the same for the villages and the towns.' The papyrus is tattered and the prefect's final ruling in the case is not preserved, but it is already clear that he will rule for the villagers when he adds, 'The force of the laws increases [rather than the opposite] with the passage of time.' After half a century the legislation promulgated by Septimius Severus was still protecting the Egyptian peasantry against at least some administrative abuses by the metropolites.[14]

A member of the boule was called bouleutes (plural, bouleutai). We encounter bouleutai in scores of extant papyri and we even know several dozen of them by name, but we still do not know how a man was named to the boule, or what the qualifications were for membership. We do know that once admitted a man was styled bouleutes for the rest of his life, but that does not necessarily imply a lifetime of service in the council. It seems likelier by far that, as in the case of the magistracies, the title was retained as a lifetime honorific once a councilman had served a tour of active duty. He might, of course, serve more than one term.

It is logical to suppose that the bouleutai were chosen from the élite class of the metropolis. But was the boule made up of them alone, or were all male metropolites eligible? And how many members did the boule have? These, too, are questions to which we have no answers.

Like the magistrates in towns throughout the Roman Empire, the councilmen paid a 'fee for the honour' on entering office. A recently published papyrus of AD 233 has disclosed that the bouleutic fee at Oxyrhynchus was 10,000 drachmas or more, a sum which in those days would have bought half a dozen unpretentious town houses or paid the hire of twenty farm labourers for a year. Obviously, only a man of considerable means could afford to be a councilman.

It is time to turn from the public life of our local gentry to look at the patterns of their private lives and daily rounds. There too, as in their expenditures on public office, an air of affluence emanates from the pertinent documents – at least before the middle of the third century. Take, for example, the houses they lived in. The documents tell us that town houses were usually two- and even three-storeyed. They tell of houses with separate wings or drawing-rooms for men and women, they mention porticoed entrances, loggias, and exedras for taking the winter sun or enjoying the respite of a summer evening, they call our attention to towers and penthouses and various other features designed for comfort or elegance. Some houses did double duty by using rooms on the street as shops, an arrangement familiar to us today from the ruins of Pompeii and Herculaneum; a recently published papyrus from Arsinoë is an offer to rent a corner house that has three shops in front and two on the side street. [15]

Dimensions are rarely given in the documents, neither for individual rooms nor for houses as a whole, but we do find mention at Oxyrhynchus of a house as small as fifteen square metres and, at the other extreme, one that covered a surface area of over a hundred square metres. House walls were made of the basic building material used in Egypt from time immemorial, sun-dried mud brick. With no significant amounts of rainfall to cause their deterioration, structures made of such material could last indefinitely. Outer walls were usually several brick-courses thick; for inner walls two courses were generally regarded as sufficient. Interior wall surfaces were plastered, and frequently decorated in bright colours, with mythological and religious scenes the great favourites. Stone, available from numerous quarries in Egypt but expensive in comparison with mud brick, was used sparingly in private houses, mostly for thresholds and the lintels of entrance doorways. When a rich Oxyrhynchite speaks of his 'stone house', the reference is probably to a house whose outer walls were made elegant with a stone facing, rather than to a house built entirely of stone.[16]

A town house of any size or elegance would have its own private water supply from a well sunk in the courtyard. As sun-dried brick would simply dissolve in the water, the well would be built of stone or, more often, of fired brick with or without a stone facing.

The living and sleeping quarters were normally on the ground floor. The cellars, often of vaulted construction, served principally for storage, as did also some of the upstairs rooms. A papyrus of *c*. AD 200 contains the following inventory.

List of household goods.

In the cellar: basin, bronze, 1; tankard, tin, 1; cup, tin, 1; wooden measure, ironclad, 1; small washtub, 1; lampstand, bronze, with shade, 1.

In the storerooms: small dish, tin, 1; cups and saucers, tin, 3; small lamp, bronze, 1; cloak, gold-coloured, 1; counterpane, ditto, 1.

In the upper rooms: kettle, bronze, 1; cup, tin, 1; saucepan, bronze, 1; small colander, bronze, 1; mixing bowls, 2; pruning knives, 3; dish, tin, 1; pitcher, bronze, 1; measure, bronze, 1; wooden measures, ironclad, 2; cloaks, gold-coloured, 3; large counterpane, linen, 1; pillows, green, 2; counterpane, coloured, 1; mattresses, stuffed, 2; bedcover, 1; couch, 1; chest, 1; small container(?), bronze, 1.[17]

The items in the above list were probably extras, or spares, of utensils and furnishings that were in active use in the ground-floor rooms. The chest, couch, and other items towards the end of the list sound very much as if there was a guest bedroom upstairs. Clothing, almost totally absent from the list, was presumably kept in the living-rooms and bedrooms of the ground floor. The four cloaks in the storerooms were presumably heavy overgarments put away till the following winter.

What did our gentry wear in the way of clothing? The sandals and shoes on their feet might be made of anything from papyrus rind to leather, and would be likely to be decorated with beads or other bright objects or colours. The garments on their bodies also showed a marked preference for colour, especially greens, reds, and — the apparent favourite — all shades of blue. The tunics worn next to the body were usually made of linen, the outer garments of linen or wool. It was thought till fairly recently that cotton was introduced from India much later than the Roman era, but three papyri in the Michigan collection have produced the evidence that cotton was not only used but even grown in Egypt at least as early as the second century. Silk fabrics, mostly of Chinese manufacture along with some of Indian origin and possibly some from Persia (surely a souce in later centuries), were imported for use as decorative effects, such as collars and borders, in the garments of the affluent.[18]

Information about the size of families occurs in a variety of contexts, most particularly in wills and inheritances, divisions of property *inter vivos*, and the census declarations that every householder was required to file every fourteen years. The metropolitan households that we encounter in the papyri contain as many as five children, with two or three the average number. The actual birth-rate was obviously much higher than those figures would imply, for the numbers must be increased — though we cannot tell by just how much — to allow, first, for an extremely high rate of infant mortality, which prevailed all through antiquity; second, for the Greek custom of exposing unwanted neonates to die; and third, for the fact that census declarations do not include grown children who have left the household. On the other hand, the household often included one or more married children with their spouses and offspring; in some we also find a parent or collateral relation; and most have a slave or two, with every fourth metropolitan household in the extant documents showing two or more. In one such 'extended family' we find a husband aged 50 and his wife-sister aged 54; their four sons aged 29 to 9 and a daughter aged 7; the wife of the eldest son and their 1-year-old twin sons; the wife of the second son and their two sons, ages illegible; three nephews aged 34 to 19; the eldest nephew's wife with their 1-year-old daughter; a 44 year-old man, presumably this baby's maternal grandfather, with his 52-year-old wife-sister and their 8-year-old son; three brothers, aged 52 to 26, of the second son's wife, and the wife-sister, aged 23, of the youngest of these three brothers. All these people, seventeen adults and seven children, are declared to be living in one-tenth of a town house![19]

All through antiquity life expectancy at birth averaged about twenty-five to thirty years. If those figures seem unrealistically low to us, it must be remembered that the high infant mortality rate is averaged in. Recent analyses and computer projections of data from Roman Egypt show that from adolescence onward the survivors were halved every ten years of life, that is of all persons reaching the age of fifteen only half would survive to be twenty-five, and only one-fourth would live to be thirty-five. These data go far toward explaining why we find in Roman Egypt so many widowed households, second marriages, and half-brothers and -sisters.

In only two of the dozens of extant census declarations does a metropolitan family have more daughters than sons (and then only one and two more, respectively). A Greek custom which the metropolites continued was that of discarding unwanted neonates with the rest of their refuse. Egyptians, whose religion forbade infanticide, often rescued babies left thus to die. The law allowed them to adopt foundlings or raise them as slaves. The origin of such children was often memorialized in the names they were given, Kopreus and its many variants, meaning 'off the dunghill'. In a letter written on 17 June in the year 1 BC and much quoted since its publication in 1904, a man named Hilarion, on business in Alexandria, writes to his wife-sister, Alis:

> Know that I am still in Alexandria. And do not worry if they all come back and I remain in Alexandria. I ask and beg you to take good care of our baby son, and as soon as I receive payment I will send it up to you. If you are delivered of child [before I get home], if it is a boy keep it, if a girl discard it. You have sent me word, 'Don't forget me.' How can I forget you? I beg you not to worry.

That casual, matter-of-fact Greek attitude toward the exposure of newborn infants is strikingly illustrated also by an agreement drawn up in Alexandria in the year 8 BC. In it a young woman, recently widowed after only a year and a half of marriage, acknowledges that she has received back from her mother-in-law the dowry which she had brought to her late husband, and she reciprocally renounces all claims upon his estate, including the following language: 'although she is pregnant, she will make no claim regarding [the expense of] her childbed, since she has been satisfied [monetarily] for that, but she retains the right to expose the infant and to unite herself to another man.'[20]

It must not be thought that only female neonates were exposed to die, but all the evidence indicates that they suffered that fate much more often than did male infants. The major consideration that made daughters less desirable additions to families than sons was, of course, the need eventually to provide them with dowries. For an affluent family, however, the bestowal of a rich dowry was a form of social éclat. In AD 127, for example, one bride's parents sent her off with an elegant trousseau consisting of a pair of ear-rings weighing 3 minas 14½ quarters, a brooch of 8 quarters, plus other jewellery making a total weight of 5 minas; also two dresses (one red the other rose-coloured), a robe, and a mantle, together worth 560 silver drachmas (about five times what such garments would be worth if plain and ordinary); and 1,800 drachmas in cash, making a dowry with a stated total value of 4,100 drachmas.

Most young men were married by the age of eighteen or twenty. Their brides were usually some years younger; and many girls were already married and mothers at fifteen or sixteen. A marriage contract, as extant examples reveal, usually included the pious wish that the couple might 'live together blamelessly, observing the duties of marriage, the husband supplying his wife with the necessities of life according to his means.' In the urban Greek milieu the reciprocal duties of the spouses were often spelled out in greater detail, as follows:

he shall not ill-treat her nor cast her out nor insult her nor bring another woman into the house, or else he shall straightway pay the value of the dowry increased by half; she shall fulfil her duties to her husband and to their common life, and shall not spend a night or a day away from the house without permission, nor dishonour nor injure their common home, nor have dealings with another man, or else, if tried and found guilty of any of those offences, she shall be deprived of the amount of the dowry.[21]

Divorce appears to have been both easy and frequent, and especially frequent — then as now — in the more youthful marriages. When a union ended in divorce the husband was obligated to give back all the objects of the dowry and the accompanying gifts (if any), or else to pay back their value in money. But, then as now, divorce was not always by mutual accord. The following somewhat enigmatic letter is probably best understood as the plea of a husband eager to take back the wife who has left him; Kolobos ('bobtail') may be the name of the man she ran off with.

Serenus to Isidora, his sister and wife, very many greetings. Before all else I pray that you are well, and every morning and evening I do obeisance in your name before [the goddess] Thoëris, who loves you. I want you to know that ever since you left me I have been in mourning, weeping at night and lamenting by day. After I bathed with you on Phaophi 12th I had neither bath nor oil-rub till Hathyr 12th [thirty days later], when I received from you a letter that can shatter a rock, so much did your words upset me. I wrote you back on the instant, and sent it on the 12th with your letter enclosed. You say in your letter, 'Kolobos has made me into a prostitute', but he told me, 'Your wife sends you this message: "[Remind him] it was he himself who sold my necklace, and it was he himself who put me on the boat."' You're just saying that so people won't believe my rebuttal. But look, I keep writing you and writing you. Are you coming [back] or not coming? Tell me that.[22]

A marriage might also be terminated by action of the woman's father, who had the legal right, traceable in its origin to the law of classical Athens, to remove his married daughter from her husband even against her will, and thereafter to give her in marriage to another. But in the centuries of Roman rule in Egypt the 'inhumanity of the law', as it was characterized in a test case, was attenuated on humanitarian grounds. In that case, which was decided in AD 186 after dragging on through legal skirmishing for the better part of two years, the daughter, resisting her father's orders to leave her husband, cited the following precedents. In AD 128 the then prefect of Egypt laid down a new deciding factor: 'It matters with whom the married woman wishes to live'. In another such case five years later, an epistrategos, citing that prefectural ruling, 'ordered that the woman be asked what her wish was. She replied, "To remain with my husband", and he so ordered.' And a year or two after that a legal expert in an advisory opinion to a lower court went so far as to state flatly that the woman, 'having been given away in marriage by her father, is no longer in her father's power'.[23]

The 'typical' metropolite household consisted of parents, children, possibily some collateral relations — and slaves. Most households, it seems, had at least a slave or two, and many had more. On the other hand, the ownership of very large numbers of slaves was exceptional; we recently learned, for example, of a family of Alexandrian notables, elevated to Roman citizenship, where the father and three sons together owned something like a hundred slaves.[24]

Most slaves, it is clear, were employed in domestic service or trained in income-producing skills (ch. 7). The relative absence of slaves in agricultural production — a feature common to almost all ancient societies — resulted in part from the fact that the free peasantry, most of whom lived at a level of bare subsistence, offered the farm operator a ready source of seasonal labour that was palpably cheaper than that of slaves, who required both an initial outlay of capital and year-round maintenance. The other major factor was that, unlike Italy and north Africa with their plains and prairies, the narrow Nile valley, a fertile river bottom hemmed in on both sides by deserts, simply did not offer the broad expanses conducive to the rise of latifundia that could be exploited economically with slave labour. Some sizeable estates — other than the emperor's — did develop in the third and later centuries, but during the Principate the dominant pattern in Egypt was one of small, even tiny, units cultivated by owners or tenants (chs. 4 and 6).

On the source as well as the utilization of slaves the evidence from Egypt is illustrative of conditions prevailing throughout the empire. In the second century BC Rome's expansionist wars had dumped captives by the tens of thousands into the slave-markets. When adult slaves could be had so cheaply, slave-owners saw little inducement to rear slave offspring. With the mortality rate so high in the early years, the child might easily die before reaching an age at which his labour could bring the owner some return on his investment. In the first two centuries AD, however, foreign wars were fewer, and the numbers of war captives available for purchase fell sharply. In consequence, slave-owners turned to encouraging slaves to bear children, and the specification that a slave was 'houseborn', or 'native', begins to appear in the papyri. Prospective buyers might find that designation reassuring as to a slave's durability under local conditions, in contrast to an imported slave whose origins and previous history could not be verified. There is no evidence to tell us whether the native slave would in fact fetch a higher price, but a curiously worded provision in the code of regulations administered under the Privy Purse appears to ban their export from Egypt.

Small numbers of slaves continued at all times to be imported into Egypt from elsewhere in the empire and from regions beyond the frontiers. Among the places mentioned in the papyri are Thrace, Phrygia, Osrhoenia, Galatia, Lycia, Pamphylia, Arabia, Ethiopia, and Mauretania. Also, as already mentioned, abandoned infants could be picked up 'off the dunghill' and raised as slaves. The Roman government in fact encouraged the raising of such foundlings as slaves by penalizing their adoption as sons or daughters of the rescuers. As stated in section 41 of the rules of the Privy Purse, 'If an Egyptian rears a child that has been exposed on a dunghill and adopts it, a fourth of his estate is confiscated at death.'

The ethic that informed the metropolites' treatment of their slaves resembles what we call *noblesse oblige*. It is clear from the extant documents that many slaves were taught to read and write, in numbers that bespeak something more than mere mercenary motives on the part of their masters. Three or four generations of slaves in the service of the same family also testify to conditions of humane treatment, whose culminating manifestation, of course, was the grant of freedom. Manumission was often ordered by the owner in his or her last will and testament, as a reward for a lifetime of faithful service. In a will drawn up in AD 156, for example, the testator grants freedom upon his death to four slaves 'for their goodwill and affection', and leaves to his heirs 'my other slaves and any offspring they may hereafter produce'. Often, too, slaves would be freed during their owner's lifetime, and some slaves, those with employable skills, were able to purchase their freedom with savings from the portion of their earnings that their masters allowed them to keep. The grant or purchase of freedom through the agency of a temple, under the aegis of its god or gods, was a common practice.[25]

To conclude this chapter, let us address ourselves to the following question: What do the papyri tell us about the level of literacy of metropolite society? One kind of evidence comes from literary papyri. A glance at a list of the surviving texts suffices to reveal that the works of all the major, and of many minor, Greek authors continued to be copied and recopied in Egypt all through the centuries of Roman rule, and for several centuries thereafter. Obviously there was a clientele ready to buy such books, or to borrow them and have copies made for their own libraries. Homer, referred to by Greeks throughout antiquity as 'The Poet', was far and away the all-time favourite, both for adult reading and in the schoolroom. To date there have been published some seven hundred papyri and ostraca bearing Homeric texts, ranging from single or several verses, quoted in one context or another, to whole books, especially of the *Iliad*. Next in frequency are Demosthenes, Euripides, and Hesiod, each with close to a hundred surviving fragments.

The evidence from provenience is also significant. While the papyri found at villages such as Tebtynis and Karanis do include some bits of literature, the overwhelming preponderance of literary and Biblical finds comes from the ruins and refuse heaps of the towns. There is little hope of making such discoveries in or near Alexandria: aside from the destruction of ancient objects wrought by the normal wear and tear of the continuous occupation of a site, the papyri committed to the soil of the Delta region, with the exception of some dozens found preserved in a carbonized state, have long since rotted away in the damp. At Antinoopolis, an expedition in the winter of 1913-14 unearthed 206 Greek papyri, of which 148 are literary or technical (medicine, astrology, etc.) in content. Panopolis, a nome capital in Upper Egypt, is very probably the source of our only completely preserved comedy of Menander and of major portions of three of his other plays, as well as the source of the oldest papyrus codices of New Testament books and other Christian writings, the earliest of them dating from *c.* AD 200. But far and away the richest source of papyri of all types has been Oxyrhynchus. The excavations conducted there at the turn of the century and subsequently have yielded up an opulent treasure that includes what appear to be the remains of at least two private libraries. Hundreds of literary texts from Oxyrhynchus, some known and some new, have already been published, with hundreds more still to come.

Occasionally a document will give us a glimpse of how bibliophiles in the metropoleis went about building up their private libraries through buying, borrowing, and copying. One such papyrus records a payment to a scribe for making a copy of Aristophanes' *Plutus* and Sophocles' *Third Thyestes*. Another tells of a son in Alexandria shipping boxes of books to his father in Oxyrhynchus. In still another we read the following postscript to a letter:

Make and send me copies of Hypsikrates' *Butts of Comedy*, Books 6-7. Harpokration says they are among Polio's books (but it is likely that others too have acquired them), and he also has the prose epitomes of Thersagoras' *The Myths of Tragedy*.

A second postscript adds:

According to Harpokration, Demetrios the bookseller has them. I have written Apollonides to send me some of my own books, which you will presently be shown by Seleukos himself. If you find any beyond what I already own, make copies and send me them. Diodoros and his friends also have some I don't own.

Commentators have suggested the possibility — unfortunately not provable — that the first-named collector in the above letter was the Valerius Pollio of Alexandria who is known to have compiled an Attic lexicon and to have had a son named Diodoros.

Two other papyri, one in Florence the other in Milan, are specially interesting with respect to books and collectors. The first was used originally to record the taxes on some parcels of land. When that record was no longer needed, an Oxyrhynchite, perhaps a dealer in books, wrote on the back a list of books that he apparently was instructing someone to buy. He wanted twenty of Plato's dialogues, which he listed by title, four works by Xenophon, and 'all you can find' of Homer, Menander, Euripides, and Aristophanes. In the second papyrus the writer tells of receiving the following 'edifying' books from Alexandria: Boethos, *On Training*, Books 3–4, Diogenes, *On Marriage, On Freedom from Pain, On the Uses of Parents, On the Uses of Domestic Slaves,* Books 1–2, Poseidonios, *On Persuasion*, Book 3.[26]

No doubt a certain element of ostentation, then as now, entered into the accumulation of specially big or specially choice libraries, yet the overriding impression we receive is that books were sought essentially to be read and reread. The metropolites' devotion to classical tradition included the performance of both classics and new compositions in stage festivals and prize competitions. A recently published fragment of Euripides, dating from the third century AD, contains marginal instructions for the actors. An account of more or less the same period shows payments of 496 drachmas to an actor and 448 drachmas to a reciter of Homer — impressive sums in a time when a skilled labourer, such as a mason, might expect to earn four drachmas a day.[27]

It is interesting, too, that several writers, of varying degrees of note, were born in the cities and metropoleis of Egypt. They included Athenaeus, that indefatigable collector of miscellanies, who was born in Naukratis, and the great neo-Platonist philosopher Plotinus, born into a Roman family residing at Lykopolis, in Upper Egypt. To be sure, these writers left home to pursue their careers in Alexandria and Rome, but their birthplaces, in which their formative years were spent, can hardly have been cultural wastelands.

One other element of the literary scene that deserves mention is the presence of Latin authors in the papyri. The number of Latin manuscripts is very small, and most of them date from after the third century, following the universal grant of Roman citizenship. One interesting result was the creation of a market for bilingual glossaries, aids for the Greek-speaking in coping with Latin texts.

All these evidences of literary activity and receptivity evoke the picture of a society made up of people who, generally speaking, could read and write. (Whether this was true of the women as well as the men is a question we shall look into below.) In this respect, too, the metropolites could liken themselves to the citizens of classical Athens.[28]

But the literary papyri are not the only, or even the best, evidence on the literacy of the metropolites. The best evidence is found in the non-literary papyri, the documents of everyday life. In contracts, wills, and all sorts of other papers, when an individual had not the ability to sign his name someone else signed for him or her and added, 'I, So-and-so, have written for him (her) because (s)he is illiterate.' Some thirty years ago, when a count was made, there were found in the published papyri of the first three centuries some six hundred such illiterates, of whom only three were metropolites; and those three occur in documents of the third century, when, as already mentioned, many metropolitan families were no longer prosperous and might forgo the education that had earlier been *de rigueur* in that social circle. In fact, more and more metropolite families ceased to set themselves so completely apart from their Egyptian townspeople, and intermarriages, hitherto unthinkable, began to take place. The trend is highlighted for us by an application, recently published, to enrol in the gymnasial élite of Oxyrhynchus a boy born *c*. AD 260. In the recitation of his pedigree there is the striking detail that his forebears, all five generations of them, all had Greek names, but the boy bears an Egyptian name, Patermouthis.[29]

Even so, those three illiterate metropolite men were clearly exceptional. Even in those less prosperous times the metropolitan class as a whole sent its sons to school. With regard to daughters the decision to educate or not appears to have been a personal one resting with the parents, rather than a social dictate. Half a dozen letters of the early second century tell us about the daughter of a nome strategos who was at school away from home. But at the opposite extreme we find, in a document of AD 151, a member of the 'colonist' élite of Arsinoë signing for his sister, who is illiterate. A woman who was able to write was proud of it and would often seize the opportunity to state the fact, whether it was germane to the situation or not. Here, in AD 263, is a woman named Aureila Thaisous also known as Lolliane, petitioning the prefect of Egypt to be awarded a status for which literacy was not a requirement:

women honoured with the three-children privilege are given the right to act independently and to negotiate without a male legal representative in any business they transact, all the more so women who know how to write. Therefore, as I am blessed with the honour of many children and am able, being literate, to write with complete ease, I appeal to your Highness [etc.].[30]

In the metropoleis, and even in some of the larger villages, there was no lack of teachers of the rudiments of Greek. Some of them were slaves, some women. Schooling appears to have begun at about the age of ten. We encounter a nine-year-old who cannot sign his name to the document establishing his inheritance, and a fourteen-year-old of the gymnasial élite who is learning to read and write. In a census return of AD 216 a father lists two sons, aged thirteen and ten, adding after the name of each that he is 'learning his letters'.[31]

Local schooling would teach the student to read and write, and would introduce him to the riches of the Greek classics. Education beyond that level would require a period of study in Alexandria, and many a scion of a metropolite family was sent to acquire that prestigious final polish, usually accompanied by a slave or two to see to his personal needs and comfort. But often the eagerly anticipated Alexandrian experience proved to be something of a let-down, as the young men discovered that in grim reality the great city along with its great reputation had its share of mediocrities and charlatans. Some time in the first century one such young man wrote home expressing his hope

that I may soon find a tutor, now that I have rejected Theon. Yes, I too have formed a low opinion of him because he is so irresponsible by nature. When I informed Philoxemos of your opinion he agreed, saying that the city suffered from a shortage of professors, but that Didymos, who (it appears) is a friend of his, would be sailing down and holding school, and he said that Didymos would be more attentive than the others. He has also persuaded the sons of Apollonios son of Herodes to sign up with Didymos; for since the death of Philologos, whose pupils they used to be, he has till now been looking with them for a more effective tutor. For my part, my prayers would be answered if I could find some worthwhile tutors and never have to lay eyes on Didymos even from a distance. The thing that gets me down is that he's seen fit to enter into competition with the other tutors [here], this man who was nothing but a country schoolmaster. So, realizing that there is no benefit to be had from [any available] tutor, just paying steep fees for nothing, I am relying upon my own devices. Write me quickly what you think. There's Didymos, always ready, as Philoxenos puts it, to give me his time and do everything he can for me. But I'm sure I'll do just fine, the gods willing, just listening to the public lectures, Poseidonios amongst them.

To another such boy a father writes that pressing business will delay his visit till next month, and he adds 'in your pursuit of learning concentrate all your attention on your books, and you will have benefit from them.' Lord Chesterfield would doubtless have phrased it more elegantly, Polonius more pompously and long-windedly, but in the simple sententiousness of that father of eighteen hundred years ago we recognize the timeless concern of parents for the enhancement of their children's lives.[32]

4

THE PEASANT VILLAGES
or
CONTENTED WI' LITTLE, AND
CANTIE WI' MAIR

The peasantry lived clustered together in villages and hamlets, whence they would travel on foot or on donkey back to their fields, which were often considerable distances away. In its physical appearance the village was the metropolis writ small. To the eye of the approaching traveller it first came into view as a congeries of dull, mud-brick walls blending into the landscape. As the traveller drew nearer he would perceive that the walls were those of houses in blocks of contiguous structures separated by narrow streets and alleyways. The best example to be seen today is in the Fayyum, some fifty kilometres south-west of Cairo, where the ruins of ancient Karanis were excavated by the University of Michigan in the years between the two World Wars.

The blown sands of the desert are again reclaiming the houses of 2,000 years ago [wrote a visitor of 1963, and he goes on to describe a typical house] : This house, part of a larger complex, was entered by a flight of three steps up from a narrow passage leading north out of the main street. Its wooden threshold beam was still in place at the house-door, which gave access to two rooms, each about ten by nine feet, with mud floors and plastered walls. No light was admitted to the first room except what came through the door; the sun shines bright in Egypt, and light indoors is avoided as much as possible. . . . The inner room had a niche contrived in its north wall, and a window looking out on the passage. . . . On the street side of the main room, and leading out of it opposite the outer door, was a series of granaries. This latter seems later to have been adapted as a kind of shop, perhaps with a separate opening on the alley. . . . The house had no underground chambers or vaults, as many of the dwellings had, nor was there a court-yard to hold the ovens, the grinding mill, or the animals.[1]

Herodotus, in the fifth century BC, had been struck by the Egyptian farmers' practice of keeping domestic animals inside the house, and had jumped to the conclusion that they were the only people to do so.[2]

For most of the population the village was their home from the cradle to the grave. But farmers who prospered would oftentimes seek social betterment and a more cultured existence by removing their families to the metropoleis. There they could live in the urban-like ambience created by the metropolites and adapt their lives to the ways of metropolite culture, even though they were permanently excluded by their humble birth from admission to that privileged class. We have the informative case of one Sarapion, son of Euty-chides, who, *c.* AD 100, at the age of forty or so, took up residence in Hermopolis with his wife, Selene, their four sons and daughter, and the children's nurse. We know the family and its business activities from an archive of some 150 papyri now scattered via the antiquities market to two museums and five libraries in Europe and the United States. In the toparchy, or country district, nearest the metropolis the family owned farm properties consisting of vineyards and pastures, as well as fields where they grew grain and other crops. Those properties were near enough so that Sarapion and later his sons could exercise personal supervision over the day-to-day operations. Their flocks of sheep and goats numbered over a thousand head, from which they sold off surplusage in lots of one to seven dozen; it has been calculated that this part of their husbandry alone represented a capital of some 15,000 drachmas. As for cultivation, they extended their operations beyond the lands they owned onto nearby parcels leased from others. In one year, the documents show, they harvested a total of 230 arouras (= 156 acres, or 62 hectares), fully twenty to thirty times what a small farmer might be cultivating. In addition, Selene owned, presumably through inheritance, some land in the toparchy to the north; because of the distance from Herm-opolis they preferred to lease out that property to local cultivators, which they were able to do on advantageous terms. Finally, with substantial amounts of cash on hand from all these activities, they were able to place considerable sums at interest, in loans of between one and two hundred drachmas at a time. From all these enterprises the family's wealth kept increasing, but not without exacting a very modern-sounding price from the eldest son: a worrier by nature, he aged prematurely, a hopeless neurotic.[3]

Not every villager who prospered was drawn by the attractions of the metropolis. Many, and presumably most, were content to remain where they were, pillars of local society, living in houses that emulated those of the metropolis in size, décor, and numbers of slaves. Those who wanted to were able to attain respectable levels of education and culture: how else explain the copies of Homer, Hesiod, Euripides, Plato, and other authors found in the ruins of the villages? When they wanted entertainment their wealth enabled them to hire performers from the metropolis.

To Isidora, castanet dancer, from Artemisia, of the village of Theadelphia. I wish to hire you with two other castanet dancers to perform at my house on six days from the 24th of the month Payni by the old reckoning. As your pay you will receive 36 drachmas a day, and for the whole time 4 artabas of barley and 20 double loaves of bread. Whatever garments and gold ornaments you bring along we will keep safe, and we will provide you with two donkeys for your trip down [from the metropolis] and the same for your trip back. [Date, 11 June AD 206.][4]

In the total village population, however, such men and women of affluence and influence were relatively few in number. The overall aspect of the village was one of a teeming populace, many of them living just above subsistence level. Men, women, children, and domestic animals huddled all together in cramped and crowded quarters. How crowded is suggested by the many documents recording sales of small fractions of houses, four-fifths of one sixth in one case, and in others a tenth, a twenty-fourth, and even a forty-second part. Even in town we found seventeen adults and seven children living together in a tenth of a house.

How many people lived in a 'typical' village? That is the kind of question which, lacking statistical data, we can never answer with anything approaching precision. The best we can do is to hazard some informed guesses based on such clues as do appear. In AD 94 a village whose name is lost numbered

636 men subject to poll tax, that is men between the ages of fourteen and sixty; this suggests a total population of some three thousand. In the tax registers of Karanis for the years 172-3, the adult tax-paying males number about a thousand, which extrapolates to a total village population of between four and six thousand souls. Comparable, if less extensive, data for nearby Philadelphia point to a population in the first century of perhaps a thousand less than Karanis. At the opposite extreme from such large villages were the numerous tiny hamlets. We hear of one whose inhabitants fled, probably because of the plague that raged for several years during the reign of Marcus Aurelius, so that the number of men fell from twenty-seven to three and then to zero; in another the number fell from fifty-four to four and then to zero.[5]

How well fed was the 'average' villager? As in most agricultural societies, the diet was preponderantly one of carbohydrates, consisting mainly of the cereals and legumes that the farmers themselves grew. In addition, the wild growths of the Nile-fed marshes were a year-round source of many edibles, 'a refuge from want for the poor', in the words of Diodorus of Sicily. The marsh 'crops' included the lotus, the meal of which was made into a kind of bread, and various berries which could serve as nibbles and desserts. The stalk of the ubiquitous papyrus plant, too, was eaten, boiled or baked, or munched raw for its juice (then they spat out the pulp, even as Egyptians do today with sugar-cane or Chinese with bamboo shoots). Chickens and meat from domesticated animals provided supplements of protein and fat, as well as variety, on the tables of those who raised them or could afford to buy them. There are some mentions of milk, more of cheese. Fish seem to have been plentiful in the river, lakes, and artificial ponds, and wild fowl as well as fish in the marshes. There were almost always fees to be paid for the right to catch these, but poaching was not uncommon. A papyrus of AD 31 reports that fish to the value of 6,000 drachmas were stolen from a privately owned pond. Another, of AD 161, shows three men paying 180 drachmas for the exclusive rights to the fish in a group of such ponds for a period of seven months. Legally or illegally, there was clearly money to be made by dealing in fish. We learn from the relevant documents that some of the fish was eaten fresh and the rest preserved for future use by drying or pickling. For beverages, finally, there were grape wine and a beer made from barley.[6]

As to the quantities of food consumed, we read in one farm account that the hired hands were paid their wages in the form of two loaves of bread a day, i.e. roughly half a kilogram per person. A study of other such data reveals individual rations varying — with ages, status, etc. — from the equivalent of about 1,200 to about 5,000 calories a day. Today we consider that a man weighing fifty kilograms and engaged in the strenuous physical activity of farm labour requires a balanced diet of 2,200 calories as an absolute minimum for continued good health. Presumably many Egyptian peasants weighed fifty kilograms or more, but whether they managed to consume 2,200 calories a day every day, and in a balanced diet, is, to say the least, doubtful.[7]

What did villagers wear in the way of clothing? Like most farm populations, they had — those who could afford it — one set of 'good' clothes to be worn on ceremonial occasions. On ordinary workdays they covered themselves in commonplace versions of the shifts and cloaks that the townspeople wore. But, unlike the townspeople, the villagers went about barefoot most of the time. One result of that was a high incidence of foot ailments.

Tebtynis, a village at the southern edge of the Arsinoite nome, has been one of the most prolific sources of Greek papyri. One of the Tebtynis finds, now at the State University in Milan, includes a group of sixty-nine documents relating to one Kronion and his family in the years AD 107–53. A papyrus of AD 35 in the University of Michigan turns out to relate to Kronion's father. As this is our best-documented village family of modest means, it will be rewarding to look into this Kronion 'archive' in some detail.

Here, first, is the family tree:

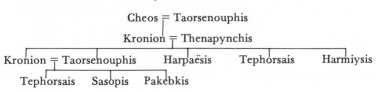

Cheos' mother was Thaësis, daughter of Psosneus. She was born in 5 BC, and was only fifteen years old when she bore Cheos (whether she produced any other children we do not know). Cheos was fifty-three when his son Kronion was born, not an unusual phenomenon in Egypt: elsewhere a man of sixty-nine and his second wife, aged fifty-two, are recorded as having a three-year-old son. Kronion's marriage to Thenapynchis produced five children — five, at all events, who survived to figure in the archive — three sons and two daughters. The first child was born when Kronion was nineteen and his wife fifteen. The four other children were born over a period of more than twenty years. This too was not uncommon. The recently published papers of one Soterichos, who lived in the village of Theadelphia in the first century, show a similar pattern. His wife bore their first son at the age of fifteen, their last child when she was forty-three. As their society knew neither incentive for, nor effective methods of, controlling the frequency of childbirth, it seems a foregone conclusion that the intervening twenty-eight years were punctuated with still births or live births followed by early death. Another woman who bore children over a span of twenty-eight years appears in the census declaration on p. 158.[8]

To return to Kronion and his family, his two eldest children entered into an endogamous marriage, Kronion jun., the first born, taking to wife Taorsenouphis, who was four years younger than himself. There is no information in the archive about where or how the family lived, other than that it was in the village of Tebtynis or its outskirts. There is a receipt attesting that in the year AD 114 Kronion paid twenty-eight drachmas toward the rental of a house, from which it would appear that even at the age of fifty he did not own a dwelling. Other documents of the period indicate that twenty-eight drachmas may well have paid an entire year's rental; but if so the house could not have been very big, and if it housed the whole family they were obviously living in one another's pockets. But such crowding, as we saw in Chapter 3, was hardly unusual.

They did own some land. Over the years Taorsenouphis managed to acquire — with saved-up pin money? — a parcel of four arouras, bringing the family holdings to a total of seventeen arouras (= 11.5 acres, or 4.5 hectares). But the family would have starved on the product of so small a farm, and they therefore cultivated additional parcels which they leased. The family's mainstay, in fact, was a farm of twenty-five arouras that they leased from its absentee owner continuously for forty years or more. To operate that farm meant they had to travel ten kilometres or more from Tebtynis and back again; it must have been an exceptionally fertile piece of land, or else they were able to have it on very favourable terms, for them to want it year after year in spite of the distance involved. In addition to those twenty-five arouras from time to time they took leases on other, smaller plots of from two and a half to twelve arouras.

Except for the affluent few, life in the Egyptian village clung in its fundamentals to the traditional practices of a natural, or barter, economy. For the taxes and certain other obligations that were payable in specie, Kronion and his likes were chronically short of cash and constantly going into short-term debt. It is thus no accident that nineteen of the sixty-nine documents of the Kronion archive relate to loans taken from one or another of the local well-to-do, loans ranging in amount from fifty-four to 373 drachmas. There are also loans in kind of twenty, forty, and fifty artabas of grain; such loans were normally repayable at harvest time with interest of fifty per cent.[9]

Through all of the above activities and devices the family of Kronion was able to live at a level somewhere between abject poverty and easy circumstances — a level that, for instance, required the men of the family to perform some of the lesser, least expensive public services of the village, an obligation not imposed upon the poorest stratum of the population (ch. 8).

As might be expected, the archive also gives us some glimpses of the personal lives of the members of the family. We discover that after producing three children and remaining married for more than thirty years, Kronion jun. and Taorsenouphis were divorced. The divorce contract, which is recited below, mentions that the marriage had been contracted without the formality of a written document — an Egyptian

custom rather like our common-law marriage. It is understandable that a sibling union could readily dispense with the
usual contractual provisions regarding dowry and such, but in
practice even endogamous marriages were usually solemnized
with marriage lines.

On 13 June of AD 138 Kronion made the following
division of his property.

[Date], in Tebtynis in the Polemon division of the Arsinoite nome.
Kronion son of Cheos (son of Harmiysis) and of Taorsenouphis, of the
village of Tebtynis, about seventy-five years old, with a scar on his
right hand, acknowledges that [to take effect] after his death he has
conveyed to his children born of his late wife, Thenapynchis daughter
of Patynis, namely to his sons Harmiysis and Harphaësis, and also to
Tephorsais, a minor, the daughter of other children, Kronion jun. and
Taorsenouphis, to the three as heirs, all that he, Kronion sen., may
leave behind, viz. belongings of every kind, furniture, implements,
household goods, etc., and all debts owing to him and anything else
of whatever kind, to each of them an equal third, and to Kronion's
other children, Kronion [jun.], Taorsenouphis and Tephorsais, as
follows: to Kronion [jun.] he assigns only forty drachmas of silver
because Kronion the father, as he declares, has suffered many wrongs
at his hands in the course of his life; and to his two daughters, Taorsenouphis and Tephorsais, aside from the gold and silver ornaments and
the clothing that he affirms he has bestowed upon them [to keep as
their own] he makes a present of a hundred(?) drachmas of silver
each. The three heirs, Harmiysis, Harphaësis and his granddaughter
Tephorsais, a minor, shall see to the funeral and burial of the declarant
Kronion, and to the payment of the aforesaid legacies and of any
private or public debts that may appear. But for as long as he shall
live the declarant Kronion is to have complete control of his affairs,
to manage as he chooses. [Signatures and seals of Kronion (who is
illiterate — someone writes for him), and of the requisite six witnesses.
Notation of the record office of Tebtynis.] [10]

There is in the above document something touching, even
poignant, in the reference to the wrongs perpetrated by
Kronion jun. They are alluded to in justification of his being
'cut off with a shilling,' but they are carefully not detailed.
To have included the bill of particulars would have amounted
to washing the family linen in public: the document was
penned by a public scribe in the presence of six witnesses,
and was later to be filed in the local office of records. Those

wrongs had recently come to a head, it would appear, and they were no doubt at the root of the divorce of Kronion jun. and Taorsenouphis, a divorce which was recorded eleven weeks later, on 30 August:

Copy of agreement. [Date], in Tebytnis in the Polemon division of the Arsinoite nome. Kronion son of Kronion, about fifty-four years old, with a scar on his left forearm, and his wife till now, who is also his sister born of the same father and of the same mother, Taorsenouphis, about fifty years old, without distinguishing mark — her legal representative being the father of them both, Kronion son of Cheos, about seventy-six years old, with a scar on his right hand — mutually acknowledge that they have annulled the marriage to each other which they entered into without written document, and that each of them is free to manage his own affairs as he chooses, and Taorsenouphis to marry another man without recrimination in any way. The jewellery — viz., one mina ten quarters' weight of gold and twenty-eight staters' weight of silver, which all the aforementioned parties agree Kronion received from his sister Taorsenouphis and which he turned into cash for his personal use — Kronion is perforce to return that to his sister Taorsenouphis in equivalent jewellery within sixty days from the present day, the said Taorsenouphis retaining the right of legal execution upon her brother Kronion and upon all his possessions. Regarding other matters relating to their marriage they will make no claim against each other on any pretext, and [in particular] Kronion will make no claim of any kind against Taorsenouphis either regarding any property she bought, since she paid the price of same from her own personal funds, or, in short, regarding any other matter, written or unwritten, to the present day. The children born of them both are sons Sasopis and Pakebkis and a daughter Tephorsais.[11]

From another document, dated two months later, we learn that Kronion had been working for some years as the steward of a woman who owned a considerable property in the vicinity. Reading between the lines we catch the hint that a middle-age romance between Kronion jun., now fifty-four, and his employer, aged forty-five, was at the root of the family's emotional distress.

Let us leave the family of Kronion to their joys and sorrows as we turn now to consider other elements of village life. Individuals, such as those from whom Kronion leased some of the fields he cultivated, owned all together only a small portion of the arable soil. Temples continued to own some land, their once vast holdings having been severely reduced by Augustus. The most extensive lands, in all categories of fertility and productivity, belonged either to the state or personally to the emperor. In the first hundred years of Roman rule quite a few members of the imperial family and court, as well as moneyed Alexandrians, found the acquisition of landed estates in Egypt to be highly profitable investments. But before the end of the first century AD those privately owned estates had all passed, by one process or another, into the emperor's possession, where they continued for over a century more to be identified by the name of the former owner, Maecenas, Antonia, Seneca, and so on. The life of the villagers was dominated by the state and imperial lands.

The state lands (officially designated as 'public' or 'royal', the latter term another of the continuations of pre-Roman terminology) were administered under the supervision of officials in the nome capitals and in the localities, by whom they were put up periodically for lease to the highest bidder. Those taking the leases constituted the category of 'public farmers'. They usually cultivated the land themselves, but they could sublet to others if they wished. Before entering upon the lease, however, they were required to provide the state with guarantees for satisfactory performance. Presumably that could take the form of posting a bond, but since few peasants had much in the way of cash the usual practice was to enlist friends as sureties.

Specially appointed stewards were in charge of the operations of the imperial estates. In some instances they would lease portions of the estate, or the rights to certain of its resources, to individual cultivators, who were then identified as 'estate farmers', or 'imperial farmers'. At other times and places the stewards would prefer to employ the system that prevailed on other large imperial estates, notably those in North Africa. In this pattern of exploitation the estate was let in large tracts to a small number of middlemen. These entrepreneurs, being men of substance, afforded the administration a guarantee of prompt payment of the contractual rentals and taxes, and, in turn, they would expect to realize a substantial profit from subleasing their tracts in smaller portions to individual 'estate farmers'. The following example of this type of subcontract was written on 10 October AD 120:

Petechon son of Hareōs to Hermias son of Sabourion, greeting. I hereby have leased from you for only the current 5th year of Hadrian Caesar our lord, for the sowing of vegetable seed, three arouras from the imperial estate land that you hold on lease in the former allotment of Apollonios son of Agathinos, at a rent of three artabas by the oil makers' measure for each aroura that appears on the survey-map of the estate inspector, viz. the parcel that was cultivated in the past 4th year of Hadrian Caesar our lord by Phinion son of Tothes. I will measure out the rent in the month Epeiph, and when you carry away your half from the threshing floor it shall be new, pure, unadulterated, sifted and measured by the seven-*metra* artaba measure of Athena that is used by the estate. You remain responsible for the rental payable to the estate. [Date.] I, Dioskoros son of Didymos, have written for him, who is illiterate.[12]

Furthermore, the state and the emperor as landowners enjoyed certain obvious advantages and powers not available to private proprietors. For one thing, any claims they might have against tenants for default or delay in the payment of rents received priority over all private liens. Then again, almost every year for one reason or another (infertility, remoteness of location, etc.) some fields would still be unleased as the sowing season approached. The private owner might then try to hire someone to cultivate the field for him, or try to attract a tenant by lowering the rental; and if he failed to make some such arrangement, he would have to reconcile himself to seeing the land lie idle that year. But state and imperial lands were immune from such mischance. In such cases the state simply imposed upon the private lands of the vicinity a pro rata obligation to cultivate its idle arouras. This was such a regular practice that conveyances of property made a point of affirming, when they could, that the land was free of such attachments. When very large tracts of state land were involved — known instances range from 210 to 859 arouras (= 584 acres, or 236 hectares) — they would sometimes be imposed in whole or in part upon a neighbouring village or villages, from which the required manpower would then have to be assigned by the local officials. What is more, when the land in question was so far away or so extensive in area that the men assigned could not perform the work of cultivation whilst living at home, the impressed manpower would be transported bodily to the work site and kept there. We have no information about how they were housed, but it seems safe to assume that they were put up either in the farmstead of the estate involved or in requisitioned lodgings near by.

In most known instances (close to fifty were collected in a recent study) the distances between the village of residence and the assigned work site do not exceed ten or twelve kilometres — a distance which, as we saw above, the men of Kronion's family were ready to travel year after year to till a field. But we also find workers from Soknopaiou Nesos at Bakchias, thirty-two kilometres away, and in two instances the distance may have been as much as forty kilometres. Some of the documents also give us information on the numbers of men and arouras involved in assigned cultivation, viz.:

AD	Men	Area cultivated	Distance away (Km)
70	3 public farmers	19 arouras	3 or 4
100–1	2 estate farmers	51 "	3 or 4
141–2	2 public farmers	13 "	6 or 7
153–4	3 public and estate farmers	37 ar. in 4 parcels	5 or 6?
215	21 public farmers	93 arouras	10 or 12?

As for the transfers of whole crews, the fact of such transfers is sufficiently well established, but numerical data are scarce. A document of AD 213–4 tells of sixty men transferred to the village of Mendes, but the record as preserved is incomplete and we cannot tell whence those men were drawn. The clearest instance, contained in a long tax roll of AD 167, concerns a huge total of 2,459 arouras (= 1,572 acres, or 676 hectares) of state and estate land at Ptolemais Nea, of which 859 arouras — more than one-third the total — were assigned to Karanis for cultivation, and the rest to landowners in Ptolemais Nea itself and in the nome metropolis. Although Karanis and Ptolemais Nea were close neighbours, probably no more than

six or eight kilometres apart, forty-four men were transferred
physically from Karanis to handle the job, no doubt because
of its size.[13]

It has been calculated that such compulsory transfers,
when added to absences for other reasons, might at any given
moment drain a village of as much as twenty or even thirty
per cent of its adult males. Of the rest, the majority were
usually away during the day — most at work in the fields,
some engaged in the transport of goods or persons. To the
approaching visitor the village might appear to be baking
somnolently in the hot sun. That illusion would quickly
be shattered when he entered the village and found all
about him a busy round of everyday activities: artisans at
work; children playing or busy helping with household
chores; housewives at their tasks, or pausing to gossip;
sudden brawls erupting over injuries real or fancied; and
in the background a thief, normally the denizen of the night,
profiting from the noise and distractions to make a swift
daytime strike and getaway.

Crimes of villainy and violence, as it happens, figure
prominently in the papyri, and the easiest victims of course
were the women, the aged, and the infirm. In the Roman
stereotype (examples occur frequently in the chapters that
follow), the Egyptians were contemned as a peculiarly
unstable and lawless society, and that prejudice has been
accepted by more than one modern writer. Yet in sober
fact there is no reason to suppose that village life was more
crime-ridden in Egypt than elsewhere. If we had papyri in
great quantities from other Roman provinces we should
expect to find a comparable picture there. The normal
quota of human greed, especially when intensified by the
pinch of poverty, constitutes a fairly universal stimulus to
illicit actions.

In the John Rylands Library, Manchester, there is a group
of twenty-eight complaints of criminal actions that were
filed between AD 28 and 42 with the police chief of the
village of Euhemeria, in the Arsinoite nome. They include
seven complaints of physical violence, three of breaking
and entering, seventeen of burglary or theft, and eight
that relate to the damage of crops by the irruption of cattle

belonging to others. Aside from their human interest, such complaints and other records from various sites give us vivid glimpses of personal and social relations in the villages, as well as of economic conditions. A few examples, chosen from the scores that have been published, follow.

To Serapion, chief of police, from Orsenouphis son of Harpaësis, headman of the village of Euhemeria in the Themistes division. In the month Mesore in the 14th year of Tiberius Caesar Augustus [AD 28] I was having some old walls on my premises demolished by the mason Petesouchos son of Petesouchos. I had left the village to fetch some victuals when Petesouchos, in the course of the demolition, found a hoard which had been secreted by my mother in a little box away back in the 16th year of [Augustus] Caesar [15 BC] − a pair of gold ear-rings weighing 4 quarters, a gold crescent weighing 3 quarters, a pair of silver armlets of 12 drachmas' weight, a necklace with silver ornaments worth 80 drachmas, and 60 silver drachmas in cash. Distracting his helpers and my people, he had his young daughter carry off the find to his house. He emptied out the aforementioned objects and then dropped the box, empty, back in my house, where he even admits he found it but claims it was empty. Therefore I ask, if you please, that the accused be brought before you to face the consequences. Farewell.

To ——, centurion, from Soterichos son of —— (son of Theon), of the village of Tebtynis. Some persons, in the manner of thieves, broke into my house in the village during the night preceding the 22nd of the present month Hathyr [i.e., today], seizing the opportunity of my sleeping away because of mourning for my daughter's husband. [They obtained entrance] by removing the nails from the doors, and they carried off everything I had in my house, a detailed list of which I will reveal when required. Therefore I submit this and ask that the due investigation be made by the proper parties, so that I may obtain relief from you. [Date, 18 November AD 176.]

To Hierax also known as Nemesion, strategos of the Arsinoite nome, Herakleides division, from Gemellus also known as Horion, son of Gaius Apolinarius, Antinoite. I appealed, my lord, by petition to the most illustrious prefect of Egypt, Aemilius Saturninus, informing him of the attack made upon me by a certain Sotas, who disdained me because of my weak vision and planned to possess himself of my property through brazen violence. I received the [prefect's] sacred subscription instructing me to appeal to his excellency the epistrategos. Sotas having died meanwhile, his brother Julius with their characteristic violence invaded some fields planted by me and carried off a not inconsiderable quantity of hay, and not only that but he also cut and stole from the olive-grove belonging to me near the village of Kerkesoucha some dried olive shoots and some heath plants, which depredations of his I learnt about when I arrived here at harvest time. In addition, not satisfied with that, he again marched onto my land, accompanied this time by his wife and a certain Zenas, bring with them a symbol of the evil eye, intending to enclose my tenant-farmer in black magic, with the result that he abandoned his farmwork after harvesting only a portion of another field of mine and they reaped the crop for themselves. After that I personally confronted Julius, taking along village officials so that they might serve as witnesses. Again, in the same way, his party aimed the evil eye at me, intending to enclose me in black magic, right in the presence of Petesouchos and of Ptollas, elders of Karanis discharging also the office of village clerk, and of Sokras, their assistant; and whilst the officials were still there Julius took the symbol of the evil eye together with the remaining crops from the fields and carried them off to his house. These acts of his I have made a matter of record through the said officials and through the collectors of grain taxes of the said village. Therefore I perforce submit this petition and ask that it be kept on file to preserve my claim against them before his excellency the epistrategos for the outrages committed by them and for the taxes to be paid to the imperial fiscus on those fields, because they wrongfully reaped the harvest. [Signature and date, 22 May AD 197.]

To Apollonios, strategos of the Arsinoite nome, from Thouonis son of Akousilaos of Ares' Village in the Polemon division. [Yesterday] as I was settling accounts with Bentetis son of Bentetis, a herdsman of [the village of] Oxyrhyncha of the said division, regarding pay and rations that he owes me, he then, wishing not to pay me but to cheat me, treated me and my wife Tanouris daughter of Heronas with contempt, right there in our aforesaid Ares' Village. And not only that but he also mercilessly rained on my wife Tanouris many blows on whatever part of her body he could reach, even though she was pregnant, with the result that she miscarried and was untimely delivered of a dead fetus and she herself is bedridden and in danger of her life. I therefore ask that you write to the elders of Oxyrhyncha to send the accused to you for the due consequences. [Date, 24 November AD 47. Signature.] [14]

It would be grossly unfair to a hard-working and long-suffering people to end this look at their village life on the depressing note of man's inhumanity to man. The very fact of community existence postulates an underlying comity amongst neighbours; organized society is simply not viable otherwise. And if the extant records are richer in instances of outrage and abuse than in evidences of harmony and co-operation, that is but a further reminder of how true it is that 'the evil that men do lives after them'. Yet the milk of human kindness did not cease to flow because life in the Egyptian village was hard. In the following letter, written some time in the first century, a man invokes his father's assistance to assure proper care of a friend's pregnant wife as she approaches full term in her husband's absence.

. . . to come up [the river] in order that he may entreat you to take good care of her, but he has no opportunity [to do so] because the office of the Arabarch has detained him and he is on the point of extricating his legacy. In fact he was about to send his brother on a fast boat to entreat you, since he is so occupied. But I said to him, 'Let me — I'll write to my father, first the essentials about her delivery, and then about your enforced absence.' Therefore please, father, go to her toward the end of Mecheir or the middle of Phamenoth, so that you will be there before she comes to term. . . . Everything has been sufficiently prepared for her childbed . . . so please, father . . . [The rest is lost.]

Equally warm are the sentiments of the following, written in the second century.

Apollonios and Sarapias to Dionysia, greeting. You filled us with joy in announcing the good news of the wedding of your fine Sarapion, and we should have come straightway on that day, most longed-for by us, to attend upon him and share your joy, but on account of the annual assizes and because we are recovering from illness we could not come. Roses are not yet in full bloom here — in fact they are scarce — and from all the nurseries and all the garland-weavers we could just barely get together the thousand that we sent you with Sarapas, even with picking the ones that ought not to have been picked till tomorrow. We had all the narcissi you wanted, so instead of the two thousand you asked for we sent four thousand. We wish you did not think us so petty as to make fun of us by writing that you have sent the money [for the flowers], when we too regard your children as our own and esteem and love them more than our own, and so we are as happy as you and their father. [Customary regards.] [15]

After reading such expressions of friendship and concern, it comes as something of a surprise to us to discover that amongst the thousands private letters that have been published the only letters of condolence, and those but a handful, relate to the deaths of children. Apparently the deaths of adults, whether young or old, were too routine a part of the human condition to call for special comment, even of a pro forma nature. The letters of condolence that we do find, are, as is still so often the case in such missives, couched in a language of affective stereotypes. One of the most revealing comes from a metropolis, but its commonplace sentiments are by no means restricted to the metropolitan community; it was sent on 14 December AD 235 to a leading burgher of Oxyrhynchus (italics call attention to the clichés).

Mnesthianus to Apollonianus and Spartiate [husband and wife], *be brave*! The gods are witness and when I learnt about my lord your son *I was grieved and I lamented as I would my own child.* He was a person to be cherished. I was starting out to come to you when Pinoution stopped me, saying that you, my lord Apollonianus, had sent him word for me not to come because you would be away in the Arsinoite nome. Well, *bear it nobly, for this rests with the gods.* [The letter then goes on to report on some business matters, and concludes:] I too have had a loss, a houseborn slave worth two talents. I pray that you fare well, my lord, togerther with my lord [your father], in the benevolence of all the gods.[16]

Let us conclude this chapter, as we did the preceding one, with a look at the cultural level of the milieu. As already noted, of the first six hundred illiterates encountered in published papyri only three were metropolites, the rest Egyptian artisans and peasants. These illiterates included priests, village headmen, estate managers, and a veteran of the armed forces — even twenty-six years of service in the army had not overcome his illiteracy. Some fifteen years ago there was published a collection of papyri surviving from the office of a village clerk who 'did not know how to write'. Having said this much, we must now add that all such designations were made with reference to the Greek language; many who were illiterate in Greek, especially members of the priestly class, could write in their native Egyptian language. The distinction is rarely expressed in so many words, but in a house sale of AD 55, for example, one of the signatures reads, 'So-and-so wrote for him because he is ignorant of Greek letters, but he does write Egyptian.' The practice of writing in Demotic, as the late Egyptian cursive is called, began to fade in the second century, though vestiges are at hand for some two hundred years after that.[17]

Often an individual is described as 'writing slowly', meaning that he could manage to indite his signature, and not much else, in clumsily traced imitations of Greek letters. It is a safe assumption that there were villagers who could do better than that, and even some who could read and appreciate Greek literature — an assumption confirmed by the fragments of the works of Greek authors found in the ruins of some villages. And finally, as we saw earlier in this chapter, the small number of wealthy villagers, seeking to plant their feet on the ladder of upward social mobility (as we might phrase it today), tended to imitate the life of the metropolites, which would include seeing to the Greek education of their sons. But the prevailing aura of the Egyptian village in Roman times remained one of illiteracy: the cultured few lived surrounded by the illiterate many. In the beginning — that is, in Pharaonic times — writing was the special province reserved to scribes, a highly respected class of skilled professionals, and something of that traditional attitude survived in the villages right into Roman times and even beyond. One still sees in the Near and Middle East the scribe sitting at a portable little table set up near a main thoroughfare, and the people come, bringing him their letters to answer, their complaints to reduce to writing, their contracts to draw up and sign. In antiquity the scribes functioned in very much the same way, and they must even have looked very much the same, except that they sat cross-legged, writing in their laps. There, 'in the street' as some contracts state, is where most of the villagers' paper work was done. The educational level of the scribes varied with the individual, but most leave the impression of being merely literate rather than highly educated. They wrote mostly in formulas and clichés, a fact which shows up in the various contracts they penned and most strikingly (to us) in the private letters, many of which are little more than the most impersonally worded collections of greetings and conventional good wishes.

The reader will not have failed to notice that this chapter is considerably shorter than the preceding one. That is because 'the short and simple annals of the poor' are soon told. However, the country folk, the vast majority of the population of the province, will be the leading actors also in most of the chapters that follow.

SUPERSTITIONE ET LASCIVIA
or
WORKS AND DAYS OF GODS AND GOBLINS

No one expressed the Roman disdain for Egyptians and their ways more passionately than did the poet Juvenal. His particular *bête noire* was one Crispinus, a *nouveau riche* Egyptian who had risen to a position of importance in Rome. But Juvenal's hatred and contempt embraced the whole people, and in his fifteenth *Satire* he holds up to ridicule that 'demented' land which worships animals. Claiming to have learnt about it on a visit to Egypt, he recounts what happened when local sectarianism stirred the hotheads from one Egyptian town to invade another at the festival of its local god: words led to blows, which led to a full-scale riot, replete with every atrocity not excluding cannibalism.

Whether Juvenal wrote in earnest or tongue-in-cheek we shall never know. Scholars have argued both positions, with neither side convinced by the arguments of the other. It is true that Plutarch and Dio Cassius also describe the Egyptians as jealously touchy about their local cults. But that is a far cry from the horror story that Juvenal tells, or concocts. Certainly the everyday reality that we encounter in the inscriptions and papyri of the first three centuries wears a totally different countenance. We see a land in which the gods of three cultures — the native Egyptian; the Greek, quite at home now after three centuries of acclimatization under the Ptolemies; and the Roman, the new arrivals — rub shoulders without noticeable friction, sometimes retaining their separate identities, but more often merging in syncretistic identification or alliance.

The Romans who took up residence in Egypt adapted easily and quickly to the Greek–Egyptian syncretisms that they found there. A good illustration is provided by an inscription of AD 11, discovered some thirty years ago in Egypt's eastern desert, along the ancient road that led from Coptus on the Nile to a port on the Red Sea. Its text reads:

With good fortune. When Publius Juventius Rufus, formerly military tribune of the Third Legion and prefect of [the mines of] Mt Berenike, was director-in-chief of the emerald and topaz mines and the production of pearls and all the mines of Egypt, Agathapous his freedman dedicated in the Ophiate region this shrine to Pan, god most great, in the name of Publius Juventius, his benefactor.[1]

The cultural mix of the inscription is worth observing in detail. The dedicant, a freedman bearing a Greek name, honours his patron and former master, who is a Roman dignitary. The text, in the Greek language, is inscribed on a stele that is Egyptian in its form and its decoration. And the god Pan, the spirit of the desert's wilderness and solitude — conditions which do cause people to 'panic' — is called by his Greek name but is pictured on the stele in the traditional profile stance of the ithyphallic Egyptian god Min.

In a letter of the second or third century we read:

Marcus Aurelius Apollonios, hierophant, to the ritual basket-carrier of [the village of] Nesmeimis, greeting. Please go to [the village of] Sinkepha to the temple of Demeter, to perform the customary sacrifices for our lords the emperors and their victory, for the rise of the Nile and increase of crops, and for favourable conditions of climate. I pray that you fare well.

Here again a manifold mixture: the priest is a Roman citizen, but the cult is not that of a Roman god; the goddess is called by the Greek name Demeter, which in the setting of an Egyptian village surely signifies Isis (the identification of the two was reported as early as the fifth century BC by Herodotus); and in her temple are performed the rites for the cult of the ruling emperors, of the river Nile, and of the gods of the weather.[2]

It was not only small villages like Sinkepha, which had neither the population nor the resources to build separate shrines for the different divinities, that went in for such 'multi-service' temples. The same cross-cultural accommodation is in evidence in the temples dedicated to Greek and Roman deities in the metropoleis. In the interior of Egypt the urban citizenry and their metropolite imitators clung, at least nominally, to the worship of the gods of the Greek pantheon as a proud manifestation of their Hellenic origins and traditions. But they were only so many Hellenic enclaves in a circumambient indigenous culture, to which, try as they might, they could not remain totally impervious. The Olympian deities remained as names but faded as realities.

The many syncretisms that resulted were mostly Greek–Egyptian, but there was also an admixture of divinities originating elsewhere, most notably in the Fertile Crescent and Asia Minor. Athena's primary identification in Egypt was with Thoëris, Zeus' with Ammon, Hermes' with Thoth, and similarly for the others. But most gods were involved in more than one such assimilation, and these took different forms or emphases in different localities. When villagers with Egyptian names call themselves priests of Hermes and Aphrodite, we realize that they are 'name-dropping', using the Greek appellatives of the privileged classes for their local native gods. One syncretism was actually promulgated as a political instrument when the first Ptolemy created the god Sarapis (or Serapis), a mystical conflation of a Greek and an Egyptian divinity purporting to symbolize the unity and equality of the two cultures — an ideal to be given lip-service in the present and realized in some utopian future. Sarapis was an instant and continuing success, with the Egyptians because of his promise of a better life, with the Greeks and their descendants because he allowed them to enjoy the luxury of endorsing the egalitarian ideal in the full knowledge that government policy was directed at perpetuating the rigidly stratified status quo. Once established as a separate entity, Sarapis too was extended into various supplementary associations, being identified in one place with Zeus, in another with the god of the Nile, and so on.

By far the most widely disseminated of the Egyptian cults was that of the goddess Isis, the bountiful, the giver of life, whose worship spread throughout the Mediterranean world, with a major centre in Rome itself. A portion of a religious book found at Oxyrhynchus lists the guises, appellations, attributes, and assimilations by which 'she of the many names' was known in different places, at home and abroad. A handful of extracts will suffice to illustrate the close to 150 different names and epithets found in the more than a hundred places listed:

at Aphroditopolis in the Prosopite nome [you are called] fleet commander, many-formed, Aphrodite; at Naukratis, parthenogenetic, joy, saviour, almighty, most great; at Hermopolis, Aphrodite, queen, holy; at Tanis, of graceful form, Hera; at Canopus, leader of the Muses; at Rome, warlike; in Italy, love of the gods.

Such profusion of identities was usually dismissed by Greek and Roman visitors as irrational and confused. 'The same goddess', remarked Diodorus of Sicily, and his words have a ring of testy impatience, 'some call Isis, others Demeter, still others Law Giver, Selene, or Hera, and some call her by all these appellations. Osiris has been called the same as Dionysus by some, Pluto or Ammon by others, Zeus by a few, Pan by many.'[3]

At Oxyrhynchus, about which our information is fullest, we can identify a considerable array of temples. Those of Sarapis and of Athena-Thoëris (the latter, we learn, having a monumental tetrastyle) were the biggest, and the town districts in which they were located were named for them. In the Thoëris district there was also a temple of Dionysus. The south-east district had a temple of Apollo, 'great god and good spirit', and one of Neotera (i.e., Aphrodite-Hathor). A southern district had a Demetrion, and three other districts each had a shrine dedicated jointly to Zeus, Hera, Atargatis (i.e., Syrian Ashtart, sometimes identified with Isis) and Persephone. Also mentioned as existing somewhere in Oxyrhynchus are temples of Isis and of the Caesars. It is particularly noteworthy that wherever the priests and priestesses of these temples appear they all bear Egyptian names.

The advent of Roman rule added the Capitoline Triad (Jupiter-Juno-Minerva) and other divinities from Italy to the preexisting Egyptian and Hellenic elements. But its most visible manifestation in the religious observances of the province was the body of ritual — ubiquitous, even if more formal than spiritual — attendant upon the worship of the Roman emperor. This embraced not only, as at Rome, the deified dead emperors, but also, as was customary in the lands of and beyond the eastern Mediterranean, the living ruler, regarded as an embodiment of divinity. Members of the imperial family were often included in the rites. Thus when Germanicus, nephew and adopted son of Emperor Tiberius, visited Egypt in AD 19 he too was automatically accorded divine honours, which, however, he rejected in a diplomatically worded edict.

Germanicus Caesar, son of [Tiberius] Augustus and grandson of the deified Augustus, proconsul, declares: I welcome the goodwill which you always display when you see me, but I find invidious and I deprecate entirely your acclamations that equate me with gods. Those are fitting only for the actual saviour and benefactor of the whole of the human race, my father, and also his mother, my grandmother [Livia]. My [position has no part] of their divinity, and if you do not obey me you will compel me to appear in public but rarely.[4]

A papyrus roll, more than two metres long, contains records of the temple of Jupiter Capitolinus in Arsinoë for a period of six months in AD 215. In that temple of the chief Roman god, a temple dominated by a statue of the ruling emperor (Caracalla), Roman holidays and a whole series of anniversaries of the imperial house, as well as the native crocodile cult, were all celebrated with local Graeco-Egyptian ceremonies. A few of many entries will suffice to illustrate.

Mechir 1 [26 Jan.]. Holiday celebrating the tenth anniversary of the accession of our lord the Emperor Severus Antoninus [Caracalla]: garlanding of all the statues of the gods, shields, and statues of men.
19 [13 Feb.]. Holiday celebrating the accession of the deified Severus, father of our lord the Emperor Severus Antoninus: garlanding of all [the statues, etc.] in the temple.
Phamenoth 18 [14 March]. Holiday with games celebrating the erection of the statue of our lord the Emperor Severus Antoninus: garlanding of all in the temple as before.
Pharmouthi 5 [31 March]. Holiday celebrating the victory and safety of our lord the Emperor Severus Antoninus: garlanding of all the shields and statues of gods and men in the temple.
9 [4 April]. Birthday of our lord the Emperor Severus Antoninus: garlanding of all in the temple as before; [list of expenditures for aromatics].
19 [14 April]. Holiday celebrating the acclamation of our lady Julia

Domna as Mother of the Invincible Armies: garlanding of all in the temple as before.

26 [21 April]. Birthday of Rome; garlanding of all in the temple as before.

[Date lost.] Care of our ancestral [crocodile] god Souchos, great, great: garlanding of all the shields and statues of gods and men in the temple.[5]

The holidays in other months, as recorded in this and other papyri, comprised the birthdays and accession days of all the emperors going back to Augustus, and also included the birthdays of such deified figures as Hadrian's Antinous (30 November), Marciana and Matidia, Trajan's sister and niece ([] August and 4 July), Germanicus Caesar (24 May), and of course Julius Caesar (12 July).

When news came of the accession of a new emperor, all the people in all the provinces were put through the ceremony of swearing an oath of allegiance to the new ruler, and the date of the accession was entered in the calendar of imperial holidays to be observed every year with appropriate rites. Here are decrees issued by prefects of Egypt on two such occasions, AD 54 and 193:

The emperor [Claudius] who was owed to his ancestors has gone to join them, a god manifest, and the emperor whom the world expected and hoped for has been designated, the good genius of the world and source of all blessings, Nero Caesar, has been designated. Therefore, ought we all wear garlands and sacrifice oxen to give thanks to all the gods. [Date.]

Mantennius Sabinus to the strategoi of the Heptanomia and the Arsinoite nome, greeting. I have ordered that there be appended hereto a copy of the edict issued by me to the most illustrious city of Alexandria, so that you may all be informed and may hold festival for a like number of days. I bid you fare well. [Date.]

Copy of edict: It is meet, people of Alexandria, that you should hold festival for the most fortunate accession of our lord the Emperor Publius Helvius Pertinax Augustus, leader of the imperial senate, father of his country, and of Publius Helvius Pertinax his son, and of Flavia Titiana Augusta [his wife], offering public sacrifice and prayer all together for his enduring rule and all his house, and wearing garlands for fifteen days beginning from today.[6]

At the opposite pole from these officially ordained celebrations were the traditional observances of the popular
religion, most of them rooted in the down-to-earth realities
of daily existence. A distinctive feature, which foreigners
usually cited with amusement or disdain, was the divine
worship accorded animals. When Octavian was acquainting
himself with his newly conquered Egypt, 'he refused to visit
Apis [the bull], saying he was accustomed to worshipping
gods, not cattle.' Juvenal's scorn, as we might expect, was
more vehement: 'Who knows not what monsters demented
Egypt worships? One part reveres the crocodile, another
stands in awe of the ibis, devourer of snakes. . . . Here they
venerate cats, there fish, and there a whole town venerates a
dog.' Even Greek writers normally given to rationalization
rarely considered that these cults may have had their origin
in a desire to propitiate wild creatures which represented
either a boon or a threat to human existence in the Nile
valley. The Greeks and Romans who came to see the great
pyramids and the labyrinth would happily make a small
detour in order to see the priests feed the crocodile who
lived in the sacred pool by his temple in Arsinoë. To them
he was a tourist attraction. But to the populace of the
Arsinoite nome he represented their tutelary god Sobk (a
name rendered in Greek as Souchos). Every village in the
nome that could do so erected a temple to him, and he was
consulted as the local oracle.[7]

The cleavage between the Egyptian population and their
social superiors was faithfully reflected also in the operation
of their temples. Very early in its history Egypt developed a
priestly class, practically a caste in its exclusivity. The ancient
Greeks never did. In their cities 'priestly office [was] open
to every man', as the Athenian orator Isocrates wrote to
Nikokles, king of Cyprus. The Roman government, as usual,
saw no reason to interfere in the continuation of those
separate cultural traditions; on the contrary, it welcomed and
fostered such aids to its policy of social stratification. 'It is
permissible', states Section 86 of the regulations of the Privy
Purse, the agency to which Augustus turned over the supervision of religious affairs in Egypt, 'for lay persons to officiate
in the ceremonies of Greek temples.' Accordingly, in the

cities and metropoleis of Egypt the temples of the Greek gods had no clergy, only officiators and administrators, a laity that the metropolites selected from their own class, in annual rotation, to see to the physical upkeep and cultic requirements of the shrines. Most of those officers corresponded to the beadles and churchwardens of today. The one who bore the lofty title of 'chief priest' was in reality one of the metropolitan 'magistrates'. After his year of service he, like the others — ex-gymnasiarchs, etc. — styled himself 'sometime chief priest' for the rest of his life. Obviously, social status rather than religious calling was involved.

In contrast, the temples of Egyptian divinities, whether called by their native or their Greek names, were served by a priestly establishment consisting of an hereditary clergy supported by several grades of acolytes. The number and frequency of Egyptian religious festivals made the rise of such a profession inevitable. Herodotus thought it remarkable that 'the Egyptians hold a festival not once a year,' as the Greeks did, 'but they have frequent festivals' for the same god. In the calendar that can be reconstructed from several papyri found in the Arsinoite village of Soknopaiou Nesos ('Crocodile-God Island'), each festival — birthday of the crocodile god; wedding day of Isis; anniversary of the founding of the shrine, etc. — calls for a celebration of anywhere from seven to nineteen days, for a grand total of more than 150 days in the year. No farming society, even one whose fields are beneficently fertilized for it by the Nile flood, can afford to take that much time off from the year-long cycle of agricultural tasks. Hence the role of the permanent clergy: the villagers would participate in some rites, and the priesthood would perform the rest in their name.[8]

Egypt's millennial history had been marked by a seesaw of royal and priestly power. After annexing Egypt to the Roman Empire Augustus instituted a system of control that effectively reduced the great wealth and curbed the political influence that the clergy had been able to arrogate unto themselves during the weak rule of the last Ptolemies. Their numbers and their temples' landholdings were severely curtailed, their personnel records and financial accounts subjected to regular audits by representatives of the Privy

Purse, and they were forbidden, on pain of rigorous punishment, to engage in any activity other than those related to divine service. (This last provision affected only the topmost echelons of the several temples. The lesser offices were usually filled by ordinary folk serving in the temples part time.) The ability of the clergy to rally popular discontent against the government was thus dissipated. Occasional flare-ups, however violent (one in Alexandria, in AD 153, actually cost the governor of the province his life), were no more than that — flare-ups, isolated local riots, foredoomed to failure (Chapter 10).

The epuration of the priestly establishment is highlighted by an edict issued in 4 BC by the prefect Gaius Turranius:

I order [the temples] to register their hereditary priests and acolytes and all the others belonging to the temples and their children, and to make clear what functions they perform. I will then scrutinize the list of the current 26th year of [Augustus] Caesar, and those not of priestly origin I will forthwith remove.[9]

Even those whose priestly status was certified were no longer automatically exempted from taxation or from the performance of compulsory public services. Instead, those privileges were thereafter allowed only to certain numbers or categories of priests. Overall numbers varied, of course, with the size of the local population and the importance of the particular shrine. At one small Arsinoite village the crocodile god was served by a mere trio of priests attended by a single acolyte, while at Tebtynis the clergy totalled eighty and at Karanis a hundred and four.

The Egyptian clergy were visibly and physically distinguished from the rest of the populace. Their heads were kept shaven (the penalty if they let their hair grow was a thousand drachmas!), they were not allowed to wear woollen garments in public, only their priestly linens, and they, alone of all the non-Jewish population, were circumcised. These and all other regulations were carefully supervised by various government agencies. A good illustration is provided by the procedure for obtaining permission for a circumcision.

The first step was the filing of an application, supported by an affidavit such as the following, which was submitted to the nome strategos *c.* AD 187 by four priests of the 'famous, tax-exempt temple of [the village of] Tebtynis':

With reference to the application presented to you by Marempsemis son of Marsisouchos son of Harpokration, priest of the said temple, requesting that his son Panesis born of Thenpakebkis daughter of Panesis be circumcised, in reply to your enquiry whether he is of priestly descent and entitled to be circumcised we declare on oath by the fortune of Marcus Aurelius Commodus Antoninus Augustus that his priestly descent and the proofs submitted for him are genuine, and that he must be circumcised because he cannot perform the sacred offices unless this is done. If not [as we have stated], may we be liable to the consequences of our oath. [Signatures.]

A particular point of the strategos' enquiry was to determine that the boy was neither adopted nor a rescued foundling, for Regulation 92 of the Privy Purse forbade such to be priests. If the strategos was satisfied as to the boy's pedigree he would so certify to a Roman aide of the governor, the high-priest of Egypt, who would then hold or waive a hearing on the application. According to the minutes of one such hearing, held in AD 171, the high-priest

enquired of the leaders and assistant leaders of the delegation, and of the scribes [and keepers] of the sacred records, whether the boy had any blemish on his body. Upon their saying that he was without blemish, Ulpius Serenianus, high-priest and minister for temple administration, by appending his signature to the letter from the strategos, gave permission for the boy to be circumcised in accordance with custom.

But in at least one case we know of, a boy with a scar on his body was apparently passed for circumcision along with a simultaneously presented unblemished candidate, and in the case of another presumably blemished candidate the hearing before the high-priest was dispensed with. In both those instances the favourable outcome was doubtless produced by the application of behind-the-scenes influence, political, monetary, or both.[10]

When an office in a temple fell vacant through lack of a successor it was sold by the state to the highest bidder. The modern reader is usually shocked to learn of this practice; to a world of churches it smacks of sacrilege. But the attitude in ancient Egypt and in many other parts of the eastern

Mediterranean was fundamentally a practical one: a priest-hood, with the privileges and perquisites thereunto apper-taining, was manifestly a thing of value, translatable into cash. There was spirited bidding, especially for the more lucrative offices, and charges of irregularities, followed by countercharges and litigation, were not uncommon.

In their physical appearance too, the temples perpetuated their separate architectural traditions, Greek and Egyptian. To the Greeks in the cities it would have been unthinkable to do otherwise than to build on the designs of their spiritual motherland; at most they might accept some technical variations dictated by local building materials and practices. In the rest of the province, except for a few Greek temples that the metropolites erected as manifestations of the Hellenism on which they prided themselves, the Egyptian style of architecture prevailed everywhere, from the small house-like temples found in many villages to the massive structures with their fortress-like pylons flanking the entrance, which one approached along an avenue flanked by sphinxes or similar recumbent figures of other animals. At Edfu, ancient Apollinopolis Magna, one may still see an almost perfectly preserved example of the pylon type, with Roman emperors depicted in its wall-reliefs in the traditional garb and attitudes of the ancient Pharaohs. At Tebtynis, one of the larger villages, almost nothing remains of the temple, but the monumental avenue flanked by sphinxes was uncovered in the excavation of fifty years ago. In a sacred enclosure near a major Egyptian temple reposed the cult animal, Apis the bull at Memphis, Sobk the crocodile at Arsinoë, Anubis the dog at Kynopolis ('Dog City'), and so on, each in the town that was the principal centre of its worship.

The river Nile on the other hand, was worshipped as a prime deity everywhere in the country, since without his waters life could not be sustained in Egypt. Paeans and prayers to the Nile at its rising can be traced over millennia. The earliest known is a hieroglyphic text of *c.* 1,200 BC; some two thousand years later we find two Byzantine versions, one of them Christian, addressed to St Senuthius; and there is even a Syriac version in a manuscript of the twelfth century. Here is a text of Roman times.

For the festival marking the rising of the most sacred Nile, the festival
with its sacred rites of abundance.
The water has come. Hail to the streams at the rising of the freshet
of Isis. Rule the streams, O Nile of many floods, of great name. From
Meroë flow down to us, gracious and welcome, and spread the fruitful
silt in your abundant freshets. May you sweeten the whole of Egypt,
fertilizing it each year in due season. Look ye how golden is the flood
to each and every one, and chorus ye thrice, in celebration of the
flowing streams, 'Rise, O Nile, mount up to the joyous six and ten
cubits [the optimum flood level] '.[11]

The goddess Isis, life-giver *par excellence* in the Egyptian
pantheon, was understandably associated with the Nile and
its life-giving waters. In the joyous procession that hailed the
annual rising, a cupful of the 'new water' dipped from the
river was carried aloft in a golden vase of Isis. A hymn in
her praise has such lines as, 'By your power all the channels
of the Nile are filled', or again, 'You induce golden-streamed
Nile and lead him in due season up over the land of Egypt, a
joy for mankind.' The rising of the Nile was celebrated up
and down the valley through most of the month of Payni,
with the 12th of that month [6 June then = 19 June New
Style] as the day of greatest solemnity. That day became so
deeply embedded in the popular consciousness that it passed
with no perceptible stress into the calendar of Christian (and
later also Arab) feasts. The rising of 'the blessed fertilizing
river of Egypt' was attributed to 'the power of Christ', and
the archangel Michael was made its patron saint. The beginning
of the annual flood is still celebrated in the Coptic Church on
19 June, the feast day of St Michael.[12]
Not all worship required temples and priests. Much of it
was conducted in the privacy of the home. With sacred niches
in houses, and with small chapels in the streets and out in
the fields, Roman Egypt must have had much the same
aspect in this regard as do some Catholic countries today.
Indoors or out, public or private, Egyptian religion was
deeply imbued with mystical and magical elements, so much
so that the rest of the ancient world regarded Egypt as the
fons et origo of the occult and of methods by which to
penetrate its secrets. The assemblage of lore that the Middle
Ages prized as the definitive repository of such arcana was

entitled *Hermętica*, that is, a body of teachings attributed to the god Thoth, the Egyptian *alter ego* of the Greek Hermes. In Roman Egypt the intervention of magical powers was sought in a variety of ways, such as prayers, curses, or invoking the help of Bes. This last was one of the lesser Egyptian divinities, portrayed as a pot-bellied, grotesque dwarf, and housed in no temple but conceived, instead, as being omnipresent. Very great trust was placed also, in the efficacy of apotropaic and salvational amulets. These have been found written on papyrus, which was then tied with a string or enclosed in a capsule for wearing on the person, and inscribed on every kind of material, including precious and semiprecious stones. The fact that amulets employing Egyptian symbols and formulas have been found in all parts of the Mediterranean world is eloquent testimony to the universality of the belief in the archetypal force of Egyptian demonolatry. And it is no secret that the use of amulets is one of the many pagan practices that survived in the Christian milieu. A particularly interesting example from the sixth century, too long to be quoted here in full, calls upon Christ, his mother, and all the saints, to preserve 'Joannia whom Anastasia bore' from a 'hateful spirit', and to 'chase away from her all fevers and every kind of chill, quotidian, tertian, quartan, and every evil'.[13]

Formulas and instructions for love charms — almost always directed, as in every culture where they have made their appearance, by males at female objects of desire — and for other magical practices have survived in large numbers. There are papyrus rolls, some of them very long, containing a seemingly endless stream of precepts and nostrums. And there are single texts, written on papyrus or inscribed on various materials, thin lead plaques being especially favoured for such purposes. One love charm on papyrus was found wrapped around a lock of hair, doubtless obtained, by fair means or foul, from the head of the beloved. A frequent practice was to tie a small clay figure, representing the love object, to the papyrus on which the charm was written. Another common practice was to place the charm on a mummy or in a tomb, in the expectation that the spirit of the deceased would be compelled by the power of the spell to do the bidding of the enchanter.[14]

Whole rolls of papyrus were filled — even long after the triumph of Christianity — with all sorts of do-it-yourself instructions for obtaining magical results. Here are two examples taken from one such roll in the British Library.[15]

When eating and drinking take the first bits and place them in a small dish in a shrine while saying, 'So-and-so, may thou be sent to serve me and hasten to carry out the god's instructions. My name is (insert). O Iao, Sabaoth, Zabarbathiao, Adonai, may she (insert name) love me (insert name) with a heavenly inextinguishable love.' Another wording: 'May she (insert name) fall in love with me at first sight, and may she not resist out of modesty, O great and powerful god.' Then, when you see her, take three deep breaths whilst looking intently in her direction, then she will smile at you. That will be the sign that she loves you.

Spell for restraining hostile spirits. Works against all enemies, accusers, thieves, fears and hallucinations in dreams. Take a golden or a silver plate and trace on it the [magical] characters and words, and having thus endowed it with potency carry it on you, pure in heart. The sign is:

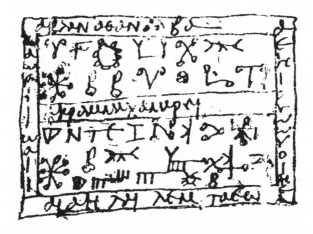

As did most other people in antiquity, the inhabitants of Egypt generally — and in some instances passionately — believed that a divinity could, and would if approached correctly, predict the future. Every god, being immortal and therefore timeless, had such oracular power, but some became more popular consultants than others: there were fashions in oracles, too. 'Amongst you', said Dio Chrysostom, addressing the people of Alexandria early in the second century, 'Sarapis enjoys particular devotion, and he displays his powers in oracles and dreams almost every day.' Another oracle, that of Zeus–Ammon in the Siwa oasis, gained prominence after Alexander the Great, interrupting his sweep of the Persian Empire, dashed across the western desert of Egypt to ask that oracle to reveal his future to him. Under the Romans its fame grew to world-wide renown.[16]

In fact, oracles everywhere grew in popularity in the first three centuries AD. At the root of that trend was the fact that the major religions tended in those days toward ever-increasing formalism, in which people continued to find pageantry and entertainment but less and less claim to their emotional commitment. By way of compensation, rich and poor alike, the mighty emperor as well as the lowly peasant, increasingly sought comfort for the spirit in various non-cultic devices. In Egypt we observe, as one manifestation of the trend, a steady decline in the number of priests in the temples: the perquisites of the calling, dependent upon offerings by the public, were becoming less and less attractive. The emphasis, in matters spiritual, shifted ever more from a community to an individual experience. Thus horoscopes, some dozens of which are extant on papyri, enjoyed an increasing vogue. But even there the subject required the services of a trained professional to unlock the astrological arcana. Hence the supreme popularity of the oracle, where the ordinary individual could converse independently and directly with the god of his choice, dealing with him face to face as it were. 'Do not think', writes a mother to her son, 'that I have been remiss about you. I consult the oracle about you every ten days without fail.' The question, it seems, was whether he should remain in Egypt or proceed to Rome on business. 'Will I be saved from this disease which is in me? Disclose this to me', asks a man of the crocodile god. Another enquiry: 'To Zeus, Helios, great Serapis and their temple-sharing gods. Nike asks if it is advantageous for me to buy from Tasarapion the slave she owns named Sarapion also known as Gaion. Give me this [reply].' And to the same gods: 'Menandros asks if it is granted to me to marry. Give me this [reply].' Before long the questions were standardized and the procedure streamlined to accommodate the crowds expeditiously. Amongst the finds from Oxyrhynchus is part of a repertory of questions, each couched in general terms, and each identified by a number; to make enquiry of the oracle all one had to do was to select the appropriate number from the menu card:

72, Shall I receive the allowance? 73, Shall I remain where I am going? 74, Shall I be sold? 75, Shall I get help from my friend? 76, Has it been granted to me to enter into a contract with another party? 77, Shall I be reconciled with my child? 78, Do I get a furlough? 79, Shall I receive the money? 80, Is the absent one alive? 81, Shall I profit from the affair? 82, Is my property to be confiscated? 83, Shall I find a way to sell? 84, Can I pull off what I have in mind? 85, Shall I be successful? 86, Shall I become a fugitive? 87, Shall I go on an embassy? 88, Shall I become a councilman? 89, Is my running away to no avail? 90, Shall I be divorced from my wife? 91, Have I been poisoned? 92, Shall I get my own back?[17]

Dreams, like oracles, were believed all through antiquity to be divine manifestations, prophetic in nature. The need to interpret their allegorical content gave rise to a flourishing profession of dream interpreters, who, armed with elaborate compilations of case histories, would, for a fee, explain the hidden meaning of day-dreams, nocturnal visions, hallucinations, nightmares. But there was one type of dream where, as with an oracle, the individual dealt directly with the god. In common with other ancient peoples, the inhabitants of Egypt believed in the healing power of certain gods, a power that was best invoked if the invalid stayed overnight in the sanctuary of the god, praying him to vouchsafe a curative dream. The most famous healing shrine of Greece, to which suppliants came even from foreign parts, was that of Asklepios, the god of medicine, at Epidauros. In Egypt the Greeks and their descendants accepted the native god of healing, Imhotep (whose name they Hellenized as Imouthes), as the counterpart of their own Asklepios. His great temple stood at the edge of the desert near Memphis, and a tale of wonders performed there by the god is found in one of the Oxyrhynchus papyri.[18]

Another significant development of the first three centuries was the spread of a new monotheism. The Jewish communities of Egypt have been described in Chapter 2. They played an important role in the commercial life of Egypt, especially in Alexandria, but their monotheistic religion did not proselytize and attracted few converts. From its home in Judaea, however, there now emerged a sect that was in a few hundred years to dominate the whole of the Roman Empire, and eventually the whole of the Western world.

Christianity came early to Egypt. It reached first the Jews of Alexandria, the community most proximate to Judaea in geography and intercourse, but before long it was spreading among non-Jews in the interior. There its reception was facilitated by the many similar elements in Egyptian religion, notably the belief in resurrection that was inherent, *inter alia*, in the highly emotional yearly celebration of Isis' restoring wholeness to the dismembered Osiris. (The annual cycle of the 'death' and miraculous 'rebirth' of vegetation was similarly mythologized in many ancient and primitive societies.)

Mark, who composed the earliest of the Gospels *c.* AD 65, is the traditional founder of the Church at Alexandria, and the first in the long line of patriarchs, as its bishops are called. By the middle of the third century there were bishops also in at least two of the nome metropoleis; by the end of that century Oxyrhynchus had two Christian churches in the list of its many places of worship. The earliest papyrus fragments of Gospels and other Christian books found in Middle and Upper Egypt date from about AD 100 or not long after. The earliest extant writing of a lay nature that we can recognize as being unequivocally Christian is a letter (now in the library of Woodbroke College, Birmingham) which, scholars are agreed, must have been written in the early part of the third century. The letter is particularly interesting because it reflects some of the Gnostic doctrines that were so widely held amongst the early Christians of Egypt, the most notable of them being the reduction of the trinity to a duality by the omission of the son (though a minority view among scholars holds that the word 'truth' is its allegorical allusion to Christ).[19]

For a hundred years or more, most outsiders regarded Christians, if they were aware of them at all, not as different from Jews but rather as a sort of lunatic fringe of that strange nonconformist people. Writing about a hundred years after the crucifixion, the biographer Suetonius reports that in AD 49 Emperor Claudius 'expelled the Jews from Rome because at the instigation of Chrestus they were constantly causing disturbances'. The spelling of the name is revealing. The word *christos* is Greek for 'anointed'. Its Messianic significance being alien to the conceptions of the pagan religions, even educated Romans like Suetonius took it to mean that 'those Jews' were obeying the orders of a leader bearing the common Greek name of Chrestos. From what they heard or saw, most contemporaries must have supposed that what brought the early Christians together was the practice of some idiosyncratic form of sorcery. Extant magical texts provide many parallels for Christian rites, concepts, and language, including the gibberish of 'speaking with tongues'.[20]

In the next two hundred years, as the numbers of Christians grew with increasing rapidity, communities in many parts of the Roman world seized upon them as convenient scapegoats to blame for all sorts of troubles and contretemps. Even those denunciations which led governors or emperors to mete out punishment had their origins in the localities, not in the Roman government. But in all that time, we hear of no such locally generated persecutions of Christians in Egypt, and if they did occur they must have been rare indeed, given the generally accommodating attitude of the population in matters of religion.[21]

The governmental organs of Egypt could not, of course, fail to carry out persecution orders if they came from the emperor. But there is no reliable evidence of any imperial law or general edict against Christianity before AD 249, recent scholarship having discarded as tendentious fiction the accounts in patristic literature of severe reprisals and martyrdoms under earlier emperors, and most particularly under the religiously tolerant, even benevolent, Severan emperors of the first third of the third century. Anti-Christian tendencies in the imperial government begin to be noticeable as the third century approached its mid-point. That hostility was stirred not so much by that cantankerous sect's stubborn refusal to acknowledge the divinity of their rulers, as by the spread of its pernicious disloyalty — as it must have appeared to the emperors — in the armed forces, where it was making converts among officers and men. In the persecution instituted by the imperial order of AD 249, but for which the brief rule of the Emperor Decius would have little claim to be remembered, every person, male and female, young and old, was required to participate in pagan worship in the presence of commissioners specially appointed in each locality to certify compliance. Those who failed to comply were punished as self-avowed Christians. Those who did comply were given certificates, several dozen of which have been found in Egypt — and only there. All are written on narrow, handy strips of papyrus. Were they, we may wonder, intended to be carried on the person, to be shown on demand? With very slight verbal variations the certificates are drawn up according to the following formula:

To the superintendents of sacrifices of the village of Theadelphia, from Aurelia Bellias daughter of Peteres, and her daughter Kapinis. We have all along sacrificed to the gods, and now in your presence pursuant to the ordinance I poured a libation and sacrificed and tasted of the sacrificial offerings, and I request that you so subscribe for us. [2d hand:] We, Aurelius Serenus and Aurelius Hermas, saw you sacrificing. [Date, 21 June AD 250.] [22]

Decius' witch-hunt resulted in many deaths, including that of the noted theologian Origen, a native of Alexandria. The persecution lasted one more year, till Decius died in a battle against Goths invading the empire. A decade later, after fitful resumptions, the persecution was officially called off by Emperor Gallienus, who had his hands full with rivals for his throne and barbarians at the gate. Egypt was allowed to return to its easy multiplicity of religious faiths and practices, and the Christians were free to pursue their own internal persecutions, disputes over dogma which often passed from verbal onslaughts into bloody ones. [23]

Another subject on which the papyri are uniquely informative is the manner in which festivals were celebrated. As we should expect, different customs and different degrees of participation are in evidence. On state occasions — the imperial birthdays, accession dates, anniversaries of victories, and so forth — the governmental organs, as we saw earlier in this chapter, conducted or ordered appropriate province-wide ceremonies. On other occasions more homely rites were led by local officials. A papyrus roll of AD 232 records that on the Egyptian New Year's Day [Thoth 1 = 29 August] the nome strategos officiated at the installation of a gymnasiarch, then conducted a sacrifice in the gymnasium and another in the temple of the Caesars, after which he departed from the metropolis 'for the rest of the nome, where he was present at the customary sacred services and procession'.[24]

In the cities the Greeks continued to hold their traditional athletic games, literary and musical contests, and dramatic festivals. The big difference from the practice of classical times was that now the performers — runners, boxers, wrestlers, and the others — were no longer amateurs but professionals, who travelled from place to place competing year after year. The most successful of them gained world-wide renown, substantial amounts of prize money, and a shower of distinctions such as honorary citizenships and tax exemptions.

In their festivals as in other respects the cities were aped by the soi-disant Hellenes of the metropoleis. Mention has already been made (p. 39) of the Oxyrhynchite who created an endowment 'for staging our ephebic contests in the same style as those currently staged at Antinoopolis'. A list covering the years AD 261-8 gives us the names — with one or two exceptions they are all Greek or Greco–Roman — of Oxyrhynchites who performed as poets, trumpeters and heralds in games modelled, it seems, on those of Naukratis. Two of the victorious heralds were only fifteen and sixteen years old, one of the poets only fifteen; it is a pity we have no sample of his *oeuvre*, the more so as a victorious poet of nineteen in the same list is notated as 'learning his letters'. It sounds as if those games were staged to display the talents of the metropolite youth before audiences of proud parents. There have also been found at Oxyrhynchus some accounts of expenditures by the town for several holiday celebrations. For a festival of Dionysus (probably), payments were made to a herald, a trumpeter, a comic (by which term they probably designated a song-and-dance man, who most likely wrote his own script), several individuals identified only by name, and a payment 'for blood of a calf' for the sacrifice. For a festival of Sarapis payments are recorded to 'a suitable dancer', a pair of pancratiasts (who performed a combined boxing and wrestling act), masseurs, a comic, a herald, 'the choreographer of the dancer', a reader [of the ritual texts], a rhapsodist, and a payment 'for titbits for the dog-headed [god Anubis] '. Another such account lists payments — for how many performances is not stated — of 496 drachmas to a mime, 448 to a rhapsodist, something between a hundred and two hundred drachmas to a dancer, an amount now lost to musicians, 76 drachmas to men who carried the sacred images of the god Nile and other gods in the processions, 8 drachmas to a herald, 4 drachmas to a trumpeter, and a number of other expenditures whose significance escapes us. Perpetuating another Hellenic tradition, the metropolites repaired often to their theatre, where they kept alive the classical Greek drama (Euripides for choice in tragedy, Menander in comedy), but also enjoyed the creations of contemporary craftsmen. A surviving example of the latter category sounds to us for all the world like a music-hall turn or a vaudeville act, running some ten minutes or less. How lavish the productions were we cannot judge, but one fragmentary account records expenditures for the theatre totalling 6,000 drachmas in two months, a sum sufficient to hire quantities of talent, even in the incipient inflation of the third century.[25]

The star athletes were elected to the Guild of Victorious Crowned Travelling Athletes under the Patronage of Herakles, an empire-wide association with its headquarters and cult centre in Rome. The most skilled poets, actors, and musicians were similarly elected to the Performers' Guild of Victorious Crowned Artistes from All over the World under the Patronage of Dionysus. We will have occasion to look more closely at these in Chapter 7.

As already mentioned, festivals in Egypt came frequently in the course of the year and often lasted for days at a time. Only the major holidays, however, commanded such elaborate ceremonies and games as those just detailed. On lesser occasions a more modest entertainment of music and dance, along the lines of what rich people enjoyed in their private parties, might be added to the prescribed rituals. Here is one such instance.

Aurelii Agathos gymnasiarch and incumbent prytanis, Hermanobammon exegetes, Didymos chief priest, and Koprias kosmetes of Arsinoë, to Aurelii Euripas actor and Sarapas rhapsodist, greeting. Come at once, in your usual way for assisting in holiday-making, to join us in celebrating our ancestral festival on the birthday of Kronos, god most great. The performances will run from tomorrow, i.e. the 10th, for the customary number of days, and you will receive your [usual] pay and presents. [Signatures.] [26]

The entertainments, however big an attraction, were — technically at least — ancillary to the religious rites of the occasion. The native rituals had as their common denominator hymns of praise, processions with the sacred images, incense and other aromatics, and offerings of cakes, honey, wine, and other comestibles (which were afterwards consumed by the temple personnel, as one of the perquisites of priestly office). Following are itemized lists of the objects carried in two such processions. The first was submitted to the nome strategos, the second to the adjutant of the local garrison; government controls apparently extended even to such details.

Articles for sacrifice in honour of the most sacred Nile on Payni 30th [24 June]: 1 calf, 2 jars sweet wine, 16 wafers, 16 garlands, 16 pine cones, 16 cakes, 16 green palm-branches, 16 green reeds, oil, honey, milk, and every spice except frankincense.

As customary, for the sacrifice of the present month Hathyr: 4 birds, 1 piglet, 8 eggs, 8 pine cones, 2 jars wine, a small amount each of honey, milk, olive oil, sesame oil, 8 flower garlands.

If each article in the first of the above lists was carried by a different person, even that small village turned out a procession with over a hundred participants, winding their way through the village streets to the delectation of paraders and onlookers alike. [27]

Holidays, band concerts, spectacles, and parades, there is nothing like them for drawing a crowd, ancient or modern. And where there are crowds, pushing and stretching to see, there are often accidents, as in the following incident.

Hierax, strategos of the Oxyrhynchite nome, to Claudius Serenus, assistant. A copy of the request submitted to me by Leonidas also known as Serenus is sent you [below], so that you may go with a public physician to inspect the corpse in question, then release it for burial and submit your joint report in writing. [Signature and date, 6 November AD 182.]

To Hierax, strategos, from Leonidas also known as Serenus, styled son of his mother Tauris,[28] of [the village of] Senepta. Late yesterday, when there was a festival at Senepta and castanet dancers performing their act were approaching my son-in-law Ploution's house, his slave Epaphroditos, about eight years old, wanting to lean out from the top of the said house to see the dancers, fell and was killed. For that reason I submit this petition, requesting, if it please you, that you despatch one of your assistants to Senepta, so that the body of Epaphroditos may be duly laid out and buried. [Same date. Signature.][29]

Holidays do come to an end, joys, contretemps, and all. The rituals and the revelry are over, the dancers and musicians receive their pay and depart, the spectators return to their homes, and the ordinary business of life resumes. For most of the population of Egypt that business was, or depended upon, agriculture. That is the subject of our next chapter.

6

ANNONAE FECUNDAM
or
THE PRODUCTION OF FOOD

The Nile

'A gift of the river' is how Herodotus (Book 2, chapter 5) characterized the alluvial soil deposited by the river in the Delta region, and his oft-quoted apothegm is applicable to life itself in the whole of Egypt. Without the life-giving water of the Nile the north-eastern corner of the African continent would have been an uninhabitable wasteland.

The land of Egypt, from Libya on the west to the Red Sea on the east, and from the Sudan (Nubia in antiquity) on the south to the Mediterranean on the north, is a vast expanse of desert that is interrupted by verdure only in the valley of the river Nile and in a string of oases to its west. There are but three arable areas of any size. That of the river valley proper ranges mostly from ten to twenty kilometres in width. The fertile Delta formed by the seven branches through which the river empties into the Mediterranean is almost an equilateral triangle some two hundred kilometres on a side. A hundred kilometres south and west of Cairo lies a natural depression into which the river pours a quantity of its water, forming a lake at the bottom. That area, today called the Fayyūm (from the Coptic word for lake), was in Hellenistic and Roman times the Arsinoite nome, which, with a superficies of perhaps 1,600 square kilometres (640 square miles) fed by a network of irrigation canals, comprised nearly ten per cent of the cultivable total. The lake, which today covers some 280 square kilometres, is but half its ancient size, the surface level having dropped some ten metres. Yet, despite the accretion of the formerly submerged land, the total expanse of farmland there is considerably less than it was in Roman times. That phenomenon is the result of a chain reaction that began in late antiquity. Economic distress, aggravated by inexorable fiscal demands, led to wholesale abandonment of cultivation, which in turn increased the tax burden on the population that remained. As more and more of the latter then found themselves in an unenviable situation, whole villages were in time deserted, especially those near the desert's edge. Their lands were largely marginal to begin with, and as they were also the most remote as well as the most elevated above the basin floor, the amount of labour required to get the irrigation water to them was disproportionately high. The water channels, lacking maintenance, silted up, the land unreached by the water was perforce left uncultivated, and so the whole vicious cycle recommenced. What man abandoned the desert quickly reclaimed and covered with its blowing sands.[1]

In summer the Nile in Egypt would overflow its banks, converting the whole valley into a broad lake. The cause of that annual phenomenon was a subject of speculation all through antiquity. In the fifth century BC. Herodotus reported that 'no one can speak of the sources of the Nile, since Africa, through which it flows, is uninhabited and desert.' He did, however, record three theories that had already by his time been advanced to explain the flood, and he added a rather fanciful one of his own. He rejected all the others, including the correct one, which had been deduced by the philosopher Anaxagoras and is also mentioned in a fragment from a lost play of Euripides. Four hundred years later, as we read in Diodorus of Sicily, various explanations, including the correct one, were still being rejected. Pliny the Elder, writing in the middle of the first century AD, remarks that 'the Nile rises from undiscovered sources', and goes on to give a description of its upper reaches that bears more resemblance to legend than to reality.[2]

What really happened, as modern explorations have confirmed, was that each spring the snows melting in the mountains of Ethiopia poured billions of gallons of water into the Nile at its sources. The ensuing surge washed down the great north-south rift-valley of the African continent, entering Egypt in early June. Today its flow in Egypt is controlled by the high dam at Aswan. In antiquity the flood rolled on, uncontrolled, reaching the area of Memphis and the Arsinoite nome some two to four weeks later. For the first month or so its penetration of the cultivable area was by what the Egyptians called, rather poetically, 'the sweat of Osiris', a process of slow infiltration or percolation which filled the hollows and marshes. About 20 July there would come a dramatic change, signalled by the heliac rising of Sirius, the Dog Star. The water, now laden with the mud and silt it had washed down from farther upstream, turned from a greenish colour to a reddish-brown; at the same time its level began to rise rapidly till it emerged from the river-bed and inundated the flood plain of the valley. It continued to rise, more slowly now that it covered a broader area, for nearly two months more. The resulting lake-like appearance of the valley, punctuated only by the towns and villages on higher ground, drew large numbers of visitors, including Roman emperors, to marvel at the sight. 'The appearance of the countryside is most beautiful', wrote the first-century philosopher and playwright Seneca, who owned sizeable estates in Egypt, 'when the Nile has spread itself over the fields.' The Nile in flood also became a frequent subject in Roman art, both in painting (as we see at Pompeii) and in mosaic, the most famous of these being the mosaic floor found at Palestrina near Rome (Plate 5).[3]

In mid-August at Elephantine, mid-September in the Arsinoite nome, that is some 100–20 days after its start, the flood began to recede. The water level was seen to drop, at first slowly, then rapidly. By the end of October the river had returned to its bed, leaving behind on the fields large quantities of sediment, a natural fertilizer rich in mineral salts and organic matter — the equivalent, modern measurements have shown, of some twenty tons of fertilizer per hectare. (As an additional bonus to the farmer, the flood had also drowned great numbers of rats.) In the following months the river continued to drop slowly in its bed, reaching its lowest point just before the onset of the next year's flood. Such was the hydrography of the Nile in an average year.

Already in prehistoric times the inhabitants of the land of Egypt were aware that the size of the crop they would obtain in any year bore a direct relationship to the height of the Nile flood. 'A rise of 16 cubits is just right', wrote Pliny the Elder in his *Natural History*. 'Less water does not irrigate all places, and a greater abundance delays too long in receding, thus cutting into sowing time by keeping the soil soaked, while the opposite makes for no sowing season at all where the soil is parched. Egypt reckons as follows: with 12 cubits it faces famine, at 13 it still goes hungry, 14 cubits bring happiness, 15 freedom from worry, 16 delight.' Pliny, who died in the eruption of Vesuvius in AD 79, adds that up to his time the lowest recorded rise was 5 cubits in 48 BC, the highest 18 cubits *c*. AD 45. A recently published papyrus provides indirect evidence of a disastrously low flood in AD 99. The result was such widespread starvation that Emperor Trajan, if we are to believe his panegyrist, Pliny the Younger, actually ordered some of the ships bringing grain from Egypt to return thither with their precious cargoes.[4]

Obviously, it would help to know in advance what to expect. Hence the invention of the nilometer. In its primitive form a nilometer was simply a rock conveniently placed in the river, or a pole placed there by man, on which was cut a column of horizontal notches, providing a scale for reading the high-water levels of the successive years. In historic times they built more ambitious structures, but on essentially the same principle. Usually it was a stone-lined well or chamber into which one descended to the river by a flight of stairs. Horizontal incisions on an interior wall would show the height of the water, measured in cubits (0.525 m) and fractions thereof. No other river had such devices in antiquity, and ancient visitors were much impressed with them — as are also present-day tourists, for some of the nilometers are still standing and visitable. Nilometers were installed for local guidance at many points along the river, often in association with a temple (the Nile, as we saw in Chapter 5, being worshipped as a god). Oxyrhynchus had two, the 'big' and 'little' nilometer. Some forty kilometres to its south, at what was the village of Akoris, there can still be read a series of inscriptions marking the peak levels of the Nile for a dozen or so years in the late third century. But the most important, the key nilometers, were the two on the island of Elephantine.

They were the first to measure the flood after it entered Egypt, and as soon as the flood peaked there the news of the maximum height was rushed by courier all the way to Alexandria, where the government bureau would then estimate the size of the crop and of the tax revenue to be expected. Some of the record levels inscribed on one nilometer at Elephantine can still be read:

Year 25 of Augustus Caesar, 24 cubits 4 palms 1 digit	[5 BC]
Year 13 of Nero Caesar, 24 cubits 6 palms 1 digit	[AD 67]
Year 10 of Domitian Caesar, 24 cubits 4 palms	[AD 91]
Year 14 of Trajan Caesar, 25 cubits	[AD 111].[5]

'There are', wrote Herodotus, 'no men in the whole world who obtain a crop from the soil with so little labour. They do not have the toil of cutting furrows with the plough, nor of hoeing, nor of doing any of the work which other men labour at for a crop. The river rises of itself, waters their fields, and after watering recedes. Then each man sows his field, lets in swine which he uses to tread down the seed, and waits for the harvest from it.'[6] Herodotus' amazement is understandable. Being a Greek, he came from a part of the world where men had to scrape and scratch with endless toil and ingenuity to wrest a yield from a thin and rocky soil. But Egyptian agriculture was nothing like the labour-free enterprise that Herodotus imagined. Egyptian farmers did indeed plough, especially intensively on land being cleared, reclaimed, or restored to production after lying fallow; they did indeed hoe and cultivate regularly; and they even piled on additional fertilizer when needed, most particularly in vegetable patches and olive orchards.

But as a first step, the floodwaters had to be directed to where they were most wanted or where they could not reach without human assistance. To that end an irrigation system was first engineered under the Pharaohs, and expanded under the Ptolemies. The system was most extensive in the broad basin of the Arsinoite nome. Under the feeble and financially strapped government of the last Ptolemies much of the system fell into disrepair for want of proper maintenance. Octavian, determined to make his newly acquired province a reliable source of grain to help feed the city of Rome, set his soldiers as well as locally conscripted labour gangs to the work of rebuilding the crumbling dikes and clearing the cluttered channels as speedily as possible. Regular maintenance was assured thereafter through the imposition of a corvée: each year every able-bodied adult male who worked the land, plus his slaves if any, was required to perform a certain quota of unpaid labour on the dikes and canals. The normal stint was five days a year, but additional days were imposed when exceptional conditions necessitated it. In Upper Egypt, and sometimes in other parts, the performance of the corvée was measured in quantities of earth moved rather than in time worked.

The degree to which the work was prescribed and monitored by a chain of command reaching from government headquarters in Alexandria to the smallest locality, is illustrated by the following circular letter, addressed to the strategoi and collectors of grain taxes in the nomes. It was dispatched from Alexandria on 1 April AD 278, the time of year when the water of the Nile was nearing its lowest level of the annual cycle. A similar reminder was no doubt issued routinely each year.

The season for repairing the dikes and cleaning out the canals having arrived, I deemed it advisable to remind you by this letter that all the farmers of your area should now set to work with all zeal on the tasks incumbent upon them for the benefit of the public as a whole and of each of them individually. Everyone, I am convinced, knows the good that comes of these labours. Therefore you must see to it that, as prescribed in the regulations, the usual overseers are chosen from amongst both magistrates and private citizens to compel, without malice or favour, every man to perform in person the labours required of him, so that the dikes are raised to the prescribed height and width and the breaks plugged up, to assure their being able to withstand the happily approaching flood of the most sacred Nile; and the canals are to be cleaned out to the customary 'standard of clearance' as it is called, so that they may easily contain the coming influx of the waters and direct them to irrigate the fields, this being for the common good. Absolutely no one is to be allowed to pay money in lieu of physical labour. If anyone dares to try anything of the sort or neglects these orders, let him know that at the risk not only of his property but of his very life he will face trial for sabotaging measures designed for the salvation of all Egypt.

The last two sentences refer to a chronic problem by which the corvée system was plagued: the opportunities it afforded for connivance, bribery, and favouritism. In a case that occurred a full two hundred years earlier, two of the village officers accused the superintendent of dikes of 'having taken four drachmas from each of fifty-nine men for them not to work on the public dikes . . . and having protected nine other men similarly.'[7]

Actually, the work would go on all through the year as needed, but, even after the preparations called for in the above letter, the greatest demands for such labour would come during the months of the flood, when it was absolutely essential to direct the precious water to where it was wanted. Normally the men were assigned to work within or near the territory of their home villages, but we know of at least three instances when they performed their five-day stint some twenty kilometres away. The dispatch of 181 men from Tebtynis to a village some twelve kilometres distant in early February, a time when the river had long since returned to its bed and was continuing to drop, must have been in response to an emergency situation — a major breach in a principal dike, perhaps, requiring a massive access of manpower.[8]

On completing his stint the worker would receive a quittance, scrawled on a bit of papyrus or on an ostracon. Here is one of the more than four hundred extant examples.

The twelfth year of Tiberius Claudius Caesar Augustus Germanicus Imperator [AD 52]. Has worked in the Porsierē navigable canal the five-day stint in fulfilment of his embankment labour of the said year, on behalf of [the village of] Soknopaiou Nesos: Psenamounis son of Harpagathos. I, Korax, have signed. I, Souchas, clerk of the royal secretary [of the nome], have signed.[9]

In many places the irrigation system had to cope with one final difficulty. Water will not run uphill. Even when it flowed freely through the channels, and also in the months of low water, it would have to be raised to higher ground by artificial means. The screw of Archimedes, called in Greek *kochlias* ('snail', i.e. spiral), was used to some extent. Diodorus emphasizes its use in the Delta, and Strabo tells that water was brought to the great legionary camp near Memphis by 150 prisoners operating screws and water-wheels. Most farmers, for whom the screw was no doubt too expensive to buy and operate, made do with one or both of two simpler devices. Originating in very early times, these still remain a characteristic feature of Egypt's rural landscape (Plates 6-7). One, called *kēlōn* ('swing beam') in Roman Egypt and *shaduf* today, is a pole mounted on a fulcrum to operate like a seesaw, with a bucket at one end that dips down into the water, and a counterweight at the other end to facilitate lifting the bucket when full. The other, called *sakkieh* today and *mēchanē* (sometimes simply *trochos*, 'wheel') then, is essentially a winch installed at a well head. An ox or other draft animal is walked round and round turning a large, horizontal, wooden wheel to which it is yoked; the notched outer rim of the wheel is geared at right angles to the hub of an endless chain of buckets, which are filled when they dip into the water below and spill their contents when, in an upside down position, they reach the uppermost arc of their circuit.[10]

Still, all man's effort and skill could not produce a normal crop in a year when the quantity of water delivered by the Nile fell below the required minimum. The vicissitudes of such total dependency on the Nile flood are well illustrated by two groups of documents from the reign of Hadrian (AD 117-38). From the months soon after his accession we have a number of applications for tax abatements. Their basis, according to a recurrent formula, is that 'along with his other benefactions our lord Hadrian Caesar ordained that royal, public and imperial-estate land should be taxed at their actual worth and not according to the old schedule.' The following application is one of the best preserved.

To Apollonios, strategos of the Seven-Village Apollinopolite nome, from Paphis son of Honēs and his brothers, of the village of Terythis. Near the said village district there are registered in the name of our father Honēs royal land as follows: taxed at [the rate of] $3\frac{1}{2}$ artabas [per aroura], $3\frac{1}{12}$ arouras, and another $1\frac{1}{2}$ arouras; at 2 artabas, $\frac{43}{64}$ aroura; at $5\frac{1}{12}$ artabas, $\frac{1}{16}$ aroura; at $4\frac{1}{12}$ artabas, 1 aroura; total, $6\frac{47}{64}$ arouras. Now, as these arouras do not produce enough for such a high tax, I am sorely burdened by the rent, and I offer, in accordance

with the orders of the most beneficent lord of the inhabited world,
Hadrian Caesar, to work the land in future at the rate of $1\frac{1}{24}$ artaba of
wheat for each aroura, with full credit to be allowed me for land
remaining uninundated [by the Nile flood] and half for land watered
by pumping, as is customary, so that I may share in the benefaction.
Farewell. [Date, 28 December AD 117.]

Toward the end of his reign Hadrian again found it necessary
to offer the farmers of Egypt a form of tax relief. His edict,
on 30 May AD 136, preserved on two fragments of papyrus
in Cairo and one in Oslo, takes note of the 'insufficient and incomplete' Nile floods in two successive years and in consequence grants a tax moratorium of two to five years.[11]

The Farmer's Almanac

As we turn now to examine into the principal crops of Roman
Egypt and the methods of their production, it will be helpful
to begin by laying out an agricultural calendar, in contradi-
stinction to the civil calendar which began on Thoth 1 [29
August]. The following is the schedule of major activities in
an average year in the vicinity of Memphis and the Arsinoite
nome, with each phase coming two to four weeks earlier in
the Thebaid.

June [Payni]	Rise of the Nile begins. Harvesting of cereal crops ends, threshing continues.
July [Epiph]	The Nile, accelerating its rise, enters the flood stage. Threshing ends.
August [Mesore]	The Nile approaches full flood. The vintage begins.
September [Thoth]	The Nile flood peaks and begins to fall. The vintage is completed. Dates are picked.
October [Phaophi]	The Nile flood is past. Sowing of cereal crops begins. Olives are gathered. The harvest of dates is at its peak.
November [Hathyr]	Sowing of cereals continues, cultivation begins. Olives and some dates are gathered.
December [Choiak]	Cultivation continues. Olives are gathered.
January [Tybi]	The olive harvest ends. The new growing season of vines and olives begins.
February [Mechir]	Preparations are begun for the grain harvest.

March [Phamenoth]	Preparations continue.
April [Pharmouthi]	The grain harvest begins.
May [Pachon]	Harvesting continues, threshing begins.

The Cereal Crops

Wheat and barley were the staple crops, the former going to make bread, the latter serving principally to make beer (the fermentation process had been discovered thousands of years before). A third cereal, called *olyra* in Greek, was apparently an ancient variety of triticum; it was regarded as an inferior product, and was accordingly grown in lesser quantities and was sometimes even fed to animals.

Then as now, a farmer was a man of all work, able to put his hand to any of the many chores that the season or the situation demanded. Prior to the Industrial Revolution the labour available to farmers was that of their own and others' bodies, and of their domestic animals, working the land with the aid of a few simple tools and machines. A few agricultural activities did, to be sure, imply a degree of specialization or expertise. When, for example, we read that vine-trimmers were hired, we may reasonably suppose that they would not be just ordinary farmhands but rather men skilled at that particular task; but they too must have done other work at other seasons of the year in order to keep body and soul together. In fact, the only ones on the agricultural scene who kept mostly or entirely to a single occupation the year round were estate managers, foremen, and some of those whose work was with the domestic animals — shepherds, cowherds, and drivers of pack animals; and even these last, we may be sure, pitched in when extra hands were needed for other tasks.

As mentioned in Chapter 4, slave labour played almost no part in agriculture. Most of the land of all categories — whether royal, public (i.e. state-owned), private, or belonging to an imperial estate or a temple — was cultivated under leases and subleases taken by tenant-farmers, either individually or in partnerships. Large estates were operated partly under such leases and partly with hired hands, some of them in steady employment, the rest taken on to meet seasonal needs.

Of the small farmers who were fortunate enough to own some land, there were those who worked their own holdings as family enterprises, while others preferred to let their fields to tenants; or if, as often happened, a man owned plots that were far apart, he might farm the ones nearest home himself and lease out the more distant ones. Sharecropping was far from unknown, but most extant leases provide for the payment of a fixed rent, in kind or in money or in both.

As is usual with legal documents, land leases followed standard forms and employed certain formulas regarded as essential for assuring validity and enforceability. The variables in the leases — aside, of course, from names, times, and places — were the term of the contract, and the degree to which the conditions and the obligations of the parties were detailed. The process of concluding a lease began with a bid, oral or written, directed to the owner or his representative. In its simplest form a lease consisted of such a written bid subscribed to by the addressee. More commonly, however, the lease was drawn up as a separate instrument. These 'deals' were normally struck just prior to or early in the sowing season, and when the lease ran for more than a single year there was commonly a provision for the rotation of crops.

To Heron son of Sarapion, minor, with his guardian Ischyrion son of Herodes and in the presence of the minor's mother Herois, from Aphrodisios son of Akousilaos, of the metropolis [Arsinoë]. I wish to lease the vineland belonging to Heron near the village of Euhemeria — eleven arouras, or however many they may be, in one parcel — for two years from the current 23rd year of Antoninus Caesar our Lord, at a total yearly rent for all the arouras of forty artabas of wheat (not including seed) by the four-choinix measure of the temple court, with no deduction or risk [to the lessor]. I will carry out the annual tasks — the work of the embankments and irrigation, ploughing, hoeing, clearing of ditches, sowing, weeding, and everything else that is required — at my own expense at the appropriate times, and causing no damage. I will sow the arouras in the first year with whatever crops I choose except safflower, and in the second year half with wheat and half with fallow growth, the annual transportation levies to be paid by me, Aphrodisios, but all the other taxes to be paid by Heron. I will pay the annual rent in the month of Payni, [in wheat] new, clean, unadulterated, and free of barley, in the village of Theadelphia, and after the term [of the lease] I will, after harvesting the crops to be sown, hand back the arouras free from rushes, reeds, couch grass, and refuse of every kind, if you agree to grant the lease. Aphrodisios, about forty years old, with a scar in the middle of his forehead. [Date, 9 November AD 159.] [12]

The mention of seed in the foregoing document reminds us of a chronic problem facing the tenant farmers — the recurrent need to borrow seed for planting, or to borrow money with which to buy it. Standard rates of interest were one per cent per month on money, and fifty per cent of the quantity on a loan in kind. Sometimes the arrangement was made with the lessor as part of the lease, sometimes the borrowing was from a third party. Tenants of state land had one advantage in this respect: they could obtain the needed amount of seed from the state granary in an interest-free loan. But then they paid the government a much greater portion of the crop than cultivators of private land paid to the landowners. When they borrowed seed from the government stock, that seemingly simple transaction was processed with enormous amounts of red tape intended to prevent, or at least discourage, fraud. Even so small a loan as one and a quarter artabas required the following lengthy authorization and the detailed procedure it prescribes:

Asklepiades, strategos of the Oxyrhynchite nome, to Heraklas also known as Herakleides, granary officer of the district of Pakerkē in the eastern toparchy, greeting. Measure out, under the joint authorization of me and Hierax the royal secretary [of the nome], from the best sample of the product of the past 13th year, for the sowing of the current 14th year of Hadrian Casear our lord, as a loan of seed for Apollonios son of Heliodoros (mother, Thais daughter of Chairemon), of the city of Oxyrhynchus, aged about 78 with a scar on his right eyebrow — you will identify him at your own risk — what he has requested for the $1\frac{1}{4}$ arouras of land that he cultivates in [carefully detailed location given] near the village of Ophis, viz. one and one quarter artabas of wheat, clean, unadulterated, free of earth, free of barley, sifted, by the public measure and the prescribed method of measurement (= wht. art. $1\frac{1}{4}$), with nothing deducted for debt or any other reason at all, which seed he shall sow on the land properly, under the observation of the usual appointees, and out of the new crop he shall repay the equal amount together with the state levies on the land. You will take from him the appropriate receipt in duplicate, of which you will send one copy to me. [Date, 14 November AD 129. Countersigned by Hierax.] [13]

Despite such careful checks and certifications, quantities of state grain managed somehow to 'disappear'. An unpublished Michigan papyrus contains a letter sent in the third century by the prefect of Egypt to the strategoi of the Arsinoite nome and the Heptanomia, chiding them for tolerating neglectful granary officers and ordering them to see to it that 'only those entitled to it receive seed for sowing'.

The inspectors referred to in the strategos' letter were appointed, as an unpaid public service imposed in rotation upon the more affluent (Chapter 8), to assure not only that all the seed was actually sown and none defalcated, but also that the sowing was accomplished in due season. One group of such inspectors filed the following statement on 11 September AD 117, that is at the time of year when in their area the land was beginning to emerge from the receding Nile flood:

To Apollonios, strategos of the Seven-Village Apollinopolite nome, from Pcheris son of Pouòris and Orsenouphis son of Peteminis, flood inspectors of the village of Naboö. We swear by the Fortune of the Emperor Caesar Trajanus Hadrianus Optimus Augustus Germanicus Dacicus Parthicus that we will cause all the land parcels listed below to be ploughed so as to be ready for sowing within three days, or else may we be liable to the consequences of our oath. [Names of nine villagers (only one of them Greek) with the size of the parcels of each, ranging from just under one to six arouras. Date. Signatures, Pcheris writing also for Orsenouphis who is illiterate.] [14]

The months that followed the sowing would demand the farmer's attention to cultivation and related tasks. Some leases, as we saw above, specify the operations in exact detail. Others, as in the following example, are equally detailed about the use of equipment that comes with the property.

Aurelius Dionysotheon or however else he is styled, ex-gymnasiarch and councilman of the city of Oxyrhynchus, has leased to Aurelius Haryotes son of Phnas and Tanechotis, from the hamlet of Monimos, for four years from the current third year out of his property near Sko and Monimos the twenty-two arouras previously cultivated by the same lessee, containing a water-wheel and its appurtenances equipped with all their wooden and iron fittings, so that he may each year sow whatever grains and grasses he chooses except woad and coriander, at a fixed annual rent of a hundred and forty-five artabas of wheat and ten artabas of vegetable seed, plus three hundred drachmas for the rental of the machine. For irrigating the land the lessee shall use the aforesaid water-wheel, providing his own draught animals and workmen and everything else required, the repairs to the wheel and the wages of carpenters and guards to be paid by the lessee, all free of every risk [to the lessor]. If in the years after this any [of the land] becomes uninundated, an adjustment [of the rent] will be granted to the lessee. The taxes on the land are to be paid by the landowner, who shall also be the owner of the crops till he receives the amounts due him each year. So long as he is guaranteed his lease the lessee shall pay the amounts due each year in the month of Payni, from the crops on the threshing floor of the hamlet of Monimos, unadulterated, free of earth, sifted, just as measured into the public granary, the wheat by the official measure of the landowner, the vegetable seed by the measure used at the landowner's oil press, and at the termination of the period he shall hand back the machine in sound condition, not counting wear and tear, or else he shall pay the value of anything he does not hand back, the right of legal execution existing upon him and upon all his property. This lease is valid. [Date, AD 223.] [15]

When time came and he paid his rent, the lessee would naturally want to have a written receipt. Here is a typical example (scores have been found).

Demetria also known as Taseus daughter of Apolonides, with my son Areios son of Nearchos also known as Menches as my legal representative, to Anoubion son of Serapion, tenant farmer, greeting. I have had measured out to me by you from the harvest of the past ninth year of Hadrian Caesar our lord all the rent for my arouras which you cultivated, and I make no claim against you for anything whatsoever, the taxes being payable by me, the owner. [Date, 10 September AD 125.] I, Areios son of Nearchos, am recorded as my mother's legal representative, and I wrote for her as she does not know how to. [16]

The contract quoted just prior to this receipt mentioned the farmer's need to hire guards. All through the growing and harvest seasons crops and equipment had to be protected not only against possible theft, but also against incursions by marauding cattle from nearby pasturages. The animals would, if allowed, happily invade a field of grain, spreading havoc as they trampled and fed. We hear complaints about unscrupulous shepherds deliberately letting their flocks into tilled fields belonging to others. In the following example the damage was caused right in the heart of the harvest.

To Gaius Julius Pholos, chief of police, from Ptolemaios son of Didymos, notary in the village of Euhemeria in the Themistes division. On the 1st of the present month of Payni of the 3rd year of Gaius Caesar Augustus Germanicus [26 May AD 39], Dares son of Ptolemaios and Seras son of Paës and Orseus (nicknamed Phelkis, 'lees') son of Herakleus, shepherds, broke into the allotment belonging to me near the village on the west side and let in their sheep and grazed down among the standing barley and sheaves to the tune of 12 artabas of barley. I therefore request that you send instructions that the accused be brought before you for the appropriate punishment. Farewell.[17]

No doubt such break-ins, whether accidental or intentional, were most frequent in years and places where the fodder to be found in the pastures was scanty. The farmers might resort to patrolling or posting guards, and such measures might do some good but could hardly provide total security. Irruptions by cattle remained an endemic phenomenon of the agricultural scene, and repeated efforts by the authorities to suppress the delict had no lasting effect. Toward the end of the third century the prefect of Egypt issued an edict in which he went so far as to threaten that 'a herdsman who lets his animals in among the crops . . . will have his animals confiscated, and he himself will suffer rigorous punishment.'[18] But it is doubtful that the edict was any more successful in curbing the depredations than earlier injunctions had been. All the evidence shows the inroads continuing as before.

The months pass. The crops have been sown, tended, protected, and the growing year draws toward its close. Now comes the busiest time of all, the grain harvest. If it has been an average year, what return can the farmer expect for his industry? Oddly enough considering how rich they are in details of agriculture, that is a question to which the papyri fail to provide a categorical answer. Egypt was in the eyes of the Greeks and Romans a place of almost legendary productivity; Herodotus, as we have seen, spoke of its fertility with awe, and the city of Rome was able to rely upon it for a third of her annual requirements of cereals. But nothing tells us in so many words what yield was expected or received from an aroura sown to grain. We are left to work with such indirect evidence as we can put together. Thus, we do know that in Italy and Sicily agriculture averaged a fivefold or sixfold return, with the most fertile areas producing up to ten- and fifteen-fold. Since the Romans marvelled at Egypt's productivity, the yield of its agriculture was presumably greater than that of Italy and Sicily. From other regions come two more bits of information. One records what looks like a fifteen-fold yield of barley for five years in a row in the Marmarica, a Mediterranean coastal strip several hundred kilometres west of the Nile Delta. The other, from a sixth-century military outpost in what is today the Negev of Israel, shows that irrigated fields in that desert area produced a yield of about sevenfold in wheat and eightfold or better in barley. Again, we should expect the legendary fertility of the Nile valley to exceed those returns. Finally, from Egypt itself there are two kinds of relevant data. First, taxes of eight and fourteen artabas per aroura (Chapter 8) obviously imply considerably higher yields. Second, the documents quoted earlier in the this chapter — and many others like them — reveal that normally one artaba of seed was sown per aroura of land, and that rent payments of six to nine artabas per aroura were common (in at least one instance a sixteen-fold rent payment is recorded). If, as the evidence of the extant metayage agreements suggests, the stipulated rent fell in the range of a third to two-thirds of the crop expected, the leases cited above point to average yields in the range of nine to twenty-seven times the quantity of seed planted. That range also accords well both with the implications of the data from outside Egypt, and with reasonable differentials in fertility from marginal lands at one extreme to prime fields at the other.[19]

For the harvest many additional hands were needed, some to guard (as we have just seen) the standing crops and harvested sheaves against theft by humans and damage by animals, the rest to do the actual harvesting. Day labourers were hired from wherever they could be found, some from so far away that it was necessary to offer them a bonus of as much as half the regular wage for their long trek to and from the work site.

The sheaves were gathered, tied, and loaded on donkeys or camels for transportation to the village threshing-floors (the larger estates had their own private ones). In one surviving account a man lists his expenses for this phase of the work during four days in Pachon (May). He hired sheavers, to each of whom he paid a daily wage of three and a half drachmas; in this season of great demand such labour could obtain almost the wage of a skilled artisan. For the hire of donkeys he paid two drachmas per animal per day; but the donkey-drivers — a job almost anyone, even boys, could perform — received an obol less. The donkeys, each carrying eight sheaves trussed together, made eight or nine trips a day from the field to the threshing-floor; that number would vary for other farmers, of course, with the distance to be traversed.[20]

How the busy traffic at the threshing-floor was regulated we do not know. Presumably it was a case of first come first served. In any case, it was at this point that the farmer ceased to have complete control of his crop. Now the grain from privately owned land belonged technically to the landowner until the lessee paid his rent. And now is when there came to the fore the overriding interest of the state in the collection of that portion of the crop that would come to it as taxes. The villages were required to appoint guards to protect the grain lying on the threshing-floor against theft, and inspectors to check the grain for adulteration and other imperfections. The men of the locality had to take turns performing those services without pay (Chapter 8). In one papyrus, for example, we read of villagers appointed to the following duties: 'for threshing-floor guard-duty; for crop guard-duty; to see to it that the grain measured out for taxes is clean and unadulterated; to assist the collectors of grain in guarding the public granaries and keeping them well sealed.'[21]

The last mentioned of those duties reminds us that the farmers' responsibilities respecting the crop did not end at the threshing-floor. They also had to deliver some of the grain to the local granary, which was prepared both to receive the quantities delivered to the state for taxes and to store, for a fee of course, grain for the account of private parties. Some lessors, as we have seen, stipulated to receive their rent at the threshing-floor and had it removed from there. Others —

probably most — employed the services of the local granary. A common provision of land leases called for the lessor to pay the costs of transporting his rent portion of the crop, while the lessee paid for transporting the amount due for taxes. Delivery at the granary was certified in a written receipt, examples of which are provided by hundreds of ostraca and papyri. Here is one of the simpler formulations, in an example of AD 180.

There have been measured into the public granary, of wheat from the crop of the past 19th year of Aurelius Antoninus and Commodus Caesars our lords, thorugh the grain collectors for the western toparchy, to the credit of Sarapion son of Charisios, of Episemos' Place, 4 artabas of wheat (= wht. art. 4). [2d hand:] I, Diogenes, grain collector, have signed [certifying] the 4 artabas of wheat.[22]

Even depositing the grain he owed for taxes in the public granary did not fully discharge the farmer's obligation in the matter. Later on he had to help move that grain from the granary to a nearby river port for loading on boats which would float it down the river to Alexandria (whence it would be transhipped to Rome). We will take a closer look at that phase of the tax collection in Chapter 8.

Finally, what of the chaff separated from the grain? Was it left behind on the threshing-floor for the wind to blow away? Hardly. In an agricultural economy no element of the biomass is wasted. In Roman Egypt the chaff was bundled up separately and removed for use as a fuel — for example, to heat the water in the public baths and army camps.

The Cash Crops

The cereal crops were the broad base of Egyptian agriculture, but they were far from being the only crops that the Egyptian farmers raised. Agriculture in Roman Egypt was, in fact, broadly diversified.

Many tracts of land, large and small, were devoted to viticulture. Like the Greeks and the Romans, the Egyptians in their legends and ceremonies celebrated the vine and its fruit as the gift of a god, in their case Osiris. The vine is in evidence in Egypt already in prehistoric times, and it continued to be grown there until suppressed in accordance with the Islamic tenets of the Arab domination. In the Roman period there are mentioned more than a dozen different varieties, including some acclimatized from stock imported from parts of the Greek world (Chios, Cilicia, etc.).

Unlike the open fields of grain, the vineyards were frequently walled around for protection against marauding animals and humans. Often, too, they were established in conjunction with date palms, in whose broad shade the tender vines would find protection against the direct rays of the hot Egyptian sun. The seasons of viticulture dovetailed conveniently with those of the cereal crops. In January and February, well after the sowing season of the cereals, came the time for pruning old vines, ploughing the ground for new plantations, and setting out or layering new shoots. In similar wise, the vintage, occurring in August and September, came well after the completion of the grain harvest. The ripe grapes were collected in baskets and carried to long troughs made of wood or stone, where they were trodden by human feet — with a flutist sometimes employed to enliven the monotonous work. The mash resulting from this treatment was put through a press, the liquid drained off and put up in leak-proofed ceramic containers. (The ancient practice of rendering the porous clay jars impermeable by lining their interiors with pitch is doubtless the origin of the resinated wine so popular in Greece today.) Exposure to the sun followed, either at once or after some months in the jars. The heat and resulting evaporation left the wine thicker and — at least to the local taste — sweeter. It was then clarified, repacked into fresh containers, and was now ready for consumption. Wine not intended for immediate consumption was stored away in containers labelled with the year of the vintage.

A detailed description of the operations involved in the exploitation of a vineyard is found in the following tender addressed on 21 December AD 280 by three men to Aurelius Serenus also known as Sarapion, a prominent landowner living in Oxyrhynchus.

We voluntarily undertake to perform under lease for one year more from Hathyr 1 of the current 6th year all the vine-tending operations in the vineyard and the adjoining reed plantation belonging to you near the village of Tanais, of whatever area each is, we Aurelius Ktistor and son, performing half, and I, Peloios, the other half, the said operations being: in the vineyard, pulling up reeds, collecting and removing them and throwing them outside the mud walls, propagating as many vines as necessary by layering, hoeing, scooping, and trenching around the vines, the stakes for the vines to be supplied by you the landowner but the attendant labour by us, also the remaining operations after the aforesaid to be performed by us, namely cultivating, pinching off excess shoots, fostering growth, distancing, tying [to the stakes], thinning foliage as needed; and in the reed plantation, two cuttings of each bed, watering, and continuous weeding; and further we undertake to work side by side with you in the vineyard and the reed plantation directing the donkeys bringing earth so as to assure that the earth is dumped where required, and we will test the jars to be used for the wine to be sure they are sound, and when they have been filled with wine we will store them in the sunning place, keep them oiled, move them, strain the wine into fresh jars, and guard them as long as they are stored in the sunning place, our pay for all the aforesaid operations being four thousand five hundred drachmas of silver, ten artabas of wheat and four jars of wine at the cask, which payments we are to receive in instalments as the work progresses. And we will likewise undertake to lease for one year the produce of the date palms and all the fruit trees which are in the old vineyard, for which we will pay separately a rent of one and a half artabas of fresh dates, one and a half artabas of pressed dates, one and half artabas of walnut dates, one-half artaba of black olives,[23] five hundred choice peaches, fifteen citrons, four hundred summer figs [picked] before the Nile flood, five hundred winter figs,[24] and four large, fat white melons, Furthermore, we will in consideration of the aforesaid wages also plough the adjoining fruit orchard to the south of the vineyard, and will do the watering, weeding, and all the other seasonal tasks, with only the staking and earth-spreading to be done by you, the landowner. [There follows the customary promise to do all the work properly and to return the land at the end of the lease in good condition and free from unwanted growth. Date.] [25]

Olives were another major crop, also grown in Egypt from time immemorial. Pruning and planting were accomplished simultaneously with those operations in the vineyards, and the crop was harvested in the period from late October to the end of January, that is — as in other Mediterranean lands — well after the vintage and well before the farmer had to busy himself with the grain harvest. In a papyrus of AD 177 we read of an orchard of thirty-six olive trees in an area of two arouras; this computes to approximately a hundred trees per hectare, which is not too different from the density found in parts of Greece today. Like vineyards, many olive orchards were interspersed with date palms, and walled for protection against invasion by cattle in nearby pastures. A complaint to the police written in AD 34 tells of an orchard, presumably unwalled, in which marauding cattle destroyed two hundred young plants by nibbling away their succulent heads.[26]

In the production of grains and grapes, as we have seen, the individual cultivator, with additional hired help as needed, was able to handle the harvest and its sequents himself. Not so with olives. While small quantities were consumed fresh or pickled, the bulk of the crop was destined for the production of olive oil. This required an olive press, a factory-like installation that was beyond the means of the average farmer. The cultivator of an olive orchard would take his crop to the operator of a press, either selling him the crop outright or paying him (in money or in kind) for his service.

Other oleaginous plants grown in abundance were castor, flax (for linseed oil), safflower, and sesame. Oils were much in demand throughout antiquity, serving, as they did, three major needs of daily existence. The best qualities, especially of olive oil, served as body rubs after exercise and bath, and in medicinal uses. The medium grades were consumed as food, both as cooking oil and as the 'butter' of antiquity, while the poorest grades fuelled the wicks of their lamps for lighting.

Ubiquitous in Egypt from very early times to the present, the date palm was grown either by itself in discrete stands or, as we have already observed, interspersed with vines and olives. From its fronds they fashioned brooms and plaited basketry. The fruit could be eaten fresh or dried. Dates ripened from September to December, but the harvest was at its height in October, when the vintage was over and the olives were only just beginning to ripen. Of several varieties grown, that known as the Syrian date appears to have been specially prized.

Of the other fruits grown the most important were the

were the citron, the peach, and the pear. Occasionally we encounter apples, carobs, nuts, and pomegranates.

The principal vegetable crops were beans, garlic, lentils, peas, and vetch. These leguminous products introduced some variety into, but as they too consisted essentially of carbohydrates did not significantly enrich, the basic diet of cereals.

The domestic animals, too, had to be fed. Their fodder consisted mainly of grass, plus some chickling. These were grown in permanent pastures, and in arable fields in the years when they were allowed to rest between cereal crops. The grasses were usually available as green fodder all the year round, but a quantity was also cut, dried, and stored away as hay to be used as needed. Vetch, barley, or triticum was sometimes mixed in as a feed supplement.

There were, finally, several important crops whose prime purpose was other than nutritional. Wool, shorn from sheep, will be discussed when we consider the domesticated animals. Flax had a double utility: its seeds yielded linseed oil, and from the fibres of its stalk linen was made. A small quantity of cotton, which was called (as in German today) 'tree wool', was also produced (p. 53). Egypt was also famous as the place where they manufactured a very fine textile called *byssos*, which may have been — scholarly opinions differ — either a sheer cotton or, more likely, a lawn linen.

A cash crop of prime importance was the papyrus, a versatile aquatic plant that was grown especially in the marshes of the lower reaches of the Nile and in its Delta. By 3000 BC or earlier the Egyptians had discovered how to make a writing 'paper' by pressing together strips cut from the pith of the plant. As far as we can tell, the plant was grown commercially only in Egypt. From Alexandria the 'paper' was exported to the rest of the Mediterranean world till the early Middle Ages, when the spread of Arab conquest brought with it the use of rag paper, made according to a process the Arabs had acquired from the Chinese.

In Egypt itself the papyrus plant served a variety of other purposes as well. The stalks were lashed together and the bundles fashioned into light but strong boats of very shallow draught; poled through the marshes like present-day punts, these served kings and courtiers for sport, fishermen and fowlers for their livelihood. (The buoyancy and serviceability of papyrus boats were recently demonstrated in dramatic style when the explorer Thor Heyerdahl had a large version built and sailed it across the Atlantic.)[27] The graceful feathery crown of the plant was made into garlands to adorn statues of gods and kings. The stalk, when young and tender, was eaten — they either chewed it raw for its juice, spitting out the pulp, or they boiled or baked it. The ligneous root served both as firewood and for making furniture and utensils. And the fibres of the rind, which was removed in the paper-making process, were woven into a wide range of products: baskets, mats, pillows, coverlets, sails, rope, wicks, even garments and sandals (particularly elegant examples of which have been found in Egyptian tombs).

The papyrus plant could, it seems, be harvested all the year round. One document granted the right to pick from January to August. Another, also from the Arsinoite nome, records the payment on 9 November AD 174 for 20,000 stalks of papyrus. A contract from the time of Augustus shows us the lessees of a papyrus plantation in the Delta harvesting daily in the six months from late June to late November. That same contract gives us a glimmer of the numbers of plants that could be obtained from a single plantation — numbers that stagger our imagination when we reflect that in classical antiquity Egypt supplied the writing-paper for the whole Mediterranean world. The lessees of the plantation borrowed two hundred drachmas, a sum on which the normal interest would amount to two drachmas a month. In lieu of interest they agreed to sell to their creditor at less than the market price a portion of their daily harvest up to a total of 20,000 one-armful loads and 3,300 six-armful loads of papyrus stalks.[28]

In 5 BC another papyrus plantation located in the Delta was leased for a period of two years. Here the peak harvest months appear to have been March to the end of August; at any rate, the rent payable in that period was more than double that to be paid in the other six months. The lessees also agreed, as the first of several conditions, not to pay their hired hands more than the wage-scale prevailing in the area. This suggests a cartel-like arrangement amongst the plantation owners to keep their profits high by not engaging in competitive bidding for the available labour supply.[29]

Domestic Animals

Some animals were raised to provide motive power for agricultural operations. Others were raised as sources of food, thus adding a modicum of meat protein and fat to the monotonous basic diet of carbohydrates. Some animals served both purposes, and all animals supplied, in their excrement, a valuable organic fertilizer supplementing that of the Nile silt.

The principal transport animal of ancient Egypt was the donkey. Next in frequency was the camel. Everything needed for or produced by the land — farm implements, loads of dung, sacks of seed and of crops, jars of wine and oil — moved on the backs of those beasts of burden, as did people, especially in going to and from work sites.

There are extant from the centuries of Roman rule some three score sales of donkeys, and half as many of camels. From these we learn that in the second century (for which the data are most abundant) a donkey could cost — depending on its age, sex and general condition — anywhere from fifty to 350 drachmas, a camel from 200 to more than 800 drachmas. The lowest of those prices represents two to four months' wages of a hired hand, or the cost of six or seven artabas of wheat, enough to feed a family of four for two months. Still, as the animals were practically indispensable even for small-scale farming, even poor peasants would save and skimp in order to own at least one or two. The penurious peasant who could not afford any would have to hire transport animals as needed from a commercial stable-keeper, or make an arrangement with a private party, as like as not the owner of the land he worked on lease.

The principal, almost the only, employment of horses was as cavalry mounts. The very few in private ownership were a luxury that the wealthy enjoyed for sport.

The beasts of burden were also used occasionally as draught-animals, but the really heavy loads were drawn by oxen.

Hitched singly or in pairs, the ox pulled the plough, turned the water-wheel, hauled the construction materials.

Comprising the large cattle, along with the oxen, were the other bovines, cows and bulls. The latter were also worked as draught-animals, and of course they were needed for stud. Together with cows and calves they also served as sacrificial animals in the major ceremonials (rites of lesser importance used smaller animals), small portions of the animal going for burnt offerings to the gods, the rest reserved for human consumption after the ceremony. Cow's milk was consumed mostly raw, being regarded as inferior to that of sheep and goats for making cheese. This was also a Greek prejudice, as we read in Aristotle, but the Romans held the cheese made from cow's milk to be the most nutritious of all.[30]

The smaller animals were sheep, goats, and pigs. Initially these last were used for such tasks as treading seed into the soil and tramping out grain on the threshing-floor. In Egyptian religion, as in Jewish, the flesh of pigs was regarded as unfit for human consumption, and even as late as the third century swine were barred from sacrificial use in Egyptian cults. But pork was a favourite food of Greeks and Romans, so much so that when Caracalla in AD 215 expelled the non-resident Egyptians from Alexandria (ch. 10), he included the pig merchants among the groups exempted from the expulsion order. In time, as we might expect, the influences of the Roman presence made the taboo against eating pork less and less potent for the native population. As with the bovines, we have no data on the numbers of pigs raised, or on their relative importance in the food supply. We do know, however, that in the third and fourth centuries meat figured more prominently in the diet, especially that of the army.

For sheep and goats we do have some figures in farm records and in the reports that owners were required to file annually for tax purposes. A few examples should suffice to convey the general impression. In 8 BC a man reported owning 566 sheep and 25 goats; they were divided into five flocks, each with its own shepherd. In AD 118 one individual owned 559 sheep, 209 lambs, 10 goats, and a ram; these were divided into several flocks, the male animals being kept separately under their own herdsman. The prosperous Sarapion whose acquaintance we made earlier (p. 66) owned over a thousand sheep and goats. In one village the animal census showed a total of 4,241 sheep and 336 goats; in another, 829 sheep and 28 goats.[31]

Several breeds of sheep are named in the documents: Egyptian, Arabian, Ethiopic, Euboean, Milesian, Xoitic. A special class were the 'leather covered'. These were not a distinct breed, but a select group kept wrapped in animal skins whilst their wool was growing. Originating in Asia Minor, this practice spread to Greece and Italy as well as to Egypt; it was believed to render the wool softer and silkier. Growing two coats a year in Egypt, sheep were shorn in January or February, and again in September. The summer wool appears to have been in greater demand, but whether that was because of higher quality or smaller yield, or simply because it was advantageous to have the wool to work on in advance of winter, we cannot tell. The preference for cheeses made of sheep's and goat's milk has already been mentioned. We read in several papyri of 'large cheeses', which obviously implies that there were small ones, and of 'dry cheeses', which implies moist ones; but most references are simply to cheese, without descriptives.

The small farm animals even rendered a final service after death: after they were slaughtered their skins were tanned and put to the many uses of leather. One of the commonest uses consisted of sewing two or more skins together to make containers for carrying liquids. Goatskins were preferred for that purpose, but skins of sheep and pigs were used as well.

Fowl appear to have been abundant. We find mentions of chickens, geese, and pigeons, but with few details. As we see from wall paintings in Egyptian tombs, geese were a favourite food already in Pharaonic times. The practice of stuffing them to fatten them continued all through antiquity. Gooseherds appear not infrequently in papyri of Roman date, and at least two metropoleis had a district named Gooseherds' Quarter. About hens and roosters we can say only that, as is still their wont today, they seem to have been all over the place. As for pigeons, the Egyptian strain was reputed in antiquity to be outstandingly prolific. Dovecotes have occasionally been found in excavations, and they are mentioned in a number of documents of the first to third centuries. Some were operated as sizeable business enterprises, others were small structures built into or onto private houses. Pigeon guano was a specially prized fertilizer, and was thought to be particularly beneficial in viticulture; some leases of vineyards actually specify that the fertilizer to be applied must be pigeon dung.

Agriculture was the basic and dominant economic activity of Egypt, engaging the lives of the vast majority of the population. But there were many other tasks to be done, and it is to those that we turn in the next chapter.

TRADES AND PROFESSIONS
or
THE PRODUCTION OF GOODS AND SERVICES

In this chapter we will look at those of the specialized occupations which figured most importantly in the everyday life of Roman Egypt.

The production of foodstuffs, as we saw in the last chapter, required relatively few specialists. However, even a primitive agricultural society quickly develops the need for supplementary services. In the prehistory of many (if not most) cultures, potters and basket-makers — that is, providers of receptacles for the storage and transportation of produce — were generally the first specialized workers to make their appearance. Thereafter it was a relatively quick and easy step from the weaving of basketry to the weaving of textiles for clothing and other kinds of covers.

We also saw in the last chapter that Egypt was famous for two of its manufacturers, linen and papyrus. In the third century, presumably in response to overseas demand, Egypt expanded its production of glass and became, along with Syria, a major exporter of that commodity. We have few details about the craftsmen who produced glass and papyrus, because those were manufactured principally in the Delta region, whence few records have survived. The weaving of textiles, on the other hand, is well documented because, while it gave rise to a certain number of sizeable factories, it remained basically a 'cottage industry', practised throughout the land. In the thousands of papyri found in the ruins of the up-country towns and villages we find information on many facets of the textile industry.

The weavers of the much-prized linens were the aristocrats of the craft, which was handed down from one generation to the next, with weavers often co-operating to train one another's children. Boys and girls from other households, both free children and slave, were also taken on as apprentices, generally starting between the ages of ten and thirteen. The period of apprenticeship was usually from one to three years, but it could run a year or two longer. The following contract, dating from the late second century, is typical of the score or so that survive.

Platonis also known as Ophelia daughter of Horion, of Oxyrhynchus, with her brother Platon as her legal representative, and Lucius son of Ision and Tisais, weaver, of Aphrodiseion in the Small Oasis, mutually acknowledge that Platonis also known as Ophelia has apprenticed her female slave Thermouthion, a minor, to Lucius for four years from the first of next month (Tybi) of the current year to learn the weaver's trade, on the following terms: she will feed and clothe the girl, and will place her at the teacher's disposal every day from sunrise to sunset to perform all the orders given her by him relating to the aforesaid trade, wages for the first year being eight drachmas a month, for the second year twelve drachmas a month, for the third year sixteen drachmas a month, and for the fourth year twenty drachmas a month; the girl will take eighteen days a year off for holidays, and for any days that she does not work or is sick she will remain with the teacher an equal number at the end of the period; the taxes on trades and apprenticeship are to be paid by the teacher; and Lucius. . . .

The rest of this papyrus and its text are lost, but we know from other such contracts that the terms would normally go on to obligate Lucius to do a thorough job of training the apprentice, 'as well as he knows the trade himself'. There would follow a clause providing for penalties in case of breach of contract by either party.[1]

Extant papyri record apprenticeships to a builder, coppersmith, mat-plaiter, nail-maker, piper, wool-carder and wool-shearer. But, beyond these actual instances, any trade or skill was presumably learnt through an apprenticeship. Amongst the dozens of slaves belonging to a very rich Roman family residing in Alexandria there were six trained as stenographers, two copyists or secretaries, a scribe, a cook, a barber, and a repairman. We do in fact have a contract for a slave apprenticed to a shorthand writer.

Panechotes also known as Panares, ex-kosmetes of Oxyrhynchus, represented by his friend Gemellus, to Apollonios, shorthand writer, greeting. I have placed with you my slave Chairammon, to learn the signs which your son Dionysios knows, for a period of two years, not counting holidays, from the present month Phamenoth of the eighteenth year of Antoninus Caesar our Lord, at a fee agreed upon between us of 120 drachmas; of which sum you have received a first instalment of forty drachmas, and you will receive the second, another forty drachmas, when the boy has memorized the whole syllabary, and you will receive the third, the remaining forty drachmas, at the end of the period, when he can without error take down and read back prose of every kind. If you perfect him within the period I will not wait for the aforesaid terminal date, but I do not have the right to remove the boy within the period, and he shall remain with you after the period for as many days or months as he may not have worked. [Date, 1 March AD 155.] [2]

Artisans who appear frequently in the papyri of Roman date are builders, stonecutters, brickmakers, bricklayers, and carpenters; potters and metal workers; bakers and butchers; barbers and shoemakers; dyers, fullers, and embroiderers, who enhanced the products of the weavers. Then there were the merchants and storekeepers, most of whom dealt in single products, one selling oils, another vegetables, another wool, still another fruits, and so on. Here and there we also encounter an 'everything emporium' (*pantopōleion*, as it is still called in Greece today) — what the United States and Canada call a general store. A list of items sold in one such emporium, apparently in the course of a single day, includes smoked fish (the most popular item), rope, mattresses, farina, wrought iron, legs for a couch, purple dye, fish baskets, and candle wicks. [3]

Such were the craftsmen and tradesmen who served the most important needs of day-to-day existence. And at the 'fine of their fines' there were the undertaker, the embalmer, and the grave-digger.

Let us look more closely now at the building trades. Ordinary construction, as we saw in Chapters 3 and 4, was of sun-dried brick. Kiln-fired brick was produced for special needs, as for example to give a well an impermeable lining. The more sumptuous public buildings, such as temples and theatres, were built of or (usually) faced with stone. The production of each of those materials was a special occupation, as was the use of each in construction.

The Greek word for brickmaker means, literally, 'brick dragger' (as also in the German *Ziegelstreicher*), an apt description of the essential operation in making sun-dried brick, that of mixing thoroughly, with a hoe or similar implement, the mud and the binder. Getting the mixture just right was the important step, requiring a skill born of experience; after that there was no great trick to pouring and packing the mixture into the moulds. In one instance we read that in the area 'between the village and the road leading to the metropolis' there was a brickyard spread over two and a quarter arouras, that is an area of more than 6,000 square metres. The cost of brick, and of their transport and laying, was calculated in units of ten thousand. One builder's account of bricks used in the course of a job shows 2,200 bricks delivered and laid — by how many men is, unfortunately, not recorded — in an average day.[4]

The Nile provided mud for bricks everywhere, but stone had to be brought from the quarries. Those lay mostly in Upper and Middle Egypt, in the desert between the Nile and the Red Sea. In that seemingly foresaken wasteland Nature's bounty comprised, along with metals and precious and semi-precious stones, abundant deposits of limestone, sandstone, basalt, granite (red, grey, and black), and porphyry. This last, after centuries of moderate use, attained in late antiquity the status of an imperial purple, especially favoured for pillars, statues, and decorative objects. There was relatively little marble in Egypt, and that little was of rather indifferent quality compared with that which the Greeks had found and put to such brilliant use in the Aegean world. But the urban Greeks of Egypt and their metropolite imitators were doubtless none too sorry about the inadequate supply of local marble; having to import it when they wanted it for some conspicuous display gave them a continuing tie to the homeland. For more ordinary purposes, such as the paving of their streets, the Alexandrians were content to get their cobblestones from the quarry at Akoris, south of Oxyrhynchus. All such mineral deposits, it should be added, were the property of the state.

Digging out the rock and ore was, to put it mildly,

unpleasant work. In the desert the blazing sun of day is often followed, especially in the winter, by biting cold at night. Furthermore, most mines and quarreries were isolated outposts, remote from 'civilization'. Manpower for work under such conditions was obtained in one of two principal ways, either by the government's leasing the works to a contractor, who then attracted workers by offering premium wages, or through the use of convicts. The gentry were exempted from condemnation to work in mines and quarries. That demeaning and cruel punishment was deemed suitable only for lower-class criminals and slaves, notable among them being captives from the Jewish revolts and, later, Christians. Each mine and quarry was policed by a garrison of soliders, usually under the command of an officer holding the rank of centurion.

Subatianus Aquila [prefect of Egypt] to Theon, strategos of the Arsinoite nome, greeting. Niger, slave of Papirius, condemned to the alabaster quarry for five years by his Honour Claudius Julianus, now that he has completed the term of his sentence, I [hereby] release. Goodbye. [Notation of receipt. Date, 27 December AD 209.] [5]

Architectural remains and written records, mostly on ostraca, have been found at several of the desert outposts. They give us vivid glimpses of the conditions of life for the soldiers stationed there and the civilians who came there on business. In one particularly pathetic letter a soldier looks forward to a furlough before he has to settle in to eighteen more months of boring isolation and relative inactivity. How precious a chit like the following must have been!

You have ten days' furlough, Ammonas. You have two additional days in which to return.[6]

But our concern in this chapter is not so much with the operation of the quarries as with their products.

From the quarry the broken rock was transported overland to the Nile, where it was loaded onto barges specially built or adapted for carrying stone; and after being carried up or downstream as required, it had once again to be taken overland from the nearest river port to the work site. Obelisks and other huge monoliths — fortunately not your everyday product — presented special problems when it came to moving them. As Pliny the Elder wrote of one such, eighty cubits (42 m) long, 'It was a much greater undertaking to transport and erect it than to quarry it.'[7]

Details about the artisans who worked with stone and about the uses to which it was put are available to us in a variety of documents, including some accounts of repairs to temples that are particularly interesting for their great detail. A small sample should suffice for purposes of illustration.

To the mason, for dressing and fitting stones for the corner above the foundation	6 dr.
To the stonecutter, for cutting 100 stones for the corners of the gateway colonnade	10 dr. 3 ob.
To hire of five donkeys to bring the lime from the harbour of Bousiris to the city	[] dr.
Cost of gravel, including transportation from the harbour to the kiln	[] dr.
To the kiln stoker, for preparing, firing and [afterwards] cleaning out [the remains of] plaster and gravel from the kiln	6 dr.
For carrying the fired gravel from the kiln to the work site	[] dr.
Freight charge of the boat bringing sand for mixing with the lime	2 dr.
For bringing the sand from the harbour to the work site	2 dr.
To plasterers, for stuccoing	16 dr.
Cost of chaparral wood bought from the government, needed for the work on the doors of the Isis temple	50 dr.
Cost of carpenter's glue for the door of the gateway, $3\frac{1}{4}$ minae [weight]	19 dr. 4 ob.[8]

Timber has always been scarce in Egypt, and that fact is reflected in the singularly high cost of the wood in the account just quoted. The native chaparrals, acacia, sycamore fig, and tamarisk, were put to use in boat-building, and they were adequate for doors and windows, as were the woods of dead or dying fruit trees. Even the trunks of palm trees were put to use: sawn into boards, they were employed especially for roofing, where their light weight would be an advantage. But heavy construction lumber had to be brought in from abroad. An attempt, early in the reign of the Ptolemies, to acclimatize the fir in Egypt apparently did not succeed in creating a domestic source of that wood. Pine and fir beams, such as the ones (a third of a metre wide by a fifth of a metre thick) that were used in the reconstruction of the gymnasium of Antinoopolis in AD 263, were no doubt regularly imported from Syria and Asia Minor.[9]

We turn now to the methods and personnel of the transportation trades. Donkeys and camels were the ordinary overland 'vehicles', and their drivers belonged to a trade that was, if not highly skilled, still essential to the economy. The typical carrier was the owner-driver of his own animal or string of animals, but many were merely employees of entrepreneurs owning large stables. For a few months in each year their services were practically pre-empted by the requirements of moving the harvest from fields to threshing floors, thence to the farmsteads and granaries, and finally from the granaries to the river ports for lading on boats. The rest of time the animals were available for private hire. Wheeled vehicles were generally reserved for loads too heavy for the animals' backs.

At many points tolls were levied on overland traffic passing in either direction. Toll payments were receipted on chits of papyrus, more than three hundred of which, emanating from a dozen or more different stations, are known. The following examples were issued at Arsinoite villages from which trails crossed the desert to Memphis.

Paid at the toll house of Soknopaiou Nesos, for the 1% [toll] and the ½% [goods tax]: Sarapion exporting on one (1) camel vegetable seed, six art. paying five dr., and on one camel and two donkeys wheat, twelve art. paying three drachmas. [Date, 26 November AD 162.]

Paid at the toll house of Philadelphia, for the desert patrol tax: Diogenes exporting fresh dates, one donkey load, and wheat, one donkey load. [Date, 16 September AD 147.][10]

Some of the desert routes were major traffic arteries, notably those leading from Coptus in Upper Egypt to Myos Hormos ('Mouse Harbour') and to Berenike (named for a Ptolemaic queen), Red Sea ports through which the trade with India, Arabia, and East Africa was funnelled. Along those routes, the first some 150 kilometres in length and

the second more than twice that, watering stops and caravan-
serais were maintained at convenient intervals; fortunately,
the desert had a good supply of fresh water not too far
below the surface. The opening of still another such route is
recorded in an inscription of AD 117:

The Emperor Caesar Trajanus Hadrianus Augustus [his many other
titles follow] opened the new Hadrian Way from Berenike to Antinoopolis through safe and level country, with stations of plentiful water,
rest stops, and guard-posts along the route.[11]

The tolls collected no doubt went, at least in part, toward
the maintenance of those services, most particularly the
services of the desert police, who protected travellers and
caravans against robber bands. Here are a few of the charges
in a tariff posted at the Coptus toll-house in AD 90.

For a skipper in the Red Sea trade	8 dr.
For a guard	10 dr.
For a sailor	5 dr.
For an artisan	8 dr.
For prostitutes	108 dr.
For sailors' women	20 dr.
For soldiers' women	20 dr.
For a permit for a camel	1 obol
For seal on permit	2 ob.
For a donkey	2 ob.
For a covered waggon	4 dr.
For a funeral, round trip	1 dr. 4 ob.[12]

On goods moved by boat similar charges were levied at
points along the river for tolls or berthing. Collectors of
tolls and customs dues had the right to search for contraband,
a privilege which could, however, easily be abused, especially
in out-of-the-way places. A prefect of Egypt whose name is
lost took note of the problem in issuing the following edict:

I am informed that tax-farmers have employed remarkably clever
devices against persons travelling through the country and, in addition,
are fraudulently demanding charges not due them and are deliberately
holding up persons who are in a hurry so that they will buy from them
a speedier departure. I therefore order them to desist from such greed.
[The rest is lost.]

On the inspection of cargoes we have the following fragment:

if the customs collector asks that the boat be unloaded, the merchant shall unload. If anything is found other than what he declared, it shall be liable to confiscation; but if nothing is found, the customs collector shall reimburse the merchant for the expense of unloading . . . and he shall receive from the tax farmers a written certification, so that he may not again be so molested. [The rest is lost.]

The following was not found in Egypt, but it has the ring of empire-wide applicability.

The tax farmer has the right of search. Undeclared articles shall be confiscated. The person of a Roman matron may not be searched.[13]

Overland transport was often only a stage preceding or following shipment by water. The water-borne commerce of Egypt comprised both river traffic and overseas transfers, but as the shipping on the Mediterranean and Red Seas occupied only an exiguous segment of the population our survey will concentrate on that which directly affected the lives of all, the river traffic.

In sheer volume the movement of grain to Alexandria (whence most of it was transhipped to Rome), and of foodstuffs and fuel to supply the army of occupation, overshadowed all else. A state-owned fleet of barges, operated by crews either hired or impressed, formed the nucleus of the grain fleet on the Nile. But the bulk of the tonnage consisted of privately owned boats, which the nome strategoi would requisition when they were needed for government service.

By its very nature river traffic was a more complex activity than overland transport. It was not only that one cargo vessel carried the loads of scores and even hundreds of donkeys and camels, but even a simple river-boat was a craft that could be operated only by men trained to the requisite skills. Then too, there was a whole series of landing stages and other facilities to be maintained for the needs of the river traffic. The boats on the Nile ranged in size from one-man punt-like skiffs made of papyrus stalks lashed together (p. 128) to vessels some twenty metres long by three metres in beam, having a rated capacity of 18,000 artabas, or about 500 tons. The larger of them also had a square sail to help in working their way up-river, as well as oars which were used both to pull against the current and to speed a downstream journey. According to one source, in summer, with the etesian winds blowing from the north, a laden cargo-boat could make forty kilometres a day sailing south against the current. Basically the gear of such vessels corresponded, on a smaller scale, to that of the larger, seagoing ships of the time. In a contract drawn up in AD 212 an owner gives a long-term lease on

the boat of Greek type belonging to him, of four hundred artabas burthen more or less, fully decked and overspread with mats, complete with yard, linen sail, ropes, containers, rings, blocks, two steering oars with tiller bars and brackets, four oars, five boat poles tipped with iron, companionway ladder, landing plank, winch, two iron anchors with iron stocks, one one-armed anchor, fibre ropes, tow line, mooring lines, three loading chutes, one measure, a balance, sailcloth, a round-bottomed two-oared skiff with all the usual gear and an iron spike.[14]

Obviously, it took a considerably greater capital to own a cargo boat, even a relatively small one, than to own a donkey or a camel. For that reason skippers who owned the craft they operated were comparatively few. More typically the boat was owned by a man of means — usually a metropolite, a Greek or a Roman — who had bought it as an investment. He would then engage a skipper, who would take charge of operating the boat, hunting up cargoes to carry, and signing on the needed crews. In the following instance, dating from AD 221, the boat is owned and operated by two inhabitants of Oxyrhynchus. A fellow townsman charters

the self-propelled light boat that they own, fifteen cubits long, fully equipped and with crew sufficient for a voyage up-river to Tebennouthis and down again from Tebennouthis to Oxyrhynchus, charter price for the round trip to be five hundred drachmas of silver, one metretes of wine, ten boxes(?) of veal, ten metretai of olive oil, and three metretai of radish oil, of which the owners acknowledge that they have received a hundred drachmas on the spot, and they will receive the rest upon unloading in Oxyrhynchus on the return from Tebennouthis. The owners are to have the boat ready for loading on the second of next month, Phaophi . . . and sail it with all caution, not sailing by night or in storms, and anchoring each day in the most secure anchorages. . . . The owners are to deliver the cargo intact, whole and free of any damage incurred during shipping. The said owners will wait in Teben-nouthis for the charterer till the tenth of the said month Phaophi, after which they will sail away as indicated above. This charter is valid. [Mutual consent. Date.] The owners will be paid fares for four passengers. [Signature.] [15]

There are few mentions of bridges in Egypt, although the Romans undoubtedly built or rebuilt some, if only to facilitate the movement of their troops. But the transfer of people and goods across the Nile and the larger irrigation canals, as well as over the valley floor in the flood season, was mainly by ferry. We have no details about the craft used for that purpose, but they must have been relatively small and of shallow draught, and it seems that they were generally operated by their owners, who obtained a concession to ply their routes by the payment of a licence fee or an income tax.

In many trades the workers were organized in guild-like associations. Extant documents inform us of the existence of 'guilds' of donkey-drivers, fullers and dyers, weavers, potters, glassmakers, hieroglyph carvers, river pilots, skippers, shoe-makers, salt merchants, and others whose occupations are not recorded in the surviving portions of the relevant papyri. Guilds of bread-makers, bronze welders, beer merchants, oil merchants, and many others, are mentioned in documents of the fourth century and later, and while some of those were doubtless newly created (under the socioeconomic policies of the Dominate), the rest are likely to have been in existence earlier as well. A half-dozen papyri dating from the first century of Roman rule enlighten us on some of the inner workings of these organizations. There was a written set of by-laws, similar on the whole to those of the artisans' and burial societies (*collegia*) that proliferated all over the Roman Empire. The by-laws fixed the schedule of dues, the calendar of banquet days, and the amounts of the fines to be imposed for different kinds of misconduct, including failure to attend stated meetings. Some also dealt with the economic interests of the members, setting the prices at which they were to sell their products or furnish their services. Usually there were also provisions for procedures to be followed in amending the by-laws, for assistance to members in need, and for the funeral rites to be observed when a member died. In some guilds, if not in all, a member was expected to celebrate occasions like his marriage or the birth of a child with a suitable contribution to the association's treasury.[16]

However, in contrast with the medieval guilds, whose members banded together on their own initiative for the protection of their common interests, the guilds of Roman Egypt were created to serve the convenience of the provincial administration in dealing with the people engaged in the different trades and occupations. When, for example, the government wanted to place an order for garments or blankets for the military, it needed only to communiate with the secretary of the weaver's guild in the area concerned, instead of with dozens of weavers individually. Similarly, the existence of the association made it easier for the provincial administration to hold the group collectively responsible for the execution of the order, and collectively liable for any shortcoming.[17]

There were two sex-linked occupations: wet-nurses and prostitutes. Of the latter we have already had two mentions, one in a private letter, the other in the so-called Tariff of Coptus (p. 141); another will appear in the next paragraph, still others in Chapter 8. When the inscription containing the Tariff was discovered in 1894, early commentators jumped to the conclusion that the steep charge levied on prostitutes was evidence of an effort tax 'the world's oldest profession' out of existence. But with sobering second thoughts came the reminder that the overriding principle of Roman taxation policy was no moral dictate, but simply 'what the traffic would bear'. Seen in that light the exceptionally high fee exacted from prostitutes passing through the Coptus toll-gate looks like a reflection of how lucrative their occupation would be in an area where, aside from the few who took their women along, the men who plied and policed the lonely desert routes would be starved for female company.

But even though the takings might be attractive, a woman would normally not, it appears, enter upon a life of prostitution unless driven to it by the pinch of necessity. An episode recorded in the fourth century gives us a picture in this regard that is surely representative of the preceding centuries as well. An Alexandrian named Diodemos was on trial for the murder of a 'public prostitute' whom he had frequented. Just before sentence was pronounced the court entertained a plea for damages, or relief:

> The mother of the prostitute, one Theodora, a poor old woman, asked that Diodemos be compelled to provide her with means of support as some small consolation in her life. She said, 'It was for this that I gave my daughter to a brothel-keeper, in order that I might have some means of support. Now since, with my daughter dead, I have been deprived of my source of sustenance, I accordingly ask that some modicum be given me, a poor woman, for my support.'[18]

The other strictly female occupation was that of the wet-nurse. With infant mortality so prevalent there was never a shortage of women secreting unused milk. To such a woman might be brought the offspring of a Roman or an Alexandrian *haut mondaine* who eschewed breast-feeding as a threat to her stylish figure or her social calendar. Or the nursling might be an infant whose own mother had died, or one whose mother's milk had dried up. But in the preponderance of documented instances the nursling was a foundling that its rescuer wanted to raise to be his slave. Whether the wet-nurse herself was slave or free seems to have been a matter of genuine indifference. Expediency was the guiding consideration, with the result that we encounter not only (as we might expect) slave women nursing freeborn infants, but also free women nursing slave children. The length of time for which the nurse was hired varies, in the extant documents, from six months to three years; the median and most common period was two years. (Long by our standards, such periods of breast-feeding are still quite common in many parts of the 'third world'.) Otherwise the contracts for such service follow a fairly standard pattern, with relatively few individual variations. The nurse takes the infant to her own place of abode, promising to feed it and clothe it and do everything necessary to provide it with proper nurture. If the nursling dies within the stated time, she is obligated to take another child and nurse it, without additional pay, for the full term of the original contract. Sometimes there is a specificiation that during the term of the contract, 'in order not to spoil her milk', the nurse will not have intercourse with a man, or become pregnant, or suckle another child. Her wages, the equivalent of those of an unskilled labourer, were usually paid partly in cash (a sizeable fraction in advance) and the rest in monthly instalments of money and olive oil (the latter no doubt to protect the infant's skin against chafing and rash).

Throughout the economy, in its varied activities, small sums were usually paid in cash passing 'from hand to hand' (a standard phrase occurring in many a contract or transaction). Large sums were handled through banks. These were numerous and ubiquitous, located mostly in towns and cities, as we should expect, but in the more populous villages as well. The 'public' banks functioned primarily for the deposit and transfer of tax revenues, while practically all private and even some public business was conducted through privately owned banks. Although banking practices did not develop as far in the direction of modern systems as has sometimes been supposed, they did include, in addition to simple deposits and withdrawals, such services as payments to third parties and transfers of funds, often quite sizeable amounts, to other banks and other accounts on the strength of a simple written order. If those called exchange banks, leaseholds banks, and banks of record, specialized in the designated activities, they did not do so to the exclusion of other types of transactions. Thus, a man taking a lease of land for five years paid the rent for the whole period in advance through an exchange bank, which sounds as if it were here functioning very much like what we call a discount bank. In another instance an exchange bank appears to be serving as a bank of record in a house purchase.[19]

Such information as we have on the subject reveals, to no one's surprise surely, that bankers were generally men of wealth and high social standing. Except for a few village bankers with Egyptian names, the bankers we encounter bear Greek names, with here and there a Roman one. Most were members of the local gentry, and a few were men of considerable distinction, like one Tiberius Claudius Demetrios son of Bion, an Alexandrian who was elected gymnasiarch of his city, awarded Roman citizenship, elevated to a priest-hood, and honoured with membership in that most famous of ancient athenaeums, the Museum of Alexandria. We meet him in a receipt issued *c.* AD 50 by him and his brother Isidoros for the repayment of the impressive sum of thirteen talents (78,000 drachmas) paid back 'by Chairemon in person and through others, by previously issued drafts on the exchange bank of Narcissus son of Archias, by drafts on the exchange bank of Demetrios and Isidoros themselves, and by the draft now drawn by the said Chairemon on and paid by the aforesaid exchange bank of Narcissus.'[20] Banking was a business, it seems, in which one started rich and ended richer.

Wealth and privilege were the lot also of actors and prize athletes. They performed in the cities and towns of Egypt, and the stars at the very top of their profession toured the major cities of the Roman world, where they were also showered with honours.

Theatrical — or, as they were then called, Dionysiac — artists were, if they became sufficiently distinguished, elected to their local or regional guilds. These were units of the Sacred Society of World-wide Travelling Victorious-in-Sacred-Games Gold-Crowned Artists Dedicated to [the god] Dionysos and Our Lord [name of ruling emperor]. The society, the grand-iloquent name of which occurs in several variations (as will presently appear), had its headquarters and cult centre in Rome. Three papyri of the third century, one in Berlin, the other two in Oxford, recite the privileges lavishly bestowed upon the members of the society by Augustus and later emperors. Hadrian, for example, issued an edict confirming

the privileges granted the society, namely personal inviolability, seating precedence [in theatres, etc.], exemption from military service, immunity from compulsory public services (Chapter 8), retaining untaxed all their earnings from games and other performances, dispensation from providing sureties for their exemption from the tax for the common sacrifices, the right not to be compelled to billet strangers or to be confined under any other constraint . . . or to be liable to a death penalty.

Further confirmations were issued by Septimius Severus and Caracalla, and again by Severus Alexander. The recitation of the imperial benefactions is followed by the society's certificate of an individual's membership; in contrast to the terse, routine communications from the emperors, the society's language is fulsome and prolix. The following example bears the Egyptian date equivalent to 10 February AD 264:

The Society of World-wide Artists Dedicated to Dionysos and the Emperor Caesar Publius Licinius Gallienus Maximus Pius Felix Augustus the New Dionysos, to the [member] artists dedicated to Dionysos, victors in sacred games, gold-crowned winners, and to their [non-member] fellow contestants, greeting. Know that Marcus Aurelius Serenus son of Serenus, of Oxyrhynchus, has been inducted into the Sacred Artistic World-wide Travelling Gallienic Great Society as high priest at the 135th sacred, triumphal, international, Olympic-class games of the great festival of Antinous, and that he has paid the enrolment fee prescribed by imperial law, viz. 250 Attic drachmas, and all the sacred charges for the worship of the emperors. We have written so that you may be informed. Goodbye.

Each of the officers then signs, each repeating almost *in toto* the language of the document they are witnessing. There follows, finally, the text of a communication from the society to the council of Oxyrhynchus informing that body that Marcus Aurelius Serenus, as a member of the society, was entitled to the privileges cited.[21]

For the athletes there was a parallel organization, the Sacred Hadrianic Antoninian Septimian Society of Travelling Athletes Dedicated to Herakles, whose privileges were confirmed by the Emperors Claudius, Vespasian, and Septimius Severus as well as, presumably, by the emperors whose names were incorporated into the society's title. Then as now, a professional career in sports could lead to even greater fame and fortune than a career in the arts. Star athletes were rewarded with rich purses, honorary citizenships, and lifelong incomes, in addition to other valuable privileges such as exemption from taxation and compulsory public services. As prime examples, which come as it happens from outside Egypt, we may point to the charioteer who in twenty-four years of racing amassed something like a million and a half drachmas in prize money, or the boxing champion, undefeated after more than a hundred bouts, who was made a citizen of fourteen different cities all over the Roman world, including Alexandria and Antinoopolis.[22]

For Egypt the papyri provide, as usual, more intimate details. A document of AD 194, similar to that quoted above for the Dionysiac artists, contains the notice to society members 'that Herminus also known as Moros, boxer, is a member of our Society and has paid the prescribed enrolment fee of 100 denarii [400 drachmas] in full.' Also from Hermopolis we have an application from a victorious pancratiast to his native town for the pension of 180 drachmas a month to which he is entitled for each of two victories, 'one at the sacred triumphal games [of Hermopolis] . . . [the other] for the victory and crown which I won at the sacred triumphal world-championship Olympic-class games held in the municipality of Sidon.'[23] As to the size of that pension, we may note for purposes of comparison that in the mid-third century skilled labour and legionary soldiers, even after the fifty per cent increase granted the latter by Caracalla, were paid at the rate of about sixty drachmas a month.

What is more, not only were the privileges granted to the athletic victor for the rest of his life, but, the financial straits of the times notwithstanding, they were sometimes extended to his heirs after his death.[24]

Finally, like priesthoods or other assets, privileges attained by victorious athletes could be bought and sold. No doubt those athletes who had been showered with the rewards of repeated victories found it particularly convenient thus to convert some of their duplicate rights into cash, as in the following example of 18 April AD 212.

> Transfer from the account of Eudaimon also known as
> Nilos and Hierakion also known as Anoubion, silv. dr. 1,000
>
> [Date], through the bank of record of Anoubion son of Ammonios, [citizen] of the Matidian tribe and Kalliteknian deme, in Antinoopolis. . . .
> To Tourbon son of Apollonios son of Ammonios, of the Augustan tribe and Dioskourian deme, victor in sacred games and tax-exempt.
>
> Tourbon acknowledges that he has received from Hierakion also known as Athenodoros for the two rights of being supplied with food at public expense which he has sold to Hierakion's aforesaid sons, rights awarded

for his victories in the men's boxing event in Antinoopolis in the thirty-first year of the deified Commodus and the following thirty-second year at the great sacred games in honour of Antinous, the price agreed upon with him, namely a thousand drachmas of silver (silv. dr. 1,000), pursuant to the official record in the public archives, with all the rights thereunto appertaining. [This receipt is read aloud to Tourbon, and his acknowledgment of receipt is written for him 'because he says he does not know how to write.' Signatures of three witnesses and the buyer follow.] [25]

To conclude this chapter let us consider the practitioners of the learned professions. The only ones who appear with any frequency in the papyri are the physicians, and even they are rarely encountered in the exercise of their profession. In most cases they are mentioned in mundane contexts relating to ownership of property, payment of taxes, and so forth. Still, we do get a few glimpses of doctors at work.

At the end of Chapter 5 we saw one instance of a physician filing an official report on an accidental death. The following on a victim of assault and battery was filed by a Roman citizen residing in a village — no doubt a veteran who had been in the medical corps during his years of military service.

Copy of report. To Protarchos, strategos of the Arsinoite nome, Herakleides division, from Gaius Minicius Valerianus, who conducts a medical practice in the village of Karanis, and from Phaësis son of Zenas and Esouris son of Kastor, both elders of the village. [Regarding] the condition of Mystharion son of Kames, after visiting him in the presence of his brother Petesouchos we report to you as follows:
We swear by the fortune of the Emperor Caesar Trajanus Hadrianus Augustus that on the fifth day after he was struck above the left temple of his head I, Gaius Minicius Valerianus, treated Mystharion for a deep wound, in which I found small fragments of stone, and we, Phaësis and Esouris, observed the aforesaid wound, or may we be liable for our oath [if false]. [Signatures. Date, 22 August AD 130.]

In a letter addressed on 29 August AD 58 to a physician friend, the writer, after the usual opening amenities, comes to the point:

you sent me two prescriptions, one for the formula of Archagathos, the other for a caustic plaster. The Archagathian is fine, but the caustic omits the relative weight of resin. What I really want from you is [the

formula for] a strong caustic that can be applied without danger to
the soles. I am badly in need of one. As for the dry plaster – you wrote
there are two kinds – send me a prescription for the relaxing kind. . . .[26]

Although there is but a single mention of a midwife in
all the thousands of papyri published so far, that mention
serves to remind us that the Egyptian peasantry, like rural
populations in all times and places, largely ministered to its
own health needs. With the prime medical facilities concen-
trated in the cities and towns, villagers relied for ordinary
ailments on their own local pharmacopoeias of simples and
nostrums, developed through trial and error over the centuries.
More than a hundred medicinal recipes are written on papyri
of Roman date, remedies for everything from abdominal
complaints to zymosis. The ingredients, as we should expect
in a rural setting, derive mostly from the vegetable kingdom;
by actual count they number three times as many as those of
animal and mineral original put together, and they range
from such everyday products as wine to rarities like absinthe
and asphodel. Some recipes, we find, have a strong admixture
of magic or mumbo-jumbo in the instructions for their
application, but most are straightforward, no-nonsense
prescriptions. A few, indeed, are accurate reflections of the
best medical knowledge or opinion of the time. Remedies for
falling hair, for example, have been found in more than one
version, and one that was published over fifty years ago was
just recently recognized as being the same prescription that is
found in the works of Galen, the leading physician of the
Roman Empire. It reads:

To stop the hair from falling out.

After steeping laudanum in dry wine, alternately add oil of myrtle and
wine till it has the thickness of honey, then anoint the head before and
after bathing. It is even better to add some maidenhair fern, which
some call adiantum, half the quantity of the laudanum, and to use it
with oil of myrtle or with nard.[27]

There are two or three occurrences of the word for a vet-
erinary ('horse doctor' in Greek), and of the expression
'legionary doctor', but they occur as simple identifications, in
contexts that have nothing to do with their professional
work. Nor do we have any details concerning the training of

a physician. We do know that there never was, anywhere in classical antiquity, any formal examination to be passed or certification to be obtained before one could engage in the practice of medicine. Empirical training in the healing arts was no doubt acquired through a period of apprenticeship, and was available not only in the big cities and famous medical centres, but wherever a local doctor was willing to teach by his own example. The wide dissemination of medical books is apparent from the papyrus finds. In Middle Egypt the ruins of the city of Antinoopolis, of the nome capitals Hermopolis and Oxyrhynchus, and even of some villages, have yielded up to the excavator's spade a commentary on a treatise of Galen's, a dozen fragments from works of Hippocrates, and well over half a hundred bits of medical works hitherto unknown to us. The works of Greek medical writers are also reflected in many of the medical recipes that have been found, as in the example quoted just above. In addition, the Egyptians had a long and impressive medical tradition of their own, recorded in hieroglyphic papyri going back to the third and second millennia BC. The medical practitioner of Roman Egypt thus had a twofold armamentarium upon which to draw, and some interpenetration of the two traditions was inevitable. A good example of such commingling is seen in a recently published papyrus roll in Vienna. It is a medical book written in Demotic in the late second century AD, when it was one of the volumes in the library of the temple of Souchos, the crocodile god, in Arsinoë. The text of the volume is a heterogeneous compilation. Some of its features and elements derive from Egyptian medical writings of Pharaonic date, some of its prescriptions are clearly of Greek origin, and — most striking of all — most of its pharmacopoeia consists of Greek terms in Egyptian transliteration.[28]

We do have one other interesting sidelight on the preparation of a village doctor. It deserves our attention for a moment, even if the light it sheds is somewhat obscured by uncertainty. In his declaration for the census of AD 118 a villager records as one member of his family a son of seventeen, and gives the young man's occupation in an abbreviation for which the corresponding English would be *physi*. Do we, then, have here a seventeen-year-old engaged in the practice of medicine (as has been assumed ever since the papyrus was published, more than seventy years ago)? In the manual trades, as we saw near the beginning of this chapter, the period of apprenticeship usually ended at an even earlier age. Did the same pattern prevail in medical training? It is true that young people mature sooner in warm climates than they do among us. Does that fact offer us a sufficient basis for supposing that the village residents were content to take their complaints to one so young? He may of course have been the only practitioner in the locality. Or perhaps he had acquired a reputation for curative laying-on of hands or some other divinely inspired faculty; such practices and the belief in their efficacy were widespread in the ancient east. Then again, the abbreviation employed by the father (who gives his own occupation as scribe) may have been intended to convey that the young man was a physician's assistant, a physician-in-training, or a physical therapist. It will be interesting to see how this puzzle is finally resolved when, and if, further evidence turns up.[29]

Whether doctors' fees were high or low, we have no idea; they are never once mentioned. The same is true of lawyers. About them, in fact, we know altogether less than about doctors. They appear often enough in courtroom settings, speaking for their clients, but we have no information about how one prepared for a career in the law or at the bar. What the growing body of papyrological evidence has made clear is that the law they practised was neither Roman nor Greek nor Egyptian. Basically it was an amalgam of the last two, but Roman principles and procedures inevitably exercised an influence that could not but increase under Roman rule; and that development accelerated markedly after AD 212, when Emperor Caracalla extended Roman citizenship to virtually the entire population of the Roman Empire. The two examples that follow should suffice to illustrate the spread of Roman influences in the area of law. In the provincial law of Egypt a minor attained the age of majority at fourteen, when he was enrolled as subject to poll tax, but by the middle of the third century the age had been raised to the Roman standard of twenty-five. Again, in a recently published papyrus of AD 260-1 certain provisions for the return of a dowry upon the dissolution of a marriage clearly stem from Roman legal procedure, not the provincial practice found in similar documents of earlier date.[30]

Unlike the Roman, the provincial law was never codified, but grew by the accretion of legislation and *ad hoc* rulings. Under such conditions the training of the lawyer must have been, as it is in the Anglo-American tradition, largely a study of cases and precedents.

CENSUS, TAXES, AND LITURGIES
or
RENDERING UNTO CAESAR

Census and Cadastre

'And it came to pass in those days that there went out a decree from Caesar Augustus, that all the world should be taxed. . . . And all went to be taxed, every one into his own city.' The well-known story of the Nativity in the second chapter of the Gospel of Luke begins thus with a reference to a prosaic but pervasive institution of life in the Roman Empire, the census. But it is only in Egypt, thanks to masses of detailed information provided by hundreds of pertinent papyri, that we can observe the separate steps, the bureaucratic procedures, and the individual responsibilities, involved in the taking of the census.

Under the Ptolemies the population of Egypt was required to register annually. Augustus abandoned that system, instituting instead a census taken at regular intervals of fourteen years, the number corresponding to the age at which Egyptian males ceased to be minors and were enrolled as payers of the poll tax. The census process was inaugurated with a promulgation such as the following of AD 103.

Gaius Vibius Maximus, prefect of Egypt, declares: The house-by-house census having begun, it is necessary that all persons who for any reason whatsoever are absent from their home districts be alerted to return to their own hearths, so that they may complete the customary formalities of registration and apply themselves to the farming for which they are responsible. Knowing, however, that our city [Alexandria] does require some of the people from the countryside, I desire all who think they have a satisfactory reason for remaining here to register with Volusius Festus, divisional commandant, to whom I have assigned this matter. Those who show their presence to be necessary will, in accordance with this proclamation, receive signed permits from him prior to the thirtieth of the present month of Epeiph, and all others are to return home within thirty days. Anyone who thereafter is found lacking a permit will be punished without moderation, for I know full well that . . . [The last few words are lost.]

A comparable order was distributed throughout the province. Severe penalties were prescribed for failure to register, as we read in the rules of the emperor's Privy Purse:

58. Persons failing to register themselves and those they are required to in a house-by-house census will have one-fourth of their property confiscated, and if they are reported as having failed to register in two censuses they are fined another quarter.
60. Those who fail to register slaves forfeit only the slaves.
63. Those called to account because they failed to register in the preceding census are pardoned if a late return is filed within three years.[1]

How often that three-year grace period was invoked we do not know. We do know that the normal procedure allowed returns to be filed up to the end of the year following that of the census, and, as people are wont to do also in today's world, five out of six waited till the deadline was approaching before complying with the requisite formality. Each head of a household, whether owning or renting the premises in which he or she was domiciled, was obligated to prepare a written statement listing, by name and age, every person residing with him or her. If a house was uninhabited, the owner was required to submit a statement to that effect. The declarations for 'the house-by-house registration', as it was officially termed beginning with the census of AD 61–2 (before that it was generally referred to as 'the identity registration'), were submitted to the strategos or royal secretary of the nome. In his office a page number was written at the top of each declaration, then its left edge was pasted to the right edge of the preceding number. The resulting 'pasted together volume', as it was called, was in turn given a number, cross-indexed, and filed away with the other such rolls.

Nearly three hundred census declarations are already known, and the papyrus collections of the world doubtless contain numbers of others not yet published. The earliest that we have is for the census of AD 19-20, the latest for 243-4. The following example, for the census of 173-4, shows the standard formulation.

[Page] 99

To Apion, royal secretary of the Prosopite nome, from Pantbeus son of Petòs and [his brothers] Tithoennesis, Haronnesis and Phalakres, all four of [the village of] Thelbothon Siphtha. We register, pursuant to the orders of the most illustrious prefect Calvisius Statianus, for the house-by-house census now felicitously being conducted, the property belonging to us in the village, namely the house and empty lots of Pantbeus, Tithoennesis, Phalakres, and Haronnesis, all four sons of Petòs son of Pnepheròs.

The occupants are then listed individually: there are four brothers, born over a period of twenty-eight years, each with a wife, plus a total of nine children amongst them, all living in the one house; two of the children were born to two of the brothers in previous marriages; two of the brothers had married their own sisters; the oldest brother, aged forty-nine, has three young children by his second wife, now aged twenty-one; six of the nine children are named, as was the Egyptian custom, for grandparents, and another bears the name of a paternal aunt who had presumably died shortly before she was born. Distinguishing marks or characteristics (e.g. 'blind in one eye') are recorded for males, to serve as identifications for poll-tax purposes; since females did not pay that tax, they are here identified simply by name, relationship and age.[2]

The office of the strategos or the royal secretary would send a copy of each census declaration to the clerk of the registrant's village, town, or town district. In those local offices various kinds of derivative records were compiled, one being a roster of male minors, each of whom would later be transferred to the roll of poll-tax payers when he turned fourteen.

While extant papyri reveal details of the taking of the census in half a dozen of Egypt's nomes, they do not give us any totals for their localities or regions, let alone for the whole province. Two ancient authors do report the total population, and the closeness of their figures argues for their authenticity. At the beginning of Roman rule the population was, according to Diodorus of Sicily, seven million. A hundred years later, according to Josephus, it was seven and half million, not counting Alexandria, which may have had another half million (ch. 2).[3]

Just as the census of persons was kept up to date from year to year by the town or village clerk, so too was the cadastre which provided the necessary data for the assessment of the taxes on the land and its products. The cadastre was arranged by localities and their subdivisions, within which the separate parcels of land were listed in topographical sequence. Recorded for each parcel were (with some local variations) its tax category, the taxpayer (owner or lessee), the crops grown on it, whether and how it received the water of the Nile flood (naturally or by pumping), and its surface area as certified in an official survey. Changes in ownership would be notified and recorded as they occurred. Some changes in the tax category would result each year from the vagaries of the Nile flood. A farmer whose crop prospects were adversely affected because some of his land had not been reached by the flood, or had been eroded or otherwise damaged by it, would submit a statement to that effect and request the appropriate tax abatement. When such a declaration was received, a party of inspectors would be dispatched to the site to verify the claim. They would be accompanied by a surveyor, who would measure the affected area. Whether the claim was submitted soon after the flood had peaked or many months later when harvest time was approaching, it would be easy enough at either season for the inspectors to confirm whether the land in question had in fact been left high and dry.

Taxes and Requisitions

No ancient government and few modern ones have had a tax structure rivalling in intricacy that of Roman Egypt. There we confront a staggering array of charges and surcharges assessed upon the person, the land, occupations and services, sales and transfers, movement of goods and people, and real and personal property — a bewildering patchwork of staples and accretions. If we add up the taxes and imposts, regular and occasional, that we encounter during the centuries of Roman rule, their number comes to something considerably in excess of a hundred.

Still, the advent of Roman rule first made itself felt to the population not so much as an increase in the number of taxes, which occurred with the passage of time, but rather as an increase in the efficiency of collections, in contrast with the lax conditions under the last Ptolemies. So marked was the change that Emperor Tiberius, Augustus' immediate successor, is reported to have rebuked his governor of Egypt for sending to Rome tax revenues in excess of the prescribed quota: 'I want', he wrote, 'my sheep shorn, not skinned alive.' The rapacity of officials and collectors was a chronic complaint of provincials throughout the empire, but Tiberius' insistence on the strict accountability of his appointees apparently afforded some short-term relief. It was during his Principate, in AD 22 or 23, that at least one village in Egypt felt impelled to record its gratitude in an honorary inscription.

[Date], the assembled populace of the village of Bousiris in the Leto-polite nome unanimously resolved as follows:

Whereas Gnaeus Pompeius Sabinus, our nome strategos, is unceasing in his strenuous and beneficent care for the people of the nome and in particular is always acting for the good of the inhabitants of this village — viz., always dispensing justice in his court evenhandedly, honestly, and without bribes, in accordance with the wishes of our most divine governor of the province, Gaius Galerius; seeing to the maintenance of the irrigation dikes with all due care at the proper times, labouring night and day without favouritism till completion, so that, with the fields thoroughly irrigated, there resulted a superabundant crop; acting to protect those working on the village's dikes against fraud and chicanery, in contrast to their previous abandonment of cultivation; furthermore, conducting the sale of public lands with complete fairness, without compulsion or abuse, which is the greatest thing for the prosperity and stability of the villages; and paying off what the village owed to other functionaries of his administration, thus in fitting manner protecting the farmers from unjust treatment and penalties — for these reasons, wishing ourselves to reciprocate in favours, we have decided to honour the aforesaid Gnaeus Pompeius Sabinus, our strategos, with a stone stele containing this resolution, to erect it in the most prominent place in the village, and to give him a copy signed by as many as possible, which copy too shall be authentic.[4]

Repeatedly under Roman rule (as earlier under the Ptolemies), official pronouncements proclaimed the concern of the ruler for the welfare of his subjects and the benefactions that he showered upon them (see esp. ch. 10). But such professions of benevolence did nothing to alter the underlying realities. Among other things, the system of farming out the collection of taxes to the highest bidder — a system developed earlier, which the emperors retained practically unchanged for the first hundred years of Roman rule — was an open invitation to corruption. Once his bid had been accepted and he had contracted to pay the government the proffered lump sum, the first aim and overriding purpose of every tax-farmer was to show a profit in his enterprise. But more than one was not satisfied with that modest goal. More than one was eager to obtain the contract because he saw it as a get-rich-quick scheme; and once the contract was safely in his pocket he did not hesitate to employ any and all means, illegal as well as legal, to maximize his profit by wresting excessive and extortionate payments from his hapless and helpless victims. Such overbearing and violent behaviour was facilitated by the fact that collectors were frequently accompanied, ostensibly for their protection, by soldiers or armed guards, whom they could and did use to intimidate and maltreat the taxpayers. Already under the Roman Republic the tax-farmers, or publicans, had become a byword for rapacity and provincial misrule. Their continuing ill repute in the first century AD is highlighted by the coupling of 'publicans and sinners' in the synoptic Gospels (Matthew 9:10; Mark 2:16; Luke 5:30 and 7:34) and in the story in Luke 3:12-14:

And even tax-farmers came to be baptized; and they said to him, 'Master, what shall we do?' He said to them, 'Exact no more than what has been assigned to you.' And even soldiers would ask him, 'And what shall we do?' He said to them, 'Do not extort money by intimidation, or make false accusations against anyone, but be content with your pay.'

A vivid account of a tax-collector's razzia comes to us in the writings of Philo Judaeus of Alexandria, who died some time after AD 40.

Recently a certain collector of taxes was appointed in our area. When some of the men who apparently were in arrears because of poverty fled in fear of unbearable punishment, he laid violent hands on their wives, children, parents, and other relatives, beating and trampling and visiting every outrage upon them to get them either to betray their fugitive or to pay up on his behalf. But they could do neither, the first because they did not know, the second because they were no less poverty-stricken than the fugitive. But the collector would not let them go before he had racked their bodies with twistings and tortures or killed them off with newly contrived modes of death. . . . And when there were no relatives left, the scourge even spread to the neighbours, sometimes even to whole villages and towns, which soon became deserted and emptied of their inhabitants, who fled their homes and scattered to places where they thought they might escape detection. But then, it is hardly surprising if for the sake of their tax collection men barbarous by nature, without a taste of civilized culture, obediently carrying out the orders of their masters, exact the annual tribute not only from people's estates but also from their bodies, even to the point of imposing the risk of life upon some in lieu of others.[5]

Philo's anger and indignation, which cry out loud and clear with almost every word, doubtless infused his account with a measure of rhetorical exaggeration. But his account resides upon a basis of fact, as confirmed by many documents ranging over the entire period of Roman rule in Egypt. Here is a farmer's complaint from the year AD 193.

To Ammonios Paternus, centurion, from Syros son of Syrion also known as Petekas, of the metropolis [Arsinoë]. I and my brother delivered in the month of Payni all the taxes in grain that we owed, and likewise nine of the ten artabas adjected (p. 166) upon us in the village of Karanis. Now, on account of the one remaining artaba the grain-tax collectors Peteësios son of Tkelō and Sarapion son of Maron, and their clerk Ptolemaios as well as their assistant Ammonios, broke into my house whilst I was out in the field, and tore off my mother's cloak and threw her to the ground. As a result she is bedridden and is unable to [move about]. I therefore request that they be summoned before you, so that I may obtain justice at your hands. [Signature and date.][6]

To escape such violence it became a way of life for the powerless to appease the powerful with bribes and other *douceurs,* which sometimes amounted to sizeable sums. The relationship was called, as in present-day American usage, 'protection'. But in the privacy of his own home and his own records a man could dispense with such euphemisms, as for example in this account.

To the military policeman	2 dr. 1 ob.
Gift	240 dr.
Suckling pit	24 dr.
To the guard	20 dr.
For extortion	2,200 dr.
To the two police agents	100 dr.
To Hermias, police agent	100 dr.
Second half-year	
To the solidier, at his demand	500 dr.
[Several purchases and tax payments follow]	
To the soldier, at his demand	400 dr.[7]

Philo's picture of delinquent taxpayers turned fugitives, and of resulting depopulations, is also confirmed by many documents. Flight was traditionally the Egyptian peasantry's last resort when conditions became intolerable. In pre-Roman centuries flight was usually to the asylum of a temple, whence the refugees would be invited to return to their homes and their work when the precipitating cause was alleviated. Two important changes occurred under Roman rule. Recourse to flight rose up the social ladder as desperation drove others besides peasants to that ultimate refuge, and the resulting absences became longer or even permanent. 'Shall I become a fugitive?', as we saw (ch. 5), was among the standard questions addressed to oracles. Many fugitives made for the cities, especially Alexandria, where they might hope, as Philo said, to disappear into the melting pot; Emperor Caracalla's explusion order of AD 215 refers to 'countryfolk who have fled to Alexandria from other parts'. Others joined or formed roving bands of outlaws, preying on defenseless villages and travellers; their brigandage was a constant thorn in the side of the Roman administration (see note 26 below). Every so often, usually at census time, the government was driven to offering tax forgiveness as an inducement to the fugitives to return home; but such measures must have been at best short-lived palliatives, for the problem remained endemic.

When a man fled, his nearest relative or other concerned party would report it, usually stressing, in the hope of keeping the tax-collector away, that the fugitive had left behind no property. Several such reports are at hand from the first half of the first century, the very time when Philo was writing.

To Apollonios and Didymos, district and village clerks of Oxyrhynchus, from Menandros and Hierax, both sons of Harbichis. Orsenouphis son of Menches, coppersmith, who is registered in the census as living in the house inherited from our mother and belonging to us in Gooseherds' Lane, went off somewhere some time ago, leaving no property. And we swear by Tiberius Claudius Caesar Augustus Germanicus our Emperor that Orsenouphis has gone off, that there is no property belonging to him, and that he has not joined the army, and if [we hear that] he has joined the army [we will report it] to you. If we swear truly may it go well with us, if we swear falsely, the reverse. [The rest is lost.]

Other such depositions conclude with the request 'that he be entered in the list of propertyless fugitives from the current year on.' The town and village clerks drew up, and provided the tax-collectors with lists of 'men who have departed for parts unknown', lists that were brought up to date each year and grew longer faster when harvests were poor and times were bad. The records of the Arsinoite village of Philadelphia have survived, as it happens, for the first years of Nero's reign. In the summer of AD 55 we find forty-three men listed as 'fled leaving no property'; twelve months later the tally of the fugitives had soared to well over a hundred; soon after the number peaked, it seems, at 152; and though a partial tax forgiveness apparently induced forty-seven to return, in the autumn of AD 57 the list of missing tax delinquents still numbered 105. Those figures mean, the extant census data from the village tell us, that every seventh or eighth man of Philadelphia was a fugitive during all or part of those years. The depopulation was so severe that the collectors who were then farming the poll tax in Philadelphia and five neighbouring villages petitioned the prefect of Egypt for an adjustment of their contractual obligation. In justification of their request they say:

From their previously populous condition the aforesaid villages have now been reduced to small numbers through some men having fled leaving no property and others having died leaving no next-of-kin, and therefore we are faced with the danger of having to abandon our collectorships because of lack of resources.

Those collectors no doubt exaggerated their plight in their effort to obtain relief. But a century later a village clerk recorded the total disappearance of poll-tax payers from two hamlets, the male inhabitants of one having dwindled in number from twenty-seven to three, of the other from fifty-four to four, and eventually in both instances to zero.[8]

Thus, even without illegal abuse and extortion, for many a villager it was a constant struggle to meet his tax obligations, and arrears of one or more years are recorded in the documents almost as often as payments on time. What made the tax burden so oppressive was not only the size of the levies imposed, but also their sheer numbers. There is neither space nor need to catalogue here every one of the scores of taxes that are in evidence. A review of some of the principal ones will suffice to reveal the patterns of conception and implementation.

The role assigned to Egypt, when Augustus annexed it to the Roman Empire, was that of victualler to the city of Rome. From then on Egypt shipped to Rome a third of all the grain consumed in that city. In an average year that amounted to six million artabas, or some 135,000 tons.[9] An additional amount, on which we have no figures, retained in the province to feed the army of occupation. The individual taxpayer would, of course, be little concerned with those astronomical figures, even if he knew anything about them. His immediate and overriding concern was with his obligation to deliver the quantities of grain and amounts of money for which he was assessed.

For cereal crops the commonest tax rate on privately owned land was one artaba per aroura, but we know of instances where it was as much as twice that. In the range of presumed yeilds (ch. 6) those rates come to something very like tithes. At the other extreme, peasants who leased and cultivated plots of land belonging to the emperor's estates, which doubtless included some of the most productive land in the province, mostly paid between five and eight artabas per aroura, and there is one instance of a rate as high as fourteen and a third artabas. Between those extremes fell a variety of other categories, for example public (i.e. state-owned) land paying three and a half artabas. As a general rule, the marginal lands dependent upon irrigation paid half the rate of lands reached by the Nile flood. In all categories the grain tax was increased, usually by five to ten per cent, by one or more supplementary fees. For many cultivators there would also be the borrowed seed to be repaid. What portion of his harvest did all these charges leave the cultivator? As to that we are in the dark, but the portions must have varied greatly according to circumstances.

The government's interest in maintaining full production is obvious. Idle land produced no crops, which in turn yielded no revenue. The state was powerless to command a crop from a plot of land that remained unwatered, beyond the reach of irrigation channels or pumps. But what of usable land abandoned by cultivators who fled, what of fields which no one offered to lease and work? The government's answer was simplicity itself: it assigned such land for compulsory cultivation, either as an 'adject' to the neighbouring properties or as an 'additional assessment' upon the villages involved, whose clerks and elders then had the task of parcelling out the cultivation of those fields amongst the local farmers. Thus with a stroke of the pen the state created taxpayers for the unwanted lands; but since, in the nature of things, unwanted land was apt to be poor in quality or difficult of access, we can readily imagine how resentful the farmers would be of such additions. A guarantee that a parcel is free of such unwelcome encumbrance is a frequent element in sales or leases of land.

To pay his taxes the farmer had not only to thresh the grain and winnow it clean, but also to deliver it, or pay to have it delivered, to the state granary serving his locality. There he would be issued a receipt for each delivery, a proof of payment to be carefully preserved. Those receipts, as we see in the hundreds of them that have been found, were written sometimes on papyrus, but preponderantly on ostraca. From this fact we deduce that the taxpayer was required to provide the material on which his receipt would be written; and while the cost of papyrus was insignificant for all but the most penurious households, broken bits of pottery, as dumps like Rome's Monte Testaccio vividly remind us, were everywhere at hand in large quantities and gratis.

For each year's harvest each state granary had its own group of sitologoi ('grain collectors'), who were appointed by turns from all but the poorest of the local residents to serve, without salary and paying their own expenses, under the system of liturgies to be described in the next section of this chapter. The sitologoi were responsible for the quantity and quality of the grain from the moment they received it at the granary to the moment it was delivered to the huge store-rooms at Neapolis outside Alexandria, or dropped off, if so ordered, at a military establishment *en route*. At Neapolis the grain taxes collected from all of Egypt came under the authority of a Roman procurator, who supervised the trans-shipment to Rome.

The sitologoi received the bulk of the tax payments in the few months of and immediately following the harvest, but late payments often dragged on for two years or more. Their shipments to Alexandria continued all through the year until they had dispatched all the grain they had collected, minus whatever amount they were authorized to retain in the granary as seed to be loaned for the next sowing. The first stage of the shipments by the sitologoi was to move the grain from the granary to a designated Nile port. This was done to some extent in small boats rowed or towed along the larger of the irrigation canals. But most of the grain went overland on the backs of donkeys and camels, the standard load of the former a sack of three artabas, the latter carrying two or three times that amount. The drivers of the animal trains were also conscripted to perform that work as a liturgic service. An itemized account of deliveries to a group of river boats at the port of Oxyrhynchus on 6–14 December of AD 127 shows that that grain arrived in convoys of six to forty-two donkeys, with a day's lading totalling from 424 to 1,314 artabas.[10]

When grain was loaded into a boat at a river port, the

skipper wrote out a receipt for the benefit of the sitologoi making the shipment.

Aurelius Ammonios son of Ammonios, skipper in the Neapolis administration of three boats of 15,000 artabas burthen, to Aurelius Sarapion, sitologos of Sko district, Upper Toparchy, greeting. I have received and have had measured out to me from you the amount assigned to me by the strategos Aurelius Harpokration and the royal secretary Aurelius Nemesion also known as Dionysios, under the supervision of the overseers of lading and the others concerned, from the public granaries of the aforesaid district at the harbour of Satyros on the great river, of wheat from the harvest of the past third year, pure, unadulterated, free of earth, free of barley, sifted, by the prescribed method of measurement using the public half-artaba measure, seventy-seven artabas including supplements (= art. 77), which I will carry down to Alexandria, and I will deliver the cargo complete and undamaged to the administration at Neapolis. This receipt is valid, being done in triplicate, one copy for you the sitologos and two for the strategos, and on being asked the formulary question I so signified. [Signature. Date, AD 221.]

Each boatload or convoy was accompanied by one or more men as supercargo. Their duties were to verify the quantities at lading, and to see to it that the cargo was not tampered with *en route*. That duty, at first assigned to soldiers, was in the second century converted into still another liturgic service imposed upon the civilian population. The supercargo carried a sealed sample or samples of the shipment, with which the cargo would be compared by the recipient official at Neapolis. If adulteration were found, the damage would be charged to the sitologoi from whom the shipment came, as in the following instance.

Antonius Aelianus [procurator of Neapolis] to the strategos of the Diospolite nome in the Thebaid, greeting. As the cargo shipped down with Pausis son of Sipōs and his crew from the nome that you head, viz. 2,000 artabas of wheat, was revealed at the examination of the samples to have been adulterated, I ordered that half an artaba should be tested for barley and dirt, and it proved to contain two per cent barley and one-half per cent dirt. Accordingly, to make up the deficiency collect at your own risk from the sitologoi who shipped the wheat the total of 50¾ artabas of wheat, plus the supplementary charges and other costs, and when you have entered the credit to my administration let me know. [Date, 28 October AD 188.] [11]

Such, then, was the pattern of assessment, collection, and delivery of Egypt's basic and pervasive tax, the grain to fill the hungry bellies of Rome. It goes almost without saying that all other agricultural products were also taxed, chief amongst them being wines (including vinegar), oils, and vegetables. Those, however, were supplied to Rome from production in Italy and nearer provinces. Accordingly, except for certain quantities delivered to military establishments in Egypt itself, the taxes on those products were collected in money. One of the principal of those taxes, called the 'survey tax' — we saw earlier the key role of the surveyor in measuring the areas in and out of production — was widely assessed on vineyards at 40 drachmas per aroura (but the rate could go, in rare instances, as high as 350), on palm groves and fruit orchards at 20 to 30 drachmas per aroura, and on vegetable gardens at 20 to 25 drachmas. Another tax, called the 'revenue portion', had under the Ptolemies been collected at one-tenth to one-sixth of the crop; the Roman administration, while retaining the name of the tax, collected it in money, initially at the rate of 5 drachmas per aroura on vegetable gardens and 10 on vineyards, but in the inflation of the third century the rate was raised to a uniform $12\frac{1}{2}$ drachmas across the board. In still another category, the farmer was taxed on his domestic animals, both on his ownership and for the use of state-owned pastures, at so much per head. That is why the owner had to report the size of his flocks each year, to satisfy the tax-collector that his assessment included the annual increase of the flock.

In addition to the taxes on the various agricultural activities. there were taxes on the other pursuits and on the person. In these categories the most general tax was the *laographia* ('populace registration'), that is the poll tax. Only the most privileged classes were exempt, namely Romans, urban Greeks and Jews, members of the Alexandrian Museum, a certain number of priests of the more prestigious temples, and some of the higher non-Roman officials during their terms of office. All other male inhabitants of Egypt were subject to the tax from the age of fourteen (when a boy ceased to be a minor) to the age of sixty. The town and village clerks would know from their census records when each boy within their territory became liable for the tax and when to remove the deceased and the superannuated from the rolls. They prepared fresh rosters of taxpayers each year, and in one such roster the clerk, after listing the names of his poll-tax payers, entered his year-end tally:

Enrolled for collection in [this] year —
men paying poll tax	629
over age, turned 61 [this] year	5
died [this] year	2
Total	636.[12]

The rate of the poll tax varied from nome to nome, with metropolites enjoying the benefit of a reduced rate. From some areas the receipts issued to taxpayers — again, more often on ostraca than on papyrus — are available to us by the hundreds. Even so the annual rate of the tax cannot always be determined with certainty, for the simple reason that most payers of the tax exercised the option of paying in instalments rather in one lump sum for the year. For most of the dozen or so nomes for which we have evidence we are therefore reduced to inferring what the annual rate must have been. The most common full rate appears to have been 16 drachmas a year, with metropolites paying 8 or 12 drachmas. In parts of Thebes the corresponding figures may have been 24 and 10 drachmas. For the Hermopolite and Oxyrhynchite nomes we know the metropolite rate, namely 8 and 12 drachmas respectively, and we think it likely that the full rates were 12 and 16 drachmas. The only nome for which we have firm evidence of both rates is the Arsinoite, where the full rate was 40 drachmas and the metropolite paid 20. These were the steepest rates in all of Egypt, more than double the rates of most other areas. It has been supposed that those high rates reflect the fact that the Arsinoite, beneficiary of the most extensive and intricate irrigation system in the province, was the most productive and prosperous of all the nomes. Attractive as this explanation may be, it remains no more than a logical inference, as yet unsupported by conclusive information.

Along with his poll tax the adult Egyptian male also paid 6⅔ drachmas for the dike tax (the only money tax whose rate was uniform throughout the province), and some two drachmas for the pig tax. The first of these taxes presumably went to pay for supplies and materials needed to maintain the dikes of the irrigation system; what is clear at all events is that it was paid in addition to, not as a substitute for, the labour on the dikes required (as we saw in Chapter 6) of the peasantry. As to the allocation of the pig tax we can only speculate: one suggestion is that it provided the Greek and Roman temples with sacrificial animals, thus acting as an incentive to the Egyptian farmers to raise an animal that was anathema to their religion.

The other taxes collected in money were many and varied. The most broadly based of them was the 'handicraftsman tax'. This was assessed on every person, male and female, engaged in any occupation for wages or profit, and that included apprentices aged fourteen and over. The collection was farmed out separately for each trade. Here again the tax was paid mostly in instalments, usually by the month, so that the large numbers of extant receipts and records confront us with a bewildering mass of figures from which it is impossible to disentangle the total annual tax paid by the individual artisan. Moreover, different rates are in evidence in different places, with the Arsinoite nome once again showing the highest rate.

The artisan — in the case of an apprentice, his master — was required to notify the authorities when he took up a trade, so that he could be entered in the pertinent tax roll. He was also required to give notice on changing his occupation, and on leaving a trade, whether permanently or temporarily, he ceased to be liable for its tax. This principle was established in a test case that arose in the middle of the second century, when an artisan refused to pay the tax for the period during which he was assigned to another activity (probably a liturgy). The case came up on appeal before the prefect of Egypt, who ruled, 'If he does not practise the trade, he cannot be prosecuted for non-payment of the trade tax'.[13]

Journeymen and transients who wanted to stop and work for a while in any village or town had to obtain temporary permits from the local collector of the tax on their occupation. The pervasiveness of those controls is well illustrated by the one-day permits issued to prostitutes (one of whom was named Aphrodite) by one farmer of their tax, allowing them — obviously for a fee, though the amount is not stated — 'to go to bed with whomever you wish on this date'.[14]

Amongst the taxes on persons there were also two special assessments to compensate for the defaults of the indigent and the fugitives. Earlier in this chapter we noted the phenomenon of insolvent taxpayers driven to flee from their hopeless situation. Each such fugitive left a gap in the per capita taxes collected, and most of the fugitives, we saw, left behind no seizable assets of any kind. From the indigent, too, no tax payments could be extracted.

How, then, was the shortfall in the collection of the poll tax and the related per capita taxes to be offset? As with the abandoned lands, the government's solution was simplicity itself: it apportioned the deficit over the total number of remaining taxpayers. Such an assessment would vary from year to year with the size of the deficit and the number of taxpayers amongst whom the deficit was to be divided. In the second century, to which the bulk of the available data belongs, the 'assessment for fugitives' ranged from a high of eight drachmas per taxpayer to a low of three obols, or half a drachma, this last in a year following a census, when many fugitives would have been induced to return home by the amnesty offered in the prefect's census edict.

Business transactions were subject to still another array of taxes, and fees were charged for the registration of documents in public archives. Of broadest impact were the taxes of ten per cent on sales of real property and of slaves, two per cent on mortgages, varying amounts on sacrificial animals, and the previously described levies collected at the many toll stations. The registration of deeds and other documents, the filing of applications, and similar official paper work, all were effected to the accompaniment of fees charged for the service.

Mention has already been made of the allocation of tax revenues for the maintenance of the Roman army of occupation in the province. Since those allocations provided only for basic needs in food, fuel, and fodder, the military were authorized to requisition additional supplies and services as needed. Historically, in Occident and Orient alike, that requisitioning power has been a classic invitation to self-indulgence and extortion; supposedly the defender and protector of the people, the soldiery slips all too easily into the habit of behaving as their peremptory master. The most common abuses in Roman Egypt were demands for billets and for means of transport, to be provided of course without payment. This practice, though illegal, was so inveterate as to persist — and not just in Egypt but all over the Roman Empire — despite repeated 'cease and desist' orders from the governors of the provinces, and even from the emperor himself. In Egypt the first such promulgation that we know of was issued in AD 19 by Germanicus, the popular nephew and adopted son of Emperor Tiberius, when he was in Alexandria in the course of a tour of Rome's eastern provinces.

Germanicus Caesar, son of [Tiberius] Augustus, grandson of the deified Augustus, proconsul, declares: I am informed that in preparation for my visit requisitions of boats and animals are being made, quarters for lodging are being occupied by force, and civilians are being intimidated. I have therefore deemed it necessary to make clear that I desire no boat or beast of burden to be taken by anyone except by authorization of my friend and secretary, Baebius, and no quarters to be invaded. If they are needed Baebius himself will assign quarters fairly and justly, and for requisitioned boats and animals I order that hire be paid according to my schedule. Those who demur I desire to be brought before my secretary, who will either himself prevent civilians from being wronged or will refer the matter to me. The forcible seizure of beasts of burden as they are encountered traversing the city is hereby forbidden, for that is nothing but an act of self-evident robbery.

In AD 42 the prefect of Egypt issued a similar edict, as did the Emperor Claudius in 49, the latter castigating 'the unscrupulousness of men' in continuing this empire-wide abuse despite the 'sufficient remedies' that he had ordered.

The pack animals belonging to the emperor's estates were protected against requisitioning by identifying tags tied around their necks. One such bronze tag, found in Egypt, is inscribed:

Property of the Agrippinian-Rutilian estate of our lord the emperor, not subject to taxation or impressment.

Next we have an imperial order of AD 90 in an inscription

found in Syria some twenty-five years ago.

From the orders of the Emperor Domitianus Caesar Augustus, son of [Vespasianus] Augustus. To the procurator Claudius Athenodoros: Amongst the special problems demanding great pains I am aware that the attention of my divine father Vespasianus caesar was directed to the cities' privileges, intent upon which he commanded that the provincial territories be oppressed neither by forced rentals of beasts of burden nor by importunate demands for lodgings. But, wittingly or not . . . that order has not been enforced. . . . Therefore I order you, too, to see to it that no one requisition a beast of burden unless he has a permit from me; for it is most unjust that the influence or rank of any person should occasion requisitions which no one but me is permitted to authorize. Let nothing, then, be done which will nullify my order and thwart my purpose . . . to come to the aid of exhausted provinces, which with difficulty provide for their daily necessities; let no one, in defiance of my wish, oppress them and let no one requisition a guide unless he has a permit from me; for if the farmers are snatched away, the lands will remain uncultivated. [The rest is lost.]

On the same subject there are extant also an edict of *c*. AD 135 from the prefect of Egypt, and one of *c*. 185 from the governor of Syria. But no amount of exhortation or threat could alter the uneven match of a powerless civilian population confronted by an indulged and at times riotous soldiery. The abuse of the former by the latter remained endemic and ineradicable. In the winter of AD 216-7, the historian Dio Cassius tells us, Caracalla's troops billeted in Syria — legally in this instance — 'used up everything of their hosts as if it were their own'.[15]

Let us now see, in contrast, how requisitions were carried out when they were carried out as directed. Here, as a first example, is an order for payment issued to a bank by men appointed to the liturgic duty of collecting requisitioned clothing and coverlets.

Pay to Herakleides son of Horigas, Heron freedman of Publius Maevius, and Dioskoros freedman of the most great god Sarapis, weavers of the village of Philadelphia, for them and the other 81 weavers of the said village, on their mutual security, as advance payment for the garments that our eminent prefect Avidius Heliodoros has ordered to be manufactured:

(a) for the needs of the soldiers in Cappadocia, viz. one white belted tunic 3 cubits long by 3 cubits 4 fingers wide, weighing $3\frac{3}{4}$ minae, on account, 24 drachmas, four white Syrian cloaks each 6 cubits long by 4 cubits wide, weighing $3\frac{3}{4}$ minae, 24 dr. each = 96 dr., total 120 dr.;

(b) for the needs of the military hospital in the emperor's camp, one plain white blanket 6 cubits long by 4 cubits wide, weighing 4 minae, on account, 28 dr., making the total for this payment order 148 dr. of silver, and from this advance of 28 dr. were deducted 6 dr. to the account of the treasury;

(c) on condition that they will make the articles out of fine, soft, pure white wool without discoloration, well and tightly woven, well selvaged, good looking, with no imperfections, full value for the price paid them in advance for the articles. If any one of the articles upon delivery is rejected or is judged to be inferior, they will on their own mutual responsibility pay back the price of the rejects (together with taxes and expenses) and the deficit on the inferior ones, and they will deliver the articles without delay in the aforesaid measurements and weights, aside from any other public clothing due from them. [Date, 9 September AD 138.] [16]

Grain, too, was requisitioned.

To Damarion, strategos of the Hermopolite nome, from Antonius Justinus, soldier of double-stipend rank, dispatched by Valerius Frontinus, prefect of the Herculian division [stationed] in Coptus. I have received from the elders of the village of Terton Epa, in the Upper Patemite Toparchy, the quota imposed upon their village out of the 20,000 artabas of barley that our most illustrious prefect [of Egypt] Longaeus Rufus ordered to be purchased from the crop of the past 24th year for the needs of the aforesaid division, viz. a hundred artabas of barley by the public receiving measure and the prescribed measuring procedure (= barley, art. 100), conformably to the assessment made by the nome officials. I have issued this receipt in quadruplicate. [Date, June of AD 185. Signature.] [17]

Another such requisition states that the barley was pur-chased 'at the customary price'. There is reason to believe that the government often, perhaps always, paid less than the current market price. But the villagers would find the requisitions onerous even if they were paid full market prices, because, although originating as impositions designed to alleviate occasional shortages, those compulsory deliveries had by the middle of the second century become more or less continuous. The papyri tell us of one army unit that made its collections in regular monthly instalments spread over the whole year, and there is no reason to suppose that that unit's practices were unique to it. Furthermore, the villagers could never be quite sure when payment might be delayed or even omitted altogether.

But that was not all. Additional supplies of food, equipment, and transport were requisitioned occasionally to support the emperor's foreign wars and repeatedly for the maintenance and entertainment of important visitors and their retinues. The latter included the annual circuit of the governor for assizes and inspections as well as the royal progress of those emperors and members of their families who toured Egypt. In a report of AD 216 an inhabitant of the village of Soknopaiou Nesos tells that in the preceding year he was required to lend two camels in connection with Caracalla's tour of the country, that the animals were in due course returned to him, after which they were again requisitioned, one then being rejected as unfit, the other led away 'by Aurelius Calvisius Maximus, centurion, dispatched for that purpose pursuant to the written authorization of our illustrious prefect Valerius Datus, for the imperial service of our very brave armies in Syria', that is, for use in Caracalla's war on the eastern frontier.[18]

Even more interesting, or at any rate more detailed, is our information relating to the administrative tours of the prefect of Egypt.[19] The assessment on the individual taxpayer for those tours was collected, usually in money, by specially appointed committees, one for each product (or group of products) or service to be delivered. The relevant documents mention more than a score of different committees. One was in charge of traffic control at the prefect's headquarters, another saw to the entertainment, another to fuel and lighting, and still another to the provision of draught-animals and waggons. On the supply side the foodstuffs mentioned include bread, barley, cheese, oil, lentils, fresh fish, smoked fish, relish, vegetables, wine, fowl, geese, suckling pigs, calves, and fodder for the transport animals. Each committee member served, without salary, in an office to which he and others of his social and economic class were assigned by turns. Such compulsory services were called liturgies. We have already encountered them several times *en passant*, and it is time we looked into them in some detail.

Liturgies

In the ancient oriental monarchies the labour of the populace was regularly conscripted to serve the needs, whims, or greater glory of the ruler. That labour built the great pyramids and ziggurats, built and adorned the royal palaces, and supplied them with food. The concept that individuals might be called upon to render service for the common good first emerged in the democracies of classical Greece, most notably (as far as we know) in Athens. Such service was termed in Greek *leitourgia*, 'work for the people'. In Athens in the fifth and fourth centuries BC the men of the richest families were required to take turns, for a year at a time, defraying out of their personal fortunes the expenses of one of several state functions. Some of those liturgies related to religious observances, some to public works, and the most expensive by far — as well as the most prestigious — were the building and equipping of a trireme for the navy, and the preparation of a troupe of performers for the annual dramatic festivals. Liturgies remained an institution embedded in the administrative structure of Greek cities all through Hellenistic and Roman times. (From service to a people or community the word came to be used also for service to a deity — hence the present usage of our word 'liturgy'.)

Early in their history the Romans developed a looser concept of *munera*, of public duties, that the citizen of means and high station was expected to discharge. In Egypt the emperors, infusing the existing Greek tradition of the eastern Mediterranean with some Roman elements, elaborated a system of liturgies that was unparalleled in the ancient world for comprehensiveness, reaching as it did into the remotest hamlets and compelling service from all levels of the population.

As with taxes, there were of course groups that enjoyed exemption from liturgy — a privilege which the emperors tended on the whole to restrict more and more as time went on. Roman citizens, urban Greeks, prize athletes, members of learned professions, fathers of five children, and persons engaged in occupations defined as essential (supplying the army, for example), were exempt from all liturgies. Members of the same household were excused from simultaneous service.

Women, veterans, some priests, the aged, and the infirm were exempted from liturgies that principally involved physical labour. In other words, there were 'blue-collar' and 'white-collar' liturgies, or, as the Romans termed them, corporeal (or dirty-hand) and patrimonial (or pocket-book) liturgies.

From sparse early documentation we have the impression of an inchoate liturgic system taking shape by the middle of the first century AD. By the turn of the century the system was growing rapidly, and it was in full bloom before the second century was many years old. New liturgic offices continued to be created as long as Roman rule lasted, but the system had matured in well-defined structural patterns before the end of Trajan's Principate (AD 117). It was Trajan himself who took what was undoubtedly the most far-reaching single step when he transferred the collection of most money taxes to liturgic appointees, thus curtailing though not completely eliminating the power and abuses of the tax-farmers.

To date we know of nearly a hundred separate liturgies, some of them embracing large or small numbers of subdivisions, each with its own appointee or group of appointees. The village elders, village and town clerks and police, collectors of taxes in grain and money, transporters to move the grain from the granary to the river port and from the river port to Alexandria or to an army camp, inspectors of the Nile flood and of the fields reached or not reached by it, inspectors of sowings, of harvests, of dike work, supervisors of public works, of tax collections, of provisions for visiting dignitaries, bankers to handle public moneys, guardians of minors, and the whole roster of metropolitan councilmen and magistrates — all these and more were liturgists in the fully developed system of the second and third centuries. The term of most liturgies was either one year or three years, after which an incumbent was generally entitled to a respite of some years before being named to a liturgy again. In practice, however, the period of respite was often arbitrarily curtailed or even disregarded completely by the appointing officials when they were short of eligible nominees for all the liturgies they had to fill.

If the tax-farmer was fading from the scene it was not because the Roman government, in an access of moral indignation, was intent on drying up a notorious cesspool of corruption, but because it had found in the liturgic system a way of enjoying the benefits of the same principle on a much broader scale. The liturgists, that is the men holding liturgic office, were not only required to defray the expenses of the office, but where tax collections were involved they were also individually and collectively responsible for turning in the full quota assessed upon their districts — which meant that they had to make up any deficits out of their own pockets. That is why a minimum property qualification was set for each office, from as much as three talents (18,000 drachmas) or more for a banker serving a whole nome to as little as two hundred drachmas for a village guard. Clearly, the liturgic dragnet corralled all but the most poverty-stricken.

As soon as a liturgic appointment was announced, the designee's property was placed under lien to the state, and he was required to submit a sworn oath pledging faithful performance of the liturgy. But the Roman government, characteristically, was not content to rely upon the sole guarantees of the liturgists' own fortunes. An entire network of primary and secondary financial responsibilities informed the liturgic system. The town and village officials whose duty it was to nominate the liturgists were required, on their personal responsibility, to certify that each nominee was in fact an eligible and suitable candidate and to guarantee that the nominee would in fact serve. Sometimes, and increasingly as time went on, the nominee was in addition required to provide sureties who guaranteed his satisfactory performance of the liturgy. The regulations further provided that the nominators acted with the tacit consent of the community; consequently, in the event of a default by a nominator, the responsibility would automatically devlove upon the entire population of the locality.

For most local liturgies the nominations were to all intents and purposes self-effectuating. Procedurally they were addressed to the nome strategos, who made them official simply by endorsing them and ordering them posted for public notice. In the case of tax collectorships, however, a different procedure was employed, one intended to prevent collusion. For each of those posts the nominators had to submit the names of two or three eligible candidates; the strategos (who, being the local administrator, might after all know one or more of the candidates personally) forwarded the entire list to the epistrategos (a geographically distant and emotionally disinterested Roman), and he then selected the appointees by drawing lots. These procedural details are spelled out in the standard formulas of the nomination documents themselves.

To Apollonios, strategos of the Arsinoite nome, Herakleides division, from Petaus, village clerk of Ptolemais Hormou and other villages. As replacements for Maron son of Sabinus, Ischyrion son of Phasis, and Heron son of Hatres, the 3 collectors of money taxes of the village of Ptolemais Hormou, and [names] the 6 collectors of money taxes of the village of Syrōn, and [names] the 4 collectors of money taxes of the village of Kerkesoucha Oros, all 13 now completing the prescribed 3-year term, I with the accord and on the responsibility of the people living in the villages and farming in their vicinities, which people also as is customary mutually stand surety for the nominees, nominate the following as being of sufficient wealth and suitable, their names to be sent to our distinguished epistrategos for sortition. They are:
For Ptolemais Hormou —
    Petheus son of Ischyrion and Thaubastis,
        owning property worth   700 dr.
    Dios son of Papontōs and Thaubas,
        ditto   600 dr.

[Twenty-four more names follow for the three villages, making a total of twenty-six candidates from whom thirteen are to be chosen by lot. Each nominee has a property rating of 600, 700, or 800 drachmas.] [20]

What if, as sometimes happened, a man was appointed in error — one not liable for service because exempt or below the stated property level? If there was still time the nominating official could try to repair the damage with a substitute nomination. Otherwise he would be obligated, under his nominator's responsibility, to discharge the liturgy himself. This rule was already in effect in the mid-first century: 'the village clerk, having on his own initiative assigned compulsory cultivation to weavers in violation of previous rulings, will himself take on the liturgy or will transfer it to others at his own risk.' In a similar situation that arose in AD 244 two brothers, citizens of Antinoopolis and therefore exempt elsewhere, had been nominated to a liturgy in Oxyrhynchus, where they owned property; they filed a protest and the town clerk who had nominated them replied to the strategos, 'Upon investigation I find that they [are exempt], and upon learning that I undertook the liturgy in their place.'[21]

If the nominator's malfeasance went beyond simple oversight he could be made to pay damages. The following judgement, handed down by the prefect of Egypt against a village clerk on 11 February AD 143, brief as it is, tells the whole story.

What did you expect when you nominated to a liturgy a man of insufficient fortune? You caused him to flee and you caused his belongings to be sold [to help defray the expenses of the liturgy]. You are subject to penalties: you will pay the [prescribed] fine to the treasury, and in addition you will pay him four times what his property was sold for.[22]

Understandably, liturgy was something most people sought to avoid if they could. A *douceur* might induce a nominating clerk to overlook one's name when he drew up his slate of nominees, and he might also omit a name out of friendship. Probably no amount of regulation could have eliminated completely such collusion and favouritism, but the government tried to interpose something of a barrier by ordering that village clerks, themselves liturgists, be drawn from outside the villages that they were to serve. Some men achieved a *de facto* exemption from liturgy through the unscrupulous use of strong-arm tactics. A village clerk usually found a way to 'look out for' (as they said even then) men who made no secret of the reprisals they would visit upon him if he did not leave them off his nomination lists. Similar threats would silence the humble victims appointed to serve in place of the ruffians. Occasionally the victims would be emboldened to complain to higher authority, and a short-lived surcease from abuse would ensue. We know that an imperial edict against buying 'protection' from liturgies was issued *c.* AD 48, and some ninety years later an inquiry into charges of the same nature was conducted by the then prefect of Egypt.

In October of AD 207 a committee of twenty-five, acting as spokesmen for the state farmers of Soknopaiou Nesos, sent the following plea to their nome strategos.

We are obligated to work, each of us to the limit of his ability, on the shore land from which the Nile flood has just receded. But a certain Orseus, a violent and headstrong man, and his four brothers attacked us and prevented us from doing our work and our sowing, and they terrorized us so that we should flee from our homes as before and they alone might lay claim to the land, and so we send you this notice of their lawlessness. They do not pay their share of the monthly quotas and assessments of taxes in money and grain . . . and they have never performed liturgies because they terrify the succession of village clerks. Wherefore of necessity we fly to you for refuge and ask you, if your Honour please, to order that they be summoned before you and to hear our case against them, so that, vindicated by your succour, we can devote ourselves to the land and discharge the liturgies devolving upon us, and that Orseus and his brothers may contribute their share to the public revenues and serve in the liturgies for which they are eligible, and that we all be responsible in equal shares for the sowing of the land in question, and thus we may abide in our village giving thanks to your Honour. Farewell.[23]

At the other end of the social scene were the pillars of local society who, in a spirit of *noblesse oblige* or *pro bono publico,* voluntarily undertook liturgies from which they were legally exempt. Some of those 'good Samaritans' came to regret their gestures of altruism when they decided to relinquish the offices; their communities, they found, had come to take their generosity for granted as a permanent boon. In one case a physician had to appeal to the prefect of Egypt to order his release. In another case that we know of a woman of property took on the cultivation of some abandoned land, a liturgy from which she could have claimed exemption on the ground of her sex, and when she tried to terminate her commitment she was kicked around from administrative pillar to bureaucratic post for almost two years before she succeeded in obtaining her release.[24]

In the late second and early third centuries decades of economic recession, further aggravated by ever-increasing taxes and assessments and by requisitions imposed to sustain the internecine struggles over the imperial succession and the wars on the empire's frontiers, succeeded in undermining the fortunes of many a hitherto well-to-do family. Our description of the life of the metropolites has touched upon some of their efforts to avoid liturgic service in those troubled times, or at least to get others to share their burden. When all else failed, some men, when faced with still another call to liturgic service, preferred to surrender all their real property to the nominator and have him perform the liturgy in their place; this too was part of the nominator's personal risk. The surrendering party would, it seems, get back some fraction of the total. That detail is not spelled out precisely in the sources, but there is no doubt that such cessions of property did take place. Men were sometimes beaten or even imprisoned by local officials to make them rescind their divestment and undertake the liturgy. Emperor Septimius Severus ordered that such maltreatment cease, and that men exercising the option of ceding their property suffer no downgrading of their social status and attendant privileges. We also have the evidence of half a dozen actual cases. Here is one of them; another appears on p. 192.

To Aurelius Leonides, strategos of the Oxyrhynchite nome, from Aemilius Stephanos son of Hatres and Tasorapis, of the village of Sinkepha. This very day I learned that I have been nominated by Aurelius Amois son of Patas and Demetrous, of the same village, as being of sufficient means and eligible to succeed him in the office of collector of money taxes due from the villagers of the said Sinkepha in the current 3rd year. This is unreasonable and not in keeping with the principle of sharing the liturgy [fairly]. I therefore resign my property to him in accordance with the divine [i.e. imperial] ruling, and I declare that I own real property at . . . [The rest is lost. The year is AD 236.] [25]

As we saw earlier in this chapter, the taxpayer's last resort, when the burden of taxes and assessments became intolerable, was to take to his heels and disappear. The burden of liturgy likewise created its share of fugitives, some of whom did not even wait to be appointed but fled as soon as they learnt or suspected that they were to be nominated. In an edict issued on New Year's Day in the eighteenth Egyptian year of Antoninus Pius (29 August AD 154), the prefect of Egypt minced no words in talking about persons 'who fled from certain liturgies because of the poverty all about them at the time [and] are still living away from home in fear, as they were promptly declared to be outlaws.' He proceeded to offer them an amnesty if they returned home within three months. [26]

Doubtless many would welcome the opportunity to return home with impunity. And then the vicious cycle would begin all over again, for the amnesty might wipe away past debts and offences, but it could effect no amelioration for the future. On the contrary, the course of Roman history after the above edict — a history characterized by increasing frontier wars, decreasing political stability, declining prosperity — meant that the burden of taxes and liturgies would not be lightened but rather would become more and more onerous as time went on. The governors of Egypt, powerless to alter those underlying realities, could only proclaim new offers of tax forgiveness and amnesty whenever the disruptions caused by the fugitives reached crisis proportions. At best those edicts served as temporary abatements. All through the centuries of Roman rule, and no doubt increasingly in the troubled times of the third century, men continued to flee their homes when their fiscal burden was increased by the last straw. And the government continued to reap the whirlwind of its own sowing: loss of manpower, decline in revenues, and unremitting military alert against the roving robber bands that the fugitives swelled.

9

INSCIAM LEGUM
or
THE ADMINISTRATION OF JUSTICE

'A nation ignorant of laws' — even the historian Tacitus, politically astute and generally percipient, surrenders his critical faculties to the inveterate Roman contempt for the people of Egypt. Diodorus, a Sicilian Greek who wrote a hundred years before Tacitus, gives us a diametrically opposite judgement, noting the antiquity of Egyptian custom and law and praising the righteous principles that informed them. Legend held that the Egyptian law code was a gift from the god Thoth (who was later equated with Hermes, the lawgiver of Greek legend) to the first-dynasty Pharaoh Menes, who united Upper and Lower Egypt toward the end of the fourth millennium BC. Even if we dismiss Menes and his codification as myth, there is clear historical evidence that principles of justice had been formulated, a body of law recorded, and a system of courts developed in Egypt some two thousand years before Rome's earliest beginnings.[1]

The supreme judicial authority of the Roman Empire was the emperor. The supreme authority in a province was the governor. Roman citizens everywhere in the empire had a right of appeal to the emperor that was absolute in capital cases, and available in civil suits above a certain sum. The rest of the population of the empire had access, with rare exceptions, only to the internal judicial apparatus of their several provinces, but the governor himself would forward to Rome those cases which he judged to require the emperor's personal decision.

In addition to the prefect assigned to govern the province, there were several other high officials of the Roman administration in Egypt who exercised jurisdiction, but only in civil suits. We know their titles: *iuridicus* ('pronouncer of law'), *archidikastes* ('chief judge'), *exegetes* ('explicator', or 'adviser'), *idios logos* ('Privy Purse administrator'), and *dioiketes* ('comptroller'). But the source material regarding them is sparse, leaving us, for most of them, without clear demarcations of their particular judicial functions. One or more of them usually accompanied the prefect when he made his annual circuit to inspect the administration of the nomes and hold the assizes. On those tours he rarely travelled south of Memphis or Arsinoë (the officials of the nomes farther up the river had to come down to report to him), and he rarely dealt with cases other than those sent up to him on appeal from courts below — and only a selection of those, as we shall see presently. One result was that only a tiny fraction of the population ever had any contact with the supreme judicial authorities of the province. For most people, going to court meant appearing before the nome strategos. Even complaints addressed to higher authority were generally referred back for disposition by the strategos.

The law and judicial processes that prevailed in Roman Egypt were an experientially developed mixture of past and present. In Roman times the designation 'Egyptian', as we have already observed more than once, embraced every inhabitant of the province excepting Romans, urban Greeks, and Jews. Each of the exempt groups enjoyed the privilege of living under its own laws and ordinances. What the Roman administration called 'the laws of the Egyptians' was at the time of the Roman conquest a congeries of operative law and custom, some of it Egyptian but most of it Greek in origin. In the ensuing centuries of Roman government those principles and practices were gradually but inevitably modified according to relevant Roman law; examples of that development have already been cited at the end of Chapter 7.

The first rulers of the Ptolemaic dynasty established separate civil courts for their two cultures. Before the 'people's judges' the proceedings were conducted in the Egyptian language and according to native law, while the law of the Greeks was administered by the 'circuit judges' who travelled from one to another of the scattered Greek settlements. The two jurisdictions were not, however, restricted as to clientele. Any litigant, whether Greek or Egyptian, could choose either court, and interpreters were at hand when a language problem arose. Still, all other things being equal, disputes between Egyptians, or over contracts written in the Egyptian language, gravitated to the native tribunal, those involving Greeks to the circuit court. Retained for a time under Roman rule, that bipartite organization of the courts was abandoned toward the middle of the first century. By then the indigenous population, while preserving their native tongue in private intercourse, had become accustomed to conducting their business (or having it conducted for them) in the circumambient *lingua franca* of affairs and government, Greek.

The provincial administration had its batteries of public prosecutors, but when the plaintiff in an action was a private individual it was up to him to institute proceedings, either in person or through a representative. His first step would be to file a complaint with an appropriate authority, usually the strategos or epistrategos, both of whom had jurisdiction over cases involving personal or financial injury. Some complainants asked them for the relief or redress sought, others asked them to docket their cases for presentation to the prefect of Egypt at his next assizes. The latter group of petitioners remind us of the ageless truth of Alexander Pope's classic observation that hope springs eternal in the human breast: as the prefect generally took cognizance only of major crimes and issues without clear precedent, most cases, as we shall see, never reached him but were routinely disposed of or delegated by his staff to the strategos or some other lower court.

A typical petition is the following, addressed in AD 177 by six priests of the village of Tebtynis to their strategos.

Having a complaint against Kronion son of Sabinus for the offences which he committed against us and which we will detail at the appointed time, we ask that you summon him through one of your attendants to appear at the assizes to be held for the common good by our most illustrious prefect Pactumeius Magnus. [Signatures.] [2]

An accused awaiting trial was required to provide sureties who, much like bail bondsmen today, would guarantee his appearance in court when the case was called. In the absence of such bond he would, in the more serious cases, be kept in custody till the trial. When the strategos was ready to act on a complaint, he or his agent would issue an order for appearance. Interestingly enough, those orders, nearly a hundred of which are extant, were, strictly speaking, neither summonses served on the defendant nor arrest warrants, but instructions addressed to the local police officials. With minor verbal variations they follow a fixed formula, brief and to the point:

To the head policeman of Taæmpetei. Send Hatres son of Harseouris, Horos son of Belles, and Psenamounis son of Pausiris, [residents] of Sepho, on petition of Philinos. Mecheir 18. XXX[3]

At the trial that ensued the strategos presided in the role of examining magistrate. Oral testimony was frequently interrupted whilst affidavits, written depositions, and relevant documents, laws and precedents were read into the record. At the end of the hearing the strategos rendered his decision. This trial procedure was, as we shall see presently, modelled on that of the prefect of Egypt.

When a strategos judged that a case was beyond his competence he would refer it to the epistrategos or sometimes directly to the prefect. One hearing of which we have the record ended with the strategos ruling, 'If as you allege his Excellency the epistrategos has decided a similar case, I refer this matter for decision by him.' At the end of another hearing the strategos issued an instruction to the head policeman of a village: 'The two [defendants] are to post bond with you for appearance before his Excellency the epistrategos when he decides the matter.' Then, too, appeals could be and were taken from decisions by strategoi, but we do not know what conditions or restrictions governed the right of such appeal; presumably the plea would be one of judicial error. Where a strategos himself was accused of malfeasance or abuse, the case would obviously have to go directly to a higher authority.

The jurisdiction of the epistrategos, while broader than that of the strategos, was still limited. Cases that exceeded his authority were referred to the prefect or another of the high officials.

From the court minutes of his Excellency Vedius Faustus, epistrategos. After interrogation Faustus consulted with his coadjutors *en banc* and said to Harpokration, strategos of the Themistes and Polemon divisions [of the Arsinoite nome], 'According to my investigation and the orders of our most illustrious prefect, the decision will have to be made by him, to whom I will disclose all the steps I have taken.'[5]

When a complaint was held over for the assizes, was there any way to assure that the case would actually be heard, or at least acted upon, by the prefect himself? The brief answer is, No. One did what one could and took one's chances. But here too it was an advantage to be rich. A man who could afford a trip to Alexandria, or the services of a representative there, was not limited to the few days allotted to his nome in the annual assizes. In an inscription of the late first century a man records how 'he approached the prefect Marcus Mettius Rufus as he was passing by and handed him a petition. . . . He accepted the petition and handed it over to Claudius Geminus, administrator of the Privy Purse, for investigation.' The latter heard the case and pronounced judgement. Again, a papyrus of the late third century tells how an Oxyrhynchite had a representative, one Nemesianus, wait upon the prefect in the weeks just prior to his setting out for the assizes that would include Oxyrhynchus. At his first try Nemesianus was told to come back 'on audience day'. He returned then, only to find that it was a holiday, so court was not sitting. The next day he did get into the audience chamber, but the prefect announced that he was devoting that day to embassies and such matters. Finally, on his fourth try Nemesianus managed to accost the prefect in a grove of the palace park, and was told to submit his petition in writing. That he did, and his document was filed as 'Vol. 1, p. 81' and acted upon in due course.[6]

The 'little man', especially if he lived in the up-country, had no such luck. He would have to wait until the assize of his nome, which could mean a wait of many months for that once-a-year event. Each year the prefect came to Memphis or Arsinoë (ocassionally he chose another town, such as Coptus) in late January or early February. He usually remained there for two to three months, that is for as long as it took him to review the financial records and administrative problems of the score or so of nomes that stretched from Memphis to Egypt's southern frontier, and to dispose of the year's accumulation of litigation and appeals. As he would not be eager to prolong his stay into the hot Egyptian summer that was approaching — nor gratuitously to violate the tradition by which the ruler, in symbolic tribute, forbore to travel on the divine Nile in flood (June–October) — each nome would be allocated but a few days in the calendar of the assizes. And the volume of business to be handled was enormous. An extant petition submitted by an Oxyrhynchite at the assizes bears the file number 1,009. A papyrus in the Yale University collection tells us that in March of AD 209, when the prefect was sitting in Arsinoë, he received 1,804 petitions in the space of just over two days. That comes to something like 700 or 750 petitions a day, and if we calculate that the prefect's office remained open ten hours a day — which, we know, was the maximum allowable length of a court day in Roman municipalities — then the petitions would have been handed in at a rate of better than one a minute for the entire ten-hour period. It takes no great imagination to visualize the suppliants forming a long queue well before sun up and waiting as long as need be in order to tender the precious paper on which rode so many hopes and fears.[7]

It is obvious that in such conditions petitions of a routine nature — the vast majority — would never reach the prefect's desk. They would be processed by his clerks and aides. Only the petitions recognized by the staff as being significant or exceptional would be set aside for the prefect's personal attention, and even those would be referred by him in most instances to lower officials or temporary judges whom he created for the purpose — special referees, in effect. If the case involved soldiers, the referral would likely be to a military officer. For himself he reserved the relatively small number of cases that appeared, by their novelty or importance, to require the personal cognizance of the governor. The 1,804 petitions mentioned in the preceding paragraph were, we know, all packed up and taken back to Alexandria, where the prefect's office got around to answering them two months later.

Many papyri make reference to hearings before prefects,

and a number preserve actual extracts from the minutes of such hearings. From that body of evidence it appears that the principal areas in which the prefect found it necessary to take personal cognizance of matters in dispute had to do with military and veterans' affairs, taxes and public finances, exemptions from liturgies, property rights, public works, and crimes of violence and fraud.

The longest of the extant court minutes is contained in a papyrus roll now in the British Library. In its present incomplete, and unfortunately much fragmented, state it consists of five columns totalling 114 lines of writing. An excerpt from this procès-verbal of AD 250 has already appeared in another connection (p. 49). Here are a few samples of the other extracts from the minutes of hearings.

[Prefect: Decimus Veturius Macrinus, AD 181–3]
Macrinus said to Psais, 'Are you registered in the census?' Through an interpreter he answered, 'I am not.' Macrinus said, 'Where, then, is your name recorded?' He admitted, 'I am unrecorded. My parents died when I was little and they had not yet registered me.' After other exchanges Macrinus said, 'This is serious', and after examining the matter with his council of advisers he ordered Psais to be arrested. [The rest is lost.]

[Prefect: Servius Sulpicius Similis]
Year 15 of the deified Trajan, Phamenoth 25
[21 March AD 112] in Naukratis
Dioskoros son of Dionysios came forward and said, 'We are two brothers in liturgies, and I ask that one of us be released so he can attend to our farming.' Sulpicius Similis: 'Is your father alive?' When he answered no, Sulpicius Similis ruled, 'One will be released.'

From the minutes of Flavius Titianus, former prefect.
Year 12 of the deified Hadrian, Payni 8 [2 June AD 128],
at the court in the market-place
Antonius son of Apollonios appeared and stated through his counsel, Isidoros jun., that his father-in-law Sempronius had been incited to pick a quarrel and take away his daughter against her will. She became ill with grief, and the epistrategos Bassus reacted sympathetically and rendered the decision that Antonius should not be prevented [from keeping her] if they wished to live together. But this had no effect, for Sempronius, ignoring it, petitioned the prefect, charging [Antonius with] violence, and he received a letter ordering the parties to be

summoned. Antonius then pleaded that, if the prefect pleased, he not be divorced from a wife who held him in affection. Didymos, [opposing] counsel, replied that Sempronius' action had been taken not without reason: since Antonius had threatened to charge him with father-daughter incest, Sempronius, refusing to brook the insult, had used the power granted him according to law and instituted this action against Antonius. Probatianus added on behalf of Antonius that if a marriage was not dissolved the father had power neither over the dowry nor over the child he had given in marriage. Titianus said, 'The deciding factor is with whom the married woman wishes to be. I have read and signed.'

From the court minutes of Munatius [Felix]
Year 13 of the deified Aelius Antoninus, Pharmouthi
22 [17 April AD 150]
Glykon son of Dionysios and Apollonios son of Glykon being before the tribunal, after other remarks Archelaos, counsel, said, 'Glykon does not have the resources [for a liturgy] and he surrenders his property.' Munatius said, 'His means will be verified, and there is a rule that I have often applied — and it seems to me to be just — in the case of persons surrendering their property, namely that if taken with a view to any circumvention of creditors their action is invalid.'[8]

The relatively few petitioners and litigants who obtained a hearing before the prefect were the lucky ones in another respect as well: once the prefect had rendered his decision, that was the end of the matter, the case was closed, *res judicata*. For the complainants not heard by the prefect the judicial process could drag on and on. They had begun by waiting for the next assizes, a wait that could be as long as ten months. After the assizes it could take another few months, as in the case of the 1,804 petitions above, before the petition was answered. And even then the answer was likely to be, 'Without prejudice the epistrategos will look into the substance of your petition', or 'If you have any proofs, present them to the stragetos and he will take the necessary action', or something similar. Sometimes the strategos was instructed not to decide the matter himself but to conduct an investigation (a task he usually delegated to the royal secretary of his nome) and report back to the epistrategos or prefect — all of which, as far as the complainant was concerned, was simply piling delay upon delay.[9]

Some cases were assigned by the prefect to 'friends' as

special referees. These were men known to or recommended to him, and doubtless they often helped to speed the process, but not always. At the end of the assizes of AD 111, for example, the prefect, informed that many cases were still undecided, announced, 'If the judges I assigned are responsible for the delay, I will keep them here till they dispose of their cases.'[10]

Then again, delays were often occasioned by the parties themselves, either through purposely dilatory tactics, or through postponements for valid cause (such as the need to see to the harvest), or simply through inability to be present when the case was called. On 3 August AD 89 the subject of non-appearance elicited a new rule from the prefect Marcus Mettius Rufus.

Copy of minutes. [Date.] Certain of the parties to be heard at the assizes being called and failing to appear, Mettius Rufus ordered the herald to proclaim: 'Persons listed for my court and failing to appear are hereby put on notice that they will be called once more and if they fail to appear even then they will be tried *in absentia*.'

But the problem obviously persisted, a constant worry to litigants, an irritant to the administration. Nearly a hundred years after Rufus the then prefect, Titus Pactumeius Magnus, issued another edict on the subject.

Submitters of petitions who have received or hereafter receive instructions or replies, telling them in effect, 'Appear before me at my tribunal', are hereby placed on notice that if they do not appear within ten days of receiving the instruction or reply, they will obtain no consideration toward the application of either legal procedure or judgementary consummation. . . . If they do record such instructions [with the court clerk] I will decide their case within the said space of ten days. [The rest is fragmentary.]

The minutes of a hearing held in AD 250 contain the remark, 'The case came before the epistrategos and judgement was rendered against them after they had been called three times and failed to appear.'[11]

The strategoi and others to whom cases were referred were usually prompt in carrying out orders of the prefect. He was, after all, their all-powerful superior and they held office at his pleasure. But the complainant who emerged victorious and vindicated from the strategos' court might still encounter one last wave of delays in the obstructionism of the local officials responsible for putting the strategos' decisions into effect. Town and village clerks were past-masters at finding reasons for not executing judgements that threatened to involve them in out-of-pocket expenses, as for example in finding a replacement for someone they had named to a liturgy in violation of his rights. In one memorable instance, nearly two years after he had ruled in her favour a woman was still appealing to the strategos to compel the village clerk to comply with his order. Another case, a dispute over property, came before an epistrategos, who had to refer it to the prefect of Egypt because it was complicated by a charge of murder against the defendant's mother, since deceased; the defendant went, as ordered, to Alexandria, where she cooled her heels waiting, in vain as it turned out, for the plaintiff to appear; finally, she asked the prefect's permission to return home to Oxyrhynchus, which permission he granted with the instruction that she resubmit the matter to the current epistrategos; months, perhaps years, had elapsed, and the affair was right back where it had started.[12]

In the hundreds and hundreds of documents relating to disputes and delicts of all kinds we have amazingly little information on penalties. Then as now, complaints seeking legal action and redress were couched largely in stereotyped, formulaic language. Appeal was made to the 'even-handed justice' or 'beneficence' or 'compassion' of the judge addressed (especially if the prefect), and the relief requested was expressed in general rather than specific terms — 'appropriate punishment', 'due consequences', and the like. For really serious crimes slaves and free men of low estate might be condemned to hard labour in an army camp, mine, or quarry. We also hear of prisons and of the liturgy of guard duty there, but nothing about the inmates, and there are a few references to beatings ordered for violations of court orders. But in the main we encounter money penalties. Most litigation that we read about in the papyri had to do with private disputes, in which restitution consisted in the payment of damages for injury to person or property. In a few cases the issue was defrauding the state, a temptation which civilian and military personnel alike often found it impossible to resist. Such charges when proved resulted in fines for the guilty and substantial rewards for informers. In AD 139 a priest of Soknopaiou Nesos who had also served as a guard at the toll station there submitted a bill of particulars to the epistrategos, charging the toll-collectors with systematic defalcation over a period of four years; and when he closes with the petitioner's stock phrase, 'I submit this report in order that I may enjoy your benefaction', it is fairly obvious that the benefaction on which he has his eye is the informer's bounty.[13]

Justice delayed, our adage holds, is justice denied. On top of the burdensome taxes, legal constraints, and illegal abuses that were permanent features of life in Egypt under Roman rule, a failure to obtain speedy remedy in the courts may well have been for many the last straw that turned a marginal existence into an unbearable one. Most of the time the Egyptians suffered in silence — at least it must have sounded like silence to an inattentive and insouciant government. But the resentment was there. Most of the time it simmered beneath the surface, but now and again it would erupt in acts of individual violence or collective revolt. That is the story that Chapter 10 has to tell.

10

DISCORDEM ET MOBILEM
or
FUMAROLES IN THE *PAX ROMANA*

Tacitus' *Histories*, quoted in the title of this and some earlier chapters, is but one of several works of ancient literature that give expression to the Roman disdain for the population of Egypt as some kind of lesser beings. That judgement, rendered axiomatic by long use, found its most vituperative voice (as we have seen) in the poet Juvenal. His contemporary, the 'golden-voiced' Dio of Prusa, in the public address that he delivered in Alexandria, combined praise of that city's commercial and cultural greatness with a barrage of denunciations, threaded like a leitmotif all through the speech, of the Alexandrians for their frivolity, mindless contentiousness, boundless ambition, extravagance, mercurial temperament, abusiveness, disorderliness, turmoil, physical violence, passionate pursuit of pleasures and trivia, lack of seriousness, irrationality, folly, wickedness, and misconduct. 'No wonder', he adds, 'you are objects of contempt to your rulers.' The other Dio, the third-century Dio Cassius, without ever having visited Egypt went out of his way repeatedly in the course of his voluminous history to condemn the Egyptians, and in particular the Alexandrian mob, as fickle, turbulent, destructive, superstitious, imprudent, and disrespectful of authority. Modern writers have tended to perpetuate those stereotypes.[1]

It was Virgil, the 'poet laureate' of the then newly created Principate, who penned the classic formulation of the historic, god-given mission proclaimed for Rome by Augustus: to rule the peoples of the world for the benefit of all, enforcing the habit of peace by sparing the conquered and crushing the recalcitrant. The chosen instrument of that divine purpose was, of course, the emperor. Beginning with Augustus, one of history's grandmasters of the arts of political propaganda, imperial coinage, imperial and provincial edicts, festive anniversaries and victory celebrations, all continually trumpeted the theme — the official 'line', as we say today — of the emperor as a good shepherd, the protector of the empire's peace and harmony, of the people's good fortune and well-being, especially in their personal security and that of the all-important food supply. He is able to bestow all those boons because he is, by divine inspiration or accolade, the incarnation of all the personal and sociopolitical virtues, most especially valour, clemency, liberality, humanity, justice, devotion to duty, and wise forethought for his subjects' welfare. The reader will doubtless recall having encountered expressions of one or another of those notions in documents quoted in the foregoing chapters.[2]

In Egypt, as in the other provinces, the subjugated population generally accepted and endured the Roman suzerainty that they were powerless to displace. But embers of resentment and even of hatred smouldered beneath the placid surface of the vaunted Roman peace. Most of the time those discontents, kept alive among the provincials by the harsh imposts and contemptuous attitudes of their masters, found outlets in words of protest and mutterings of frustration. In the first century Seneca, the philosopher-statesman, who had first-hand experience of Egypt from owning estates there, remarked that that province had a positive genius for devising ways of deriding its Roman governors. The notoriously outspoken and irreverent populace of Alexandria, in whose midst the governor lived, were doubtless the ringleaders in that game of verbal vengeance, a game in which they usually knew the limits to which they could go without incurring serious punishment.[3]

At times, however, verbal ferment gave way to action. The precipitating cause of an uprising might be as serious as the pinch of famine or as trivial as an imagined indignity. The challenges to Roman might that are best known to us are the Jewish revolts. But those had unique socioreligious roots that set them in a class apart; they were accordingly, discussed in Chapter 2. In the present chapter we concentrate our attention on the Greek and Egyptian strains of hostility to Rome, strains discrete in their aetiology and most of the time in their manifestations as well, but joining occasionally when it came to open rebellion.

First, the Greek facet. Alexandria made no secret of its antipathy to Octavian even after his victory over Antony and Cleopatra was sealed by their suicides. Reciprocating in displeasure, Octavian set a precedent, which the succession of emperors upheld for over two hundred years, of refusing the Alexandrians' repeated pleas to have their own elected council, the traditional organ of self-government in Greek cities. The injury to their pride was all the greater because certainly two and perhaps all three of the other Greek cities of Egypt were allowed the privilege of local self-rule, and the resulting rancour was passed on from generation to generation. Alexandria flourished under Roman rule as the commercial crossroads between West and East. But in its political status the former queen city of the Mediterranean was now no more than the merest country town. There, in the country towns, the metropoleis of the nomes, a similar resentment rankled among the *déclassé* metropolites, who regarded themselves as authentic scions of Greek culture but were treated by the Roman government as just another group of lowly Egyptians, a somewhat privileged group to be sure, but Egyptian none the less.

Alexandrians nursed other grievances as well. There was no blinking the fact that even as a cultural centre Rome was now Number One in the Mediterranean world; Alexandria, formerly the cynosure of all eyes, now took second place. And a further goad to their rancour were the Jews, enjoying right in their midst — for the first hundred years of Roman rule, at any rate — imperial favours that they, the Alexandrians, were denied. The resentments fuelled by all these affronts, real and imagined, emanated in the creation and clandestine circulation of an 'underground' literature, of which a dozen or more tracts are thus far in evidence. As the fragments began to make their appearance in the papyrus finds, this body of tendentious literature quickly acquired the catchy, allusive title of *The Acts of the Pagan Martyrs*.

The 'martyrdoms' are all cast in the same mould of

pretended actuality. Each purports to be the verbatim record of a hearing at which an individual or a small group of Alexandrians appear before the emperor to press a suit or to answer to serious charges, usually of *lèse-majesté*. Without exception the Alexandrian heroes voice their insolent defiance of, and contempt for, the ruler of the empire, the world's most powerful figure. The dramatic dates of the several episodes range from Augustus to Commodus, or possibly to Caracalla, and, in the words of one writer on the subject, 'few if any of the emperors of the first two centuries escaped the pillory . . . of these fugitive and treasonable texts.'[4] It should be noted, further, that although the protagonists of this literature are all Alexandrians, the papyri bearing these texts were all found in the up-country, an indication of the wide circulation and continuing popularity those works enjoyed amongst the claimants to Hellenic culture in the metropoleis and villages.

An analysis of the contents of the 'martyrdoms' reveals such recurrent motifs as civic pride and anti-Semitism, but far and away the greatest emphasis is anti-Roman. Repeatedly there are served up for the reader's delectation instances, real or extrapolated, of the avarice and injustice of the Roman government, and of the tyranny and immorality of emperors and prefects of Egypt. One of the better-preserved pieces contains the following exchanges (the dramatic date is mid-first century):

The Alexandrian envoys were summoned, and the emperor postponed his hearing of their case to the morrow. . . . Second day, Pachon 6. Claudius Caesar hears the case of Isidoros, gymnasiarch of Alexandria, against King Agrippa [of the Jews] in the Lucullian Gardens [in Rome]. Sitting with him were twenty senators and sixteen consulars, and some ladies of the court also attended the trial of Isidoros.

Isidoros began, 'My lord Caesar, I beg at your knees that you give ear to the suffering of my native city.'

The emperor: 'I shall allot you this day.' All the senators *en banc* nodded their agreement. . . .

Claudius Caesar: 'You have brought about the deaths of friends of mine, Isidoros.'

Isidoros: 'I obeyed the emperor [Caligula] who was then giving the orders. You too have only to say whom you want me to accuse, and I will do so.'

Claudius Caesar: 'Are you really the son of an actress, Isidoros?'

Isidoros: 'I am neither slave nor actress's son, but gymnasiarch of the illustrious city of Alexandria. But you are the cast-off son of the Jewess Salome. . . .'

Lampon [another Alexandrian] said to Isidoros: 'What else can we do but yield to a mad king?'

Claudius Caesar: 'Those whom I previously ordered to execute Isidoros and Lampon [will now carry out the order.] [The rest is lost.][5]

In the next selection the emperor is Commodus, the time of the action *c*. AD 190.

Appian, being led away . . . turned, saw Heliodoros and said, 'Heliodioros, have you nothing to say at my being led away to execution?'

Heliodoros said, 'To whom can we speak when we have no one who will listen? Go, my son, and die. Yours is the glory of dying for your native city most dear. Do not anguish . . . I will follow you. . . .'

The emperor recalled Appian. The emperor said, 'You know whom you are talking to now, I suppose?'

Appian: 'I know. Appian speaks to a tyrant.'

The emperor: 'No, to a ruler.'

Appian: 'Don't say that! The deified Marcus [Aurelius], your father, was fit to be an emperor. Look you, in the first place he was a philosopher, secondly he was not a money-grubber, thirdly he was a lover of the good. In you inhere the opposites of those qualities — tyranny, dishonesty, boorishness.'

Caesar ordered him led away to execution. As he was being led away Appian said, 'Grant me this one favour, my lord Caesar.'

The emperor: 'What?'

Appian: 'Order that I be led to execution in my insignia of nobility.'

The emperor: 'Granted.'

Appian, taking the fillet, placed it on his head, and putting the white shoes on his feet he cried out in the middle of Rome, 'Come running, Romans. See this once-in-a-lifetime sight, a gymnasiarch and envoy of Alexandria being led to execution.'[6]

The 'martyr' literature, as we can sense from these excerpts, was more irreverent than subversive. It contained no calls to action, and it did not even indulge — as did the apocalyptic writings of Jews, Christians, and Egyptians — in the vicarious vengeance of forecasting a horrible doom for the oppressor. We can easily picture the more literate and affluent of the Alexandrians and metropolites nursing the political grievances of their classes by perusing these books in the privacy of their libraries or reading them aloud in gatherings of friends. Even when, on occasion, they did in fact send some of their leading citizens on embassies to Rome, they were venting their frustrations in words rather than deeds. Not so the Alexandrian mob, which quickly earned and long retained a reputation for being unruly, volatile, and easily inflamed.

During the first century the Alexandrians could concentrate their hostility on the Jewish community in their midst. The privileges which the Roman government allowed the Jews but denied to them were a constant irritant to the aggrieved Alexandrians. Minor clashes between members of the two groups were frequent, and from time to time those clashes flared into murderous riots, most notably in the full-scale pogrom of AD 38 and again some twenty and thirty years later. But after their revolt of AD 115-17 the Jews of Egypt, decimated in numers and stripped of their privileges, were a negligible factor, and the Alexandrians could turn the full force of their antagonism upon the Roman government, very visibly headquartered in the very heart of their city. They often mounted public demonstrations, in the streets and in the theatre, against the governor of the province and even against a visiting emperor. A revolt erupting elsewhere in the province usually found them ready to pitch in and help. Pretenders who rose to challenge emperors, from Avidius Cassius in AD 175 to Domitius Domitianus at the end of the third century, could usually count on being accepted and supported in Alexandria. Such defections had more than political significance: they also interrupted the grain shipments to Rome, threatening the capital city's food supply. But the punishments that followed the suppression of resistance only intensified the Alexandrians' hatred of the Roman rulers. The bloodiest reprisal was that wreaked by Caracalla in AD 215. We have the story from the pens of two contemporary historians, both hostile to the emperor, Dio Cassius and Herodian. As they tell it, in personal terms emphasizing the depravity of Caracalla, the outspoken Alexandrians had ridiculed the emperor for his pretensions to immortal fame and had made open mock of his public proclamation that his cold-blooded murder of his brother Geta had been an act of self-defence. Caracalla was then preparing to launch a war against Parthia, and he may well have been concerned lest the agitation in Alexandria threaten the lines of supply to his invading forces. His response to the situation was sly, swift, and savage. On his approach to Alexandria the leading citizens, as was customary, came out to the suburbs to greet him. He welcomed them with open arms, then had them put to death on the spot. After that he turned his troops loose on the city, with licence to plunder and slaughter at will. After several days he called a halt to the massacre, and in his report to the Roman senate he remarked that it was not important to know how many of the Alexandrians had perished, because they all deserved to die. He then issued a series of orders, one of which is preserved in the following copy.

All Egyptians who are in Alexandria, and particularly country folk who have fled thither from elsewhere and can easily be identified, are absolutely by every means to be expelled, not, however, dealers in pigs and river-boat men and those who bring in reeds for heating the baths. But expel all the rest, who disturb the city by their very numbers and their lack of occupation. I am informed that at the festival of Sarapis and on certain festal days — and even on other days as well — Egyptians observe the custom of bringing in bulls and some other animals for sacrifice. They are not to be prevented from coming for that. The ones to be prevented are those who flee the countryside where they belong in order to avoid farmwork, not those who converge upon Alexandria out of a desire to view the glorious city or come here in pursuit of a more cultured existence or on occasional business.
And further along: Amongst the linen weavers the true Egyptians can easily be recognized by their speech, which reveals that they are affecting the appearance and dress of others. What is more, in the way they live their manners, the opposite of urbane behaviour, reveal them to be Egyptian rustics. [7]

Up to this point we have been probing the anti-Roman feelings and actions of the Greeks and would-be Greeks of Egypt. Caracalla's expulsion order reminds us that it is time to look at the broad mass of the Egyptian population and their feelings about their Roman rulers.

Who were the 'illegals' whom Caracalla denounced as such disturbers of the peace in Alexandria? While they doubtless included a certain number of shiftless drifters, many — possibly even most — were indeed country folk who had fled to the city from the countryside. It is in characterizing their flight as motivated by a perverse desire to avoid their life of toil that Caracalla turned a blind eye to the reality. Throughout history most people, and agricultural populations in particular, have generally been content to remain in their places of origin, where they felt they belonged, as long as the conditions of life were at all bearable. For centuries and indeed millennia the Egyptian peasantry had given proof of their attachment to the land, even though most of the time it provided them with little better than a marginal subsistence. To flee, abandoning one's home — be it ever so humble — with no prospect of return, was a counsel of despair, a last resort to which men were driven, as we saw in Chapter 8, when they had lost all hope of being able to meet the inexorable demands of the Roman administration for taxes and liturgic services.

Some of the fugitives would make their way to Alexandria or some other large population centre, where they could hope to disappear with impunity into the 'melting-pot'. Others found desert hide-outs, where they formed, or joined up with, robber bands. As we saw in Chapter 7, the trade routes crossing the deserts had constantly to be protected by patrols of police and soldiery against the raids of the roving outlaws. Emperors and governors issued edict after edict on the subject, denouncing, threatening, cajoling. Such pronouncements, especially those offering an amnesty and tax forgiveness on the occasion of an approaching census, effected some temporary reductions in the numbers of the bandits on the prowl. For example, the tenant farmers of Soknopaiou Nesos whose plea we read on p. 182 began their petition as follows:

Our most divine and everlasting emperors Severus and [Caracalla], when they were sojourning in their very own Egypt, amongst the very many boons they bestowed desired also that persons abiding in other parts should all return to their own homes and have done with acts of violence and lawlessness, and in accordance with their sacred orders we came back.[8]

But as the underlying causes that drove men to flight remained unaltered, brigandage remained endemic in Roman Egypt, inveterate and ineradicable in good times, a menace increasing to near crisis proportions in bad. A dozen or so years after the imperial order that induced those peasants of Soknopaiou Nesos to return home, the prefect of Egypt sent the following letter to the strategoi of the Heptanomia and the Arsinoite nome.

I have already in a previous letter ordered you to conduct an industrious search for bandits, which, I warned, you would neglect at your peril. And now I have decided to confirm my resolve by issuing an edict, so that all throughout Egypt may know that I do not regard this task as one of secondary importance but am in fact offering rewards to those of you who co-operate and threatening peril to any who choose to disobey. I wish my edict to be publicly displayed in the metropoleis and in the most conspicuous places of your nomes, and you will be liable to penalties as well as risk [of dismissal] if any malefactor commits an act of violence and goes undetected. I bid you farewell.

But the problem, as we saw, was chronic, and the 'search and destroy' tactic was not new. When, in AD 154, the prefect proclaimed a three-months' grace period during which fugitives might return home with impunity, he added this threat to prod the recalcitrant or hesitant:

Let them know that their Excellencies the epistrategoi, as well as the strategoi and the soldiers dispatched by me for the security and tranquillity of the country districts, have been given orders to suppress incipient raids by provident and timely measures, to give immediate chase when raids have been perpetrated, and to deal with [other] malefactors caught in the act no differently than with those engaged in actual brigandage.[9]

We must not, however, let the prefects' rhetoric and air of urgency distort our sense of perspective. Although the government never succeeded in eradicating brigandage completely, the number of brigands always remained small relative to the total population, even in the worst of times. To choose the life of an outlaw demanded a hardihood beyond that of your 'average' individual. It meant permanent separation from hearth and loved ones, and capture meant certain death. Philostratos, a writer of the early third century, mentions as an ordinary occurrence how a dozen men convicted of banditry were paraded through the streets of Alexandria to the place of execution, where they were beheaded.[10]

The vast majority of the population, it is clear, simply stayed put. How did they express their disaffection? Long-suffering and quiescent most of the time, they too could be goaded beyond endurance by food shortages and by the endless taxes and requisitions. Some flare-ups of discontent were successfully contained within their localities by prompt action of the military garrisons posted about the province. Other protests expanded rapidly into more or less general revolts, in which the bandits were usually only too happy to join. Among the major disturbances was an insurrection that erupted in AD 152 and lasted over a year. Few details are recorded about the rebellion, except that it seriously endangered Rome's food supply, that it cost the life of the prefect of Egypt, and that it apparently required the personal intervention of the emperor before it was put down. Even more threatening was the outbreak of AD 172-3, which centered in the Boukolia marshes of the Nile Delta. Here too the ancient account is silent about the precipitating cause or causes, but the fact that the leader of the uprising was an Egyptian priest is suggestive of an upsurge of nationalism. The plague that was then sweeping the Roman Empire undoubtedly loosened the bonds of submissiveness by revealing the helplessness of authority. Another element that made the situation seem ripe for revolt was the fact that one of the two legions regularly stationed in Egypt had recently been withdrawn to aid in fighting Germanic tribes pressing on the Danube frontier of the empire. The hap-hazardly armed Egyptian peasants actually defeated units of the remaining Roman force and came close to capturing Alexandria. The governor of the neighbouring province of Syria, who commanded the most powerful military concentration in the eastern half of the empire, was called in to restore order — which he did less by frontal attack upon the rebels than by skilfully sowing dissension in their ranks.

Like the Greeks, the Egyptians too expressed their hatred of Rome with the pen as well as the sword. Amongst the anti-Roman writings discovered in the papyri, there are some which, though written in Greek to reach the widest audience, are clearly of native Egyptian origin. In interesting contrast to the 'martyr' literature of the Greeks, the Egyptian tracts are apocalyptic in nature, prophesying the cataclysmic downfall of their pitiless and immoral masters, after which the Egyptians, no longer downtrodden and oppressed, will enjoy a new Golden Age. The longest extant fragments come from a work which takes its title, *The Narrative* (or *Prophecy*) *of the Potter*, from a prominent element in Egyptian mythology, according to which the god Khnum, the creator, fashioned mankind on his potter's wheel.

Apocalyptic literature, growing as it does by repetition and accretion, makes free to incorporate fantasies, ideas, and clichés from other cultures, wherever it finds bits and pieces congenial to its emotional message and salvational goal. *The Prophecy of the Potter* conforms to that paradigm. Deriving ultimately from an Egyptian work of Pharaonic date, it shows in its extant Greek versions, which were still being copied and recopied at least to the end of the third century, some elements of Greek legend and history and possibly some of Iranian and Jewish origin. These are interwoven into the fabric of the narrative without derogating from the fundamentally Egyptian character of its vision of a millennium to come after the fated, inevitable overthrow of the present rulers. Of the three extant fragments the following, which was found at Oxyrhynchus, is the longest and best preserved. The Potter speaks:

As for the impious, a king from Syria will master them. . . . . And good fortune will be taken away from that people, and their kin will be humbled, and the land will be in turmoil, a mere fragment of its former self. . . . All will proceed to the same end for the profit of the one . . . and many a death will [strike] in the high places, and the city of the belt wearers will be deserted, the slaves will be freed, their masters deprived of life, their virgin daughters will perish, men will castrate their daughters' husbands and practise incest with their mothers, they will perforce violently sacrifice their male children and themselves. . . . The Tutelary Divinity will abandon their city, leaving it destitute, and will go off to god-bearing Memphis. That will be the end of our woes, when . . . the city of the belt wearers will be as deserted as my kiln because of the lawless acts they committed . . . and [justice] will return, transferred back into Egypt, and the city by the sea will be but a place for fishermen to dry their catch, because Knephis, the Tutelary Divinity, will have gone to Memphis, so that passers-by will say, 'This is the all-nurturing city in which live all the races of mankind.'

Then will Egypt be increased, when . . . the dispenser of boons, coming from the Sun, is established there by the goddess [Isis] most great, so that those then alive will pray and those previously deceased will arise in order to partake of the boons at the end of our woes.[11]

Edward Gibbon never heard of *The Prophecy of the Potter*. He had been dead ninety-nine years when the first fragment of that Egyptian tract became known. Besides, Gibbon's attention was focused on the ruling powers; Egypt entered his purview only when the Romans lost it to the Arabs. Before turning to his main business of Rome's decline he penned, to dramatize the contrast with the degradation to come, a veritable paean in praise of the empire at its apogee.

If a man were called to fix the period in the history of the world, during which the condition of the human race was most happy and prosperous, he would, without hesitation, name that which elapsed from the death of Domitian to the accession of Commodus. The vast extent of the Roman Empire was governed by absolute power, under the guidance of virtue and wisdom. The armies were restrained by the firm but gentle hand of four successive emperors, whose characters and authority commanded involuntary respect. The forms of the civil administration were carefully preserved by Nerva, Trajan, Hadrian, and the Antonines, who delighted in the image of liberty, and were pleased with considering themselves as the accountable ministers of the laws. . . . The labours of these monarchs were overpaid by the immense reward that inseparably waited on their success; by the honest pride of virtue, and by the exquisite delight of beholding the general happiness of which they were the authors.[12]

Yet it was precisely during those generally prosperous years of those enlightened 'Good Emperors' that the Roman province of Egypt was racked by its most serious disturbances — the revolts of the Jews under Trajan and Hadrian, those of the Egyptians under Antoninus surnamed the Pious and under the philosopher-king Marcus Aurelius. How many dwellers in the province of Egypt, we may wonder, would have recognized Gibbon's words as a description of the world in which they lived?

APPENDIX

THE PRICES OF GOODS AND SERVICES

The significance of an amount of money mentioned in a document is best appreciated in comparison with elements of ordinary expenditure such as would today go to make up a consumer price index. The range of some such prices, as far as we know them, is given in the following table; the figure in parentheses is the median. The extremes undoubtedly reflect seasonal factors, scarcity, and similar variables. Many of the figures from the third century reflect the inflation of that time. Prices are in drachmas.

	I cent.	II cent.	III cent.
wheat, artaba	3–11 (7)	$5\frac{1}{2}$–20 (8)	8–20 (15)
barley, artaba	3–4 ($3\frac{1}{2}$)	$4\frac{1}{3}$–11 (5)	5–20 (14)
wine, jar	$\frac{1}{2}$–7 (5)	$1\frac{1}{4}$–24 (11)	9–52 (12)
labour, daily wages*			
harvesting	$\frac{1}{3}$–$\frac{1}{2}$ ($\frac{1}{3}$)	$\frac{5}{6}$–2 ($1\frac{1}{2}$)	2–$2\frac{1}{3}$ ($2\frac{1}{6}$)
other agricultural	$\frac{1}{3}$–$1\frac{1}{2}$ ($\frac{2}{3}$)	$\frac{1}{3}$–2 ($\frac{5}{6}$)	$\frac{1}{3}$–6 (2)
household, industrial	$\frac{1}{2}$–$1\frac{1}{3}$ ($\frac{2}{3}$)	$\frac{1}{2}$–$1\frac{2}{3}$ (1)	$\frac{2}{3}$–9 (4)
foreman, manager, etc.	1	1–3	2
legionary soldier, per day	$2\frac{1}{2}$–$3\frac{1}{3}$	$4\frac{1}{3}$–$5\frac{1}{2}$	$8\frac{1}{3}$
house	180–1,500 (600)	120–6,400 (650)	125–25,000 (1,400)
farm land, aroura	12–495 ($97\frac{1}{2}$)	20–636 (160)	20–1,200 ($266\frac{2}{3}$)

	I cent.	II cent.	III cent.
slave, male	[no data]	200–2,800 (1,200)	1,600–12,000 (1,960)
slaye, female	600–2,000 (950)	700–1,500 (1,200)	2,200–48,000 (3,000)
slave, child	640	300–2,600 (700)	1,600–5,000 (2,600)

*Not including: (a) supplements of food, especially frequent in the case of farm labour; and (b) child labour, which was paid at a lower rate.

GLOSSARY

aroura — a Greek word originally meaning 'plough land'. In Hellenistic and Roman Egypt it was the unit of land measurement, equivalent to 29,825 square feet, or 0.68 acres, or 0.275 hectares.

Arsinoite nome: see Fayyūm.

artaba — the principal unit of dry measure, used for grains and other produce. Artabai of different capacities are attested, ranging from 24 to 42 choinikes (*q.v.*). The standard artaba of tax collection appears to have contained 40 choinikes, a quantity equal to some 43 litres, or 1 1/6 bushels. For the most recent discussion of the complex evidence see *Zeitschrift für Papyrologie und Epigraphik*, 42 (1981), 101.

Aurelius (feminine, -lia) — the family name of the emperor Marcus Aurelius (AD 161–80). The name was adopted, as a warrant of legitimate succession, by several of the emperors after him, including Caracalla, and it was assigned as a hereditary forename to the provincials who acquired Roman citizenship through Caracalla's universal grant of AD 212.

choinix (plural, -nikes) — a dry measure, approximately the same amount as a litre.

chous (plural, choes) — a liquid measure of about 1.5 litres.

dekaprotos — the title of the collector of grain taxes in a toparchy (*q.v.*) in the latter half of the third century.

Demotic ('popular') — the modern term for the cursive script in which the Egyptian language was written from the sixth century BC to at least the fourth century AD. Thereafter the Egyptians adopted the Greek alphabet, adapting it to the needs of their native tongue through the addition of a few non-Greek letters. In this form the language is known as Coptic.

drachma — (1) a weight, equivalent to about 3.5 grams; (2) the basic unit of Greek currency, which continued in use in the eastern Mediterranean all through the centuries of Roman rule. Originally a silver coin, the drachma in Egypt was repeatedly devalued and otherwise juggled by Roman emperors seeking a fiscal advantage. The Roman *denarius* was equated with a tetradrachm.

elders — a group of villagers performing a liturgy (*q.v.*), the chief responsibilities of which lay in the areas of policing and tax assessment. The term quickly lost all implication of age, men as young as twenty being appointed to the post.

epikrisis — the process for determining admissibility to a special status, civilian or military.

epistrategos — a Roman of equestrian rank placed in charge of one of the three administrative units in which the nomes (*q.v.*) of Egypt were grouped under Roman rule. The units (epistrategia, plural -iai) were, from north to south, Delta; Heptanomia and Arsinoite; Thebaid.

Fayyūm — the present-day name of the Nile-fed geographical depression south-west of Cairo. In Ptolemaic and Roman times the area constituted the Arsinoite nome.

Heptanomia ('seven-nomes region'): see epistrategos.

keramion ('jar') — a measure used for wine, oil, and other liquids. One size held six choes, the other eight (= *c.* 9 and 12 litres). An alternative designation of the same measure was metretes ('measurer').

kotyle — a liquid measure, equal to about half a pint, or 1/4 litre.

liturgy — anglicized spelling of Greek *leitourgia*, a term designating any of a wide array of compulsory public services and offices which all Eyptian males but the most penurious were required to discharge by turns.

medimnos — a dry measure of two artabai. See artaba.

metretes: see keramion.

metron ('measure') — perhaps another name for chous (*q.v.*).

metropolis — a nome capital. The term did not connote, as it does with us, a cosmopolitan centre, but rather approximated our county seat.

mina — (1) a weight, probably equivalent to 160 drachmas, or just under six kilograms; (2) a monetary unit equal to 100 drachmas.

nome — anglicized spelling of Greek *nomos* (plural, *-moi*), any one of some thirty administrative divisions of Egypt, each headed by a strategos (*q.v.*).

obol — originally one-sixth of the monetary value of a drachma (*q.v.*), but that relationship was distorted by imperial fiscal policies.

prefect — (1) *praefectus Aegypti*, the governor of Egypt, the appointee and vice-regal representative of the emperor; (2) *praefectus militaris*, a Roman officer in charge of a division of the armed forces.

sitologos ('grain collector'; plural, -goi) — a liturgic appointee operating a state granary. See liturgy.

stater — a weight, equivalent to 350 grams.

strategos (plural, -goi) — the title of the chief officer of a nome (*q.v.*), where he exercised judicial and administrative authority, but had no military commission and commanded no troops.

talent — (1) a weight, equivalent to some 44 kilograms; (2) a unit of monetary reckoning, equal to 6,000 drachmas.

Thebaid: see epistrategos.

toparchy — an administrative division of a nome (*q.v.*), serving chiefly for tax-collection purposes.

NOTES

Regarding Abbreviations

1. Papyri

The convention is to use *P.* for papyrus and *O.* for ostracon, followed by an identifying abbreviation, usually the site of origin as in *P. Oxy.-* (rhynchus), or the present location of the collection as in *P. Mich.-* (igan). The principal exceptions are:

BGU = the *B*erlin Egyptian Museums' *G*reek '*U*rkunden' (documentary papyri); the bulk of these are in East Berlin.

M. Chr., W. Chr. = documents published or republished in the *Chrestomathie* of L. Mitteis and U. Wilcken, Leipzig–Berlin, 1912.

SB = *S*ammel*b*uch, a continuing series of volumes in which are reprinted documents published in journals, occasional volumes, etc.

Up-to-date lists of all the principal editions, with their abbreviations, are available in the following:

J. F. Oates *et. al.*, *Checklist of Editions of Greek Papyri and Ostraca, Bulletin of the American Society of Papyrologists*, Supplement 1, 1978, with addendum to 30 June 1981.

E. G. Turner, *Greek Papyri. An Introduction*, Oxford, 1968, second (paperback) edition, 1980, pp. 156–71.

2. Other

IGRR = *Inscriptiones Graecae ad Res Romanas Pertinentes*, 3 vols., Paris, 1906–27, reprinted Chicago, 1975.

OGIS = *Orientis Graecae Inscriptiones Selectae*, 2 vols., Leipzig, 1903–5, reprinted Hildesheim 1960.

SEG = *Supplementum Epigraphicum Graecum*. Leiden, 1923–.

L–R = N. Lewis and M. Reinhold, *Roman Civilization*, 2 vols., New York, 1951–5.

INTRODUCTION

1. *Egypt Exploration Fund Archaeological Report 1896–1897*, pp. 5–9.

CHAPTER 1

1. T. C. Skeat, in the *Journal of Roman Studies*, 43 (1953), 98–100 demonstrates that Cleopatra's suicide most probably occurred on the day that the Romans counted as the 10th of August; the Roman calendar having by then fallen two days behind, our retrospective calculation would call the day the 12th. The citations in the Roman poets are: Virgil, *Aeneid*, Book 8, verse 697, Horace, *Odes*, Book 1, no. 37, Propertius *Odes*, Book 3, no. 11. The quotation from Augustus is from chapter 27 of the document we commonly designate, from its opening words, as the *Res Gestae Divi Augusti* ('The Deeds of the Deified Augustus'). The text was inscribed on the door-posts of Augustus' mausoleum in Rome, and copies were displayed inscribed on monuments in every provincial capital. The inscription in Rome has perished, but a nearly complete text survives at Ankara in Turkey (Ancyra was the capital of the Roman province of Galatia), and fragments have been found in a few other eastern provinces.

2. Justinus (a writer of the second century AD), *Roman History*, Book 34, sect. 2.

3. Polybius, *Histories*, Book 29, ch. 27. A recently published papyrus confirms 'that a permanent conquest was intended [by Antiochus] — obviously something that would trouble the Romans more than a temporary intervention' (R. S. Bagnall, *Classical World*, 76 (1982–3), 14).

4. *P. Teb.* 33 = *W. Chr.* 3 = *Select Papyri* 416.

5. The quotation is from Virgil's *Aeneid*, Book 8, verses 687–88.

CHAPTER 2

1. Pliny, *Letters*, Book 10, nos. 6–7. To describe the occupation of men like Harpocras the Romans borrowed the Greek word which translates literally as 'massage doctor'.

2. The data on the cohort are found in *BGU* 696 = *Select Papyri* 401.

3. The Oslo papyrus is published in *Proceedings of the XVI International Congress of Papyrology, American Studies in Papyrology*, 23 (1981), 329. The preceding document, written in Latin, is *PSI* 1026. Every veteran, legionary and auxiliary, received a bronze plaque, or *diploma* in Latin, certifying his honourable discharge and resultant privileges. Legionaries were Roman citizens all during their years of service; they therefore needed, and hence received, no further attestation of status when they were discharged. The case of these twenty-two petitioners was abnormal in that they were non-citizens when they began their military service and were later transferred to a legion.

Because their enlistment records would show them in the auxiliaries they felt the need for a clarifying document. A translation of *PSI* 1026 appears in L-R II, pp. 525-6.

4. The data for Soknopaiou Nesos are presented and analysed by D. H. Samuel, *Proceedings of the XVI International Congress of Papyrology, American Studies in Papyrology*, 23 (1981), 389-403, where the reader will also find the references to earlier studies relating to other places.

5. *SB* 9636.

6. The documents are *SB* 11114, and *SB* 7523 = *Select Papyri* 254. The quotation from Cicero is from his *On the Republic*, Book 2, ch. 52.

7. The evidence of the existence of a boulē in Ptolemais occurs in *SB* 9016, which preserves documents of AD 48 and 160.

8. The letter of Claudius is *P. Lond.* 1912 = *Select Papyri* 212 = *Corpus Papyrorum Judaicarum* 153 (with translation and extensive commentary); a translation appears also in L-R II, pp. 366-9. The Alexandrian's letter is *BGU* 1079 = *Select Papyri* 107 = *Corp. Pap. Jud.* 152.

9. The documents quoted are *P. Giss.* 41 = *W. Chr.* 18 = *Select Papyri* 298, and *P. Oxy.* 705 = *W. Chr.* 153. These and others that reflect the revolt and its effects are collected in *Corp. Pap. Jud.* 435-50.

10. *History of Rome*, Book 38, ch. 37.

11. *W. Chr.* 52 = *Select Papyri* 301.

12. *BGU* 1210. A longer extract appears in L-R II, pp. 380-3.

13. The quotations in this paragraph are from the following: T. Rice Holmes, *The Architect of the Roman Empire* II, p. 16; R. Syme, *The Roman Revolution*, p. 275; Horace, *Odes*, Book 1, no. 37.

CHAPTER 3

1. *P. Brem.* 23. The work of these 'committees' was a civic duty, not that of a professional police force.

2. The results of the excavation of Hermopolis are reported in G. Roeder, *Hermopolis 1929-1939*, Hildesheim, 1959. A brief summary is offered by J. Schwartz in *Ktema*, 2 (1977), 59-63.

3. The details on the buildings at Oxyrhynchus are found in *P. Oxy.* 43 Verso, those on the water supply of Arsinoë in *P. Lond.* 1177 = *Select Papyri* 406. A translation is available also in L-R II, pp. 333-5.

4. The endower of games appears in *P. Oxy.* 705 = *W. Chr.* 153. The Council of Elders appears in *P. Ryl.* 599 = *SB* 8032. For the grain distribution in Oxyrhynchus see *P. Oxy.* XL, and the additional comment in *Chronique d'Egypte*, 49 (1974), 158-62. The number of recipients was 4,000 adult males, which according to one estimate would amount

to a fifth of the town's total population.

5. *P. Oxy.* 1681 (third century) = *Select Papyri* 152.

6. *P. Oxy.* 2186.

7. The extant applications are *P. Oxy.* 3276-84.

8. The families cited for their numerous sibling unions are found in *P. Amh.* 75 and *BGU* 115 = *W. Chr.* 203 (further details below, p. 53). The wedding invitation is *P. Oxy.* 111 = *W. Chr.* 484. Examples of sibling marriages in villages will be found on pp. 70 and 158.

A 1960 Münster dissertation by H. Thierfelder does little more than cite samples of the extant documents to show that 'brother-sister marriage in Roman Egypt . . . is irrefutable' fact. The author goes on (pp. 90-4) to suggest that religious influences were more important than economic considerations, but that view has found little acceptance.

A much more sophisticated study — one which attempts to interpret the historical evidence with the aid of anthropological and genetic findings as well as modern statistical methods — is that of K. Hopkins, *Comparative Studies in Society and History*, 22 (1980), 303-54. Hopkins points out (pp. 322-3) the theoretical weakness of the argument for an economic basis for the custom, but he admits both here and later that the practitioners may well have had such a purpose. ('The parents' objective was perhaps to hold the family property together', p. 351.) Since the aleatory evidence does not enable us to 'know what factors should cause this phenomenon', he devotes the last half of his article to 'an analysis of elements in Egyptian society which . . . should help flesh out the social context in which brother-sister marriages once flourished' (pp. 327-8).

9. The edict is found in the *Codex Justinianus*, Book 5, ch. 4, no. 17. The reference to Diodorus is to his *Historical Library*, Book 1, ch. 27.

10. The documents cited are *BGU* 141, *P. Lond.* 188, *P. Mil. Vogl.* 52 and 130 introd. Another example of farm-owning metropolites occurs on p. 162.

11. The examples are taken from *P. Giss.* 32, *St Pal.* XX 18, *PSI* 1253, *P. Oxy.* 2848, *P. Grenf.* I 50.

12. *P. Oxy.* 2147. The designees took office on the Egyptian New Year's Day, the first of the month Thoth (= 29 August).

13. Certain other functions in which an exegetes appears, such as assigning guardians for orphans and women, may not have been duties of the office.

14. The hearing, held in AD 250, is recorded in *SB* 7696, a papyrus that is unfortunately poorly preserved in many places.

15. *P. Turner* 37.

16. *P. Oxy.* 243.

17. *St Pal.* XX 67 recto.

18. Cotton in Roman Egypt: *P. Mich.* 500 and the note to line 7.
19. *BGU* 115 = *W. Chr.* 203.
20. *P. Oxy.* 744 = *Select Papyri* 105, and *BGU* 1104.
21. *BGU* 1052 = *Select Papyri* 3. Mothers at fifteen: p. 70.
22. *P. Oxy.* 528 = *Select Papyri* 125.
23. *P. Oxy.* 237 contains the case of AD 186 and its precedents; the minutes of the hearing of AD 128 are reproduced below, p. 191. These and other evidences of the father's historic right are discussed in *Revue Internationale des Droits de l'Antiquité*, 17 (1970), 251-8.
24. *P. Oxy.* 3197, of AD 111.
25. An example occurs on p. 174. The document quoted in this paragraph is *P. Oxy.* 494 = *M. Chr.* 305.
26. In the order cited the documents will be found in *Aegyptus*, 2 (1921), 283-5; *P. Oxy.* 1153 and 2192; *Aegyptus*, 2 (1921), 19-20, with further comment in 44 (1964), 23-4; and *P. Mil. Vogl.* 11.
27. *P. Oxy.* 2548 and 529.
28. The level of literacy in fifth-century Athens is discussed by F. D. Harvey in *Revue des Etudes Grecques*, 79 (1966), 585-636.
29. *P. Turner* 38. An illiterate urban Greek, a citizen of Antinoopolis, occurs in a document of AD 198 published since the tally of thirty years ago.
30. *P. Oxy.* 1467 = *Select Papyri* 305.
31. *P. Flor.* 56, and 382 = *W. Chr.* 143, and *St Pal.* II, p. 27.
32. The two letters quoted are *P. Oxy.* 2190, and 531 = *W. Chr.* 482.

CHAPTER 4

1. E. G. Turner, *Greek Papyri, an Introduction*, pp. 78-9.
2. Herodotus, *Histories*, Book 2, ch. 36.
3. The family records are edited, with ample commentary, by J. Schwartz, *Les archives de Sarapion et de ses fils*, Cairo, 1961.
4. *P. Corn.* 9 = *Select Papyri* 20.
5. *W. Chr.* 63, *P. Mich.* 224, *PSI* 101 and 102.
6. Diodorus, *Historical Library*, Book 1, ch. 34; *P. Oxy.* 2234; *P. Turner* 25.
7. The data on rations are derived from T. Reekmans, *Papyrolgica Bruxellensia* 3 (1966), esp. 55-7.
8. The other families referred to are found in *P. Lugd.-Bat.* V col. v = *P. Brux.* 5, and *P. Soterichos*.
9. So too, in the case of Soterichos of Theadelphia, who has come into our purview in a very recent publication. As the editor of that archive observes (p. 23), 'Soterichos managed from one day to the next, and he could hardly build up any reserve. That is the typical situation

of the farmer of the time. But that does not make him a poor man by the standards of the time.' 'Soterichos', writes a reviewer, 'was principally a lessee, not a landowner, and he seems to have been always in debt for the capital needed for his ventures in farming. . . . At his death he left large debts, which it took his widow and children years to pay off' (R. S. Bagnall, *Bull. Amer. Soc. Papyrologists*, 17 (1980), 98).

10. *P. Mil. Vogl.* 84 = *P. Kronion* 50.

11. *P. Mil. Vogl.* 85 = *P. Kronion* 52. It has been calculated that the weights of gold and silver mentioned would be worth about 900 drachmas. As we have seen (p. 55), the dowries of the daughters of metropolites were worth several times that amount.

12. *P. Ryl.* 168. Other examples will be found in L-R II, p. 185.

13. The principal documents are *SB* 7528, *P. Iand.* 27, *P. Hamb.* 65, *P. Phil.* 15, *CPR* I 33, *BGU* 618, and *P. Bour.* 42. The most recent study of the subject is that of G. Poethke, *Papyrologica Bruxellensia* 8 (1969).

14. A typical perpetuation of the Roman view is 'a people given to turbulence' in J. G. Winter, *Life and Letters in the Papyri*, p. 113. The complaints quoted in our text are *P. Ryl.* 125 = *Select Papyri* 278, *P. Mich.* 421, *BGU* 22, *P. Teb.* 332, and *P. Mich.* 424 and 228. Another example addressed to a centurion occurs on p. 162. See also p. 121, and Chapter 6, note 10.

15. The letters quoted are *BGU* 665, and *P. Oxy.* 3313.

16. *PSI* 1248. A letter about a woman who died in childbirth appears in L-R II, pp. 408–9.

17. On Petaus, 'le scribe qui ne savait pas écrire', see *Chronique d'Egypte*, 41 (1966), 127–43. The papers from his office, 127 in number, are three-fourths in the University of Cologne, one-fourth in the University of Michigan. They are published by a German-American équipe (Hagedorn-Youtie) in *Das Archiv des Petaus, Papyrologica Coloniensia* 4, 1969. The signatory who could not write Greek but could write Egyptian appears in *SB* 5117. On illiteracy in general see pp. 62–3.

CHAPTER 5

1. *SB* 10173a = *SEG* XX no. 670.

2. The papyri quoted are *P. Mert.* 63 and *P. Oxy.* 2782. The references to Herodotus are to his *Histories*, Book 2, ch. 59 and 156.

3. *P. Oxy.* 1380 and Diodorus, *Historical Library*, Book 1, ch. 25.

4. *SB* 3924 = *Select Papyri* 211.

5. *BGU* 362 = *Select Papyri* 404.

6. Texts quoted: *P. Oxy.* 1021 and *BGU* 646 = *Select Papyri* 235 and 222.

7. The quotations are from Dio Cassius, *Roman History*, Book 51, ch. 16 and Juvenal, *Satires* 15, verses 1–8. The propitiatory worship of wild animals is, of course, a phenomenon widely observed in primitive societies.

8. The quotation is from Herodotus, *Histories*, Book 2, ch. 59.

9. *BGU* 1199.

10. The documents quoted are *P. Teb.* 293 and *BGU* 347 = *W. Chr.* 75 and 76. Approval of a blemished candidate occurs in *SB* 16 and *P. Teb.* 314.

11. The hymn is part of *P. Lond. Lit.* 239. Meroë, the capital of Nubia, refers figuratively to the sources of the Nile. It was situated on the White Nile south of its confluence with the Blue Nile, whence the river traverses more than a thousand kilometres before entering Egypt.

12. The quotations are from *SEG* VIII nos. 548, 549, and *P. Oxy.* 1830. A visitor to Egypt in the late eighteenth century reports, 'the festival of the archangel Michael . . . has given rise to a fable, which is firmly believed, as well by the Turks, as by the Cophts and other Christians of this country, viz. That the angel on that day, throws a drop of water of such a fermenting quality into the river, that it causes it to rise to such a height, as to overflow all the country. For this reason [that day] of June is called Nockta (which signifies a drop), by all the inhabitants of Egypt: and should anyone contradict this notion, he would be charged with gross ignorance; as would also be the case were he to deny the merits of the prophetical well at El Garnaus, in Middle Egypt, which, according to their opinion, shews in the first months of the year, by a miraculous elevation of its water, to what height the river will rise that season' (J. Antes, *Observations on the Manners and Customs of the Egyptians*, Dublin, 1801, pp. 78–9).

13. *P. Oxy.* 1151.

14. A clay figurine tied to a papyrus amulet is shown in Plate XXXI.1 of *Journal of Egyptian Archaeology*, 15 (1929). That charm is exceptional as expressing the desire of a man for another man. The papyrus from Hawara published in *Archiv für Papyrusforschung*, 5 (1913), 393 is a female homosexual charm.

The resort to love charms remains something of a universal even in modern times. In passing it may be interesting to note that the incantation ritual most familiar from classical literature, that in the Second Idyll of the Sicilian poet Theokritos, betrays a Thessalian origin.

15. *P. Lond.* 124 = *Pap. Gr. Mag.* X.

16. Dio, *Oration* 32, sect. 12.

17. The texts quoted are *P. Mert.* 81, *BGU* 229, and *P. Oxy.* 1149, 1213, and 1477. In this last, Question 86 refers to the desperate last resort of people who could not meet their taxes or other obligations to

the state (see ch. 8). The appeal to oracles adapted itself quickly and easily to the triumph of Christianity. Among sixth-century papyri we find, to quote but two examples of many (*P. Oxy.* 925 and 1150 = *Select Papyri* 196 and 197):

> O God almighty, holy, true, benevolent, Creator, Father of our Lord and Saviour Jesus Christ, reveal to me in the truth that emanates from Thee whether it is Thy will that I go off to Chiout. Shall I find Thee cooperative, gracious? So be it. Amen.

And again,

> O God of our patron Saint Philoxenos, dost Thou bid us convey Anoup into Thy hospital? Show Thy power and let this message have a successful outcome.

18. *P. Oxy.* 1381.

19. *P. Harr.* 107.

20. See M. Smith, *Jesus the Magician*, New York, 1978. The Suetonius quotation is from *Life of Claudius*, ch. 25.

21. The reverse appears to be asserted by the theologian Tertullian in chapter 40 of his *Apology*, written *c.* AD 200: 'If the Tiber reaches the walls, if the Nile fails to reach the fields, if the sky does not shake [to give rain] or the earth does [quake], if there is famine, if there is pestilence, at once the cry is raised, "The Christians to the lions!"' But in the light of the obvious rhetorical and generalizing character of the passage, it would be unwise to insist that the mentions of Tiber and Nile refer to specific instances.

22. *P. Mich.* 158.

23. Persecution by imperial order came to an end everywhere in the empire a generation after Gallienus' discontinuance. Early in the fourth century came the Great Persecution, followed in a few years by the Edict of Toleration (AD 311) and the next year by the conversion of Emperor Constantine to Christianity.

Origen has been called 'the most notable figure in the history of Egyptian Christianity, a daring and profound theologian, a subtle exegete, one of the greatest of Christian scholars. . . . He too was a Platonist and influenced by the Gnosticism of Egypt' (H. I. Bell, *Cults and Creeds in Graeco-Roman Egypt*, p. 97).

24. *P. Par.* 69 = *W. Chr.* 41 ii.

25. The documents cited are *P. Oxy.* 705 = *W. Chr.* 153, *P. Oxy.* 2338, *SB* 7336, *P. Oxy.* 519 = *W. Chr.* 492 = *Select Papyri* 402, and *P. Oxy.* 413 and 2127.

26. *P. Oxy.* 1025 = *W. Chr.* 493 = *Select Papyri* 359. The term Aurelii dates it after AD 212: see Glossary.

27. *P. Oxy.* 1211 = *Select Papyri* 403 (second century) and *P. Oxy.* 2797 (late third century). Pigs earlier were taboo in Egyptian ceremony: p. 131.

28. This formula usually identifies sons born to soldiers in active service. Although not allowed to contract legal marriages, soldiers quite commonly formed conjugal ties and created families (pp. 20–1). Leonidas' Greek name reflects his mother's, while his Latin Serenus no doubt comes from his soldier father.

29. *P. Oxy.* 475 = *W. Chr.* 494 = *Select Papyri* 337.

CHAPTER 6

1. How quickly the wind-driven sands can obliterate the works of man was dramatically illustrated in the exploration by G. Caton-Thompson and E. W. Gardner (*The Desert Fayum*, London, 1934, p. 141): 'It became evident that we had found an [ancient] irrigation system, of which the sand-filled channels were . . . completely merged in the desert surface.' Three and a half months were then spent in digging out some twenty-five kilometres of canals. The reporter goes on, 'Three years later . . . I took the opportunity to fly over the [area] . . . but all was bare desert, and nothing could be seen either by eye or photograph.'

On the abandonment of land by the peasants see pp. 68 and 163–5.

2. Herodotus, *Histories*, Book 2, ch. 34; the theories are detailed in chapters 20–6. The other references are to Euripides frag. 228 in A. Nauck's collection of fragments of lost tragedies (2d., 1889), Diodorus, *Historical Library*, Book 1, ch. 38, and Pliny, *Natural History*, Book 5, sect. 51.

Writing in 1788, 'during a residence of twelve years in Cairo and its vicinity,' J. Antes, *Observations on the Manners and Customs of the Egyptians*, Dublin, 1801, pp. 103–4, smugly proclaimed, 'The cause of the annual overflowing of the river is no longer a mystery; and we need not amuse ourselves with the many ridiculous fables of the ancients. The regular or tropical rains in Abyssinia, where this river takes its rise . . . is fully sufficient for this.' Ten years later, however, at a meeting of the Institute of Egypt newly created by Napoleon, Sucy, a member of the Political Economy section, read a paper on the need to explore the sources of the Nile.

3. The quotation is from Seneca's *Natural Questions*, Book 4, no. 2. So, too, J. Antes, *op. cit.*, p. 86, in the late eighteenth century: 'When the river is at its greatest height, the villages, which are commonly surrounded with a grove of date, and other fruit trees, appear as so many islands in an extensive sea, which is in some places broader than the eye can reach: this is a delightful prospect.'

4. Pliny, *Natural History*, Book 5, sect. 58, Pliny the Younger, *Panegyric*, sect. 31. Low Niles and poor harvests are doubtless to be inferred also from the depopulations described on p. 165.

5. *SB* 8392 = *IGRR* I 1290. The second nilometer at Elephantine was only recently discovered. See also Chapter 5, note 12.

6. *Histories*, Book 2, ch. 14.

7. *P. Oxy.* 1409 (= *Select Papyri* 278) and 3264. Fraud and chicanery in the assignment of dike work are mentioned in the document quoted on p. 160. We are told that Napoleon in Egypt laid great stress on the proper maintenance of the irrigation works, saying at one point, 'In no country has the government so much influence over the public prosperity. The government has no influence over the rain or snow that falls in Beauce or Brie. But in Egypt the government has direct influence on the extent of the inundation it directs. That is what made the difference between the Egypt administered by the Ptolemies and the Egypt already decaying under the Romans and finally ruined under the Turks' (quoted from F. Charles-Roux, *Bonaparte, Governor of Egypt*, London, 1937, pp. 113-4).

8. The distant assignments are found in *P. Fay.* 79, *P. Grenf.* II 53d, *P. Mich.* 381, and *SB* 5124.

9. *SB* 9567. These receipts were often 'mass produced' in advance a blank being left for the name of the recipient. In the second century the receipts also specified the month and days on which the work was performed.

10. The references are to Diodorus, *Historical Library*, Book 1, ch. 34, and Strabo, *Geography*, Book 17, ch. 1, sect. 30. In a recently published papyrus (*Scritti . . . Montevecchi*, Bologna, 1981, p. 318) the writer complains to the police chief of his village that a neighbour has smashed the base supporting the swing beam belonging to his recently deceased brother, 'thus making it impossible to draw water for the vineyard with the bucket . . . so that the vineyard has been rendered parched and dry, and in consequence suffered no little damage.'

11. The document quoted in full is *P. Brem.* 36. A translation of the edict of 136 appears in L-R II, pp. 396-7.

12. *P. Amh.* 91. The stipulation banning safflower occurs in a fair number of leases, always without explanation of the purpose, which the parties themselves obviously understood only too well. We, however, are left to speculate about the reason for the exclusion, which is to us the more puzzling as we know that safflower was in fact grown and valued for its oil (p. 127). A leading botanist, Arthur W. Galston of Yale University, to whom I put the problem, has offered the following suggestion: 'The most reasonable hypothesis, since the safflower is thistle-like, is that it is excreting from its roots and fallen leaves chemical

compounds that inhibit the growth of other plants. Such compounds, known as allelopathic substances, are often used by plants in their "chemical warfare" against neighbours in the fight for living space in harsh environments. If I had to make a guess it would be this one, but I really can't be sure.'

13. *P. Oxy.* 1024.

14. *P. Alex. Giss.* 25.

15. *P. Oxy. Hels.* 41. The provision about uninundated portions does not apply to the current year because the lease was entered into when the Nile had already risen and flooded the land in question.

16. *P. Amh.* 104 = *Select Papyri* 73.

17. *P. Ryl.* 147. Another example occurs on p. 127. Both come from the archive described on p. 77.

18. *P. Oxy.* 2704.

19. Italy and Sicily: G. Rickman, *The Corn Supply of Ancient Rome*, pp. 103-4; Marmarica: *P. Vat.* 11 recto; Negev: *P. Ness.* 82. The yields estimated nearly fifty years ago by A. C. Johnson, *Roman Egypt*, p. 59 ($4\frac{1}{4}$-10 times for wheat, seven to twelvefold for barley) continue to be used (e.g. D. Bonneau, *Publ. de la Sorbonne: Série 'Etudes'*, 14 (1979), 65), but the data cited in this paragraph argue that those figures need to be revised upward. D. Foraboschi, *Scritti . . . Montevecchi*, Bologna, 1981, pp. 155-61 regards a tenfold yield as normal, and attributes the higher yields attested to various kinds of intensive cultivation, for example raising two crops a year. The sixteen-fold rent payment occurs in *P. Teb.* 375.

20. *P. Oxy.* 1049.

21. *P. Ryl.* 90.

22. *P. Oxy.* 518.

23. Pliny tells us in his *Natural History*, Book 15, sect. 16, that 'the best time for picking, with a view to quantity and flavour, is when the olive is just starting to turn black.'

24. Pliny, *op. cit.*, Book 13, sect. 56 and Book 15, sects. 68-71, talks about 'the marvels of the Egyptian fig', which was, according to his report, very sweet, seedless, and extremely prolific. In describing early and late varieties he writes, 'The latest ripen just before winter. Moreover, there are varieties that are both early and late, producing two crops, a white and a black, ripening with the grain harvest and with the vintage.'

25. *P. Oxy.* 1631 = *Select Papyri* 18. A similar (but otherwise much less detailed) document of AD 252, *P. Berl. Leihg.* 23, specifies that a newly planted vineyard is to be cultivated three times in its first growing season.

26. *BGU* 241 and *P. Ryl.* 138. On the latter see also note 17, above.

27. T. Heyerdahl, *The Ra Expeditions*, New York, 1971.
28. *P. Med.* 6, *P. Teb.* 308, and *BGU* 1180.
29. A detailed analysis of the lease of 5 BC, *BGU* 1121 = *Select Papyri* 41, will be found in N. Lewis, *Papyrus in Classical Antiquity*, Oxford, 1974, pp. 109-13.
30. Aristotle, *History of Animals* 522c26, Varro, *On Agriculture*, Book 2, ch. 11.
31. *P. Lond.* 1171, *P. Strassb.* 24, *P. Oxy.* 807, and *P. Hamb.* 34.

CHAPTER 7

1. In most such contracts the first year of apprenticeship was without pay. In the contract quoted here, *P. Oxy.* 1647, the wage in the last year of the apprenticeship was approximately that of an unskilled labourer: see Appendix.
2. *P. Oxy.* 724 = *W. Chr.* 140 = *Select Papyri* 15.
3. *P. Oxy.* 520, of AD 143.
4. *P. Hamb.* 12 and *P. Teb.* 402.
5. *SB* 4639.
6. *P. Mich.* 203 and *O. Flor.* 1.
7. Pliny, *Natural History*, Book 36, sect. 67.
8. *P. Oxy.* 2272.
9. *P. Köln* 53.
10. *P. Ryl.* 197a and *P. Grenf.* II 50c = *Select Papyri* 383 and 382.
11. *OGIS* 701 = *IGRR* I 1142. In his *Natural History* (Book 6, sects. 102-3) Pliny enumerates eight stations on the Coptus-Berenike road, but there may have been more.
12. *OGIS* 674 = *IGRR* I 1183. The complete text is translated in L-R II, pp. 147-8. That the fee for the passage of a camel, which carries a much bigger load (p. 167), is half that charged for a donkey is doubtless explained by the fact that the camel made less use of the watering facilities along the route.
13. *P. Princ.* 20 = *SB* 8072, *P. Oxy.* 36 = *W. Chr.* 273, and Ps.-Quintilian, *Declamations* 359.
14. *P. Lond.* 1164h = *Select Papyri* 38. Forty kilometres per day: Pliny, *Natural History*, Book 6, sect. 102. On the technical details see L. Casson, *Ships and Seamanship in the Ancient World*, Princeton, 1971, esp. p. 164.
15. The papyrus, *P. Iand.* inv. 616 + 245, is published in *Zeitschrift für Papyrologie und Epigraphik*, 20 (1976), 162-5.
16. See especially *P. Mich.* 243-5.
17. A good example appears on p. 174.
18. *BGU* 1024 vii.

19. The examples cited here are *P. Oxy.* 2584 and *P. Strassb.* 34.

20. *P. Oxy.* 2471. In the third century, however, some bankers were adversely affected by the growing inflation: see the example in *P. Oxy.* 1411 = *Select Papyri* 230.

21. The documents are quoted in a conflation of *BGU* 1074, *P. Oxy.* 2476, and *P. Oxy. Hels.* 25, which relate to three different honorands (Marcus Aurelius Serenus is the subject of the third).

22. *Corp. Inscr. Lat.* VI 10048 = *Inscr. Lat. Selectae* 5287 and *IGRR* IV 1519 = *Sardis* VII 79.

23. The documents cited are *P. Lond.* 1178 = *W. Chr.* 156 and *St Pal.* V 52-6 = *Select Papyri* 306.

24. Such a grant to a grandson is *St Pal.* V 119 verso iii = *W. Chr.* 158 = *Select Papyri* 217. A translation incorporating later revisions appears in L-R II, p. 237.

25. *P. Lond.* 1164i = *Jur. Pap.* 31. Matidia was the niece of the Emperor Trajan and the mother-in-law of Hadrian, who founded Antinoopolis. The epithet Kalliteknian, 'of beautiful children', is in praise not of Matidia but of the city of Antinoopolis.

26. *BGU* 647 and *P. Mert.* 12. Archagathos was a Greek physician of the third century BC. Pliny the Elder and the Roman medical writer Celsus, as well as this papyrus, inform us that his reputation, and that of his formula, lasted for centuries. Health problems caused by callused soles are today still endemic in areas where people go about barefoot most of the time.

27. For the identification of the text see M.-H. Marganne, *Papyrologica Florentina*, VII (1980), pp. 179-83.

28. E. A. E. Reymond, *A Medical Book from Crocodilopolis*, *Mitteil. Papyrussamml. oesterr. Nationalbibl.* 10, 1976.

29. The document discussed is *P. Giss.* 43 = *SB* 10630. 'Physicians' under twenty in Asia Minor: *Phoenix* 36 (1982), 271.

30. The two Roman influences cited are discussed by me in *BASP* 18 (1981), 73-4 and by H. J. Wolff in *Zeitschr. Savigny-Stift.* 96 (1979), 258-68.

CHAPTER 8

1. *P. Lond.* 904 = *Select Papyri* 220 and *BGU* 1210. See also p. 191.

2. *P. Lugd.-Bat.* V col. x = *SB* 7460 = *P. Brux.* 10. A similarly numerous household appears on p. 53. On brother–sister marriage see p. 43.

3. Diodorus, *Historical Library*, Book 1, ch. 31; Josephus, *The Jewish War*, Book 2, sect. 385.

4. *SB* 7738 = *SEG* VIII no. 527. An instance of cheating in assignment of dike work appears on p. 113. Tiberius' rebuke, quoted earlier in this paragraph, is reported by Dio Cassius, *Roman History*, Book 57, ch. 10.

5. Philo, *On Special Laws*, Book 3, ch. 30. It hardly needs to be added that the actions described were illegal. Relatives and friends were not liable for the defaulter's taxes, as the emperor Septimius Severus found it necessary to reiterate in AD 200: 'Since many still petition to be freed from being forced, contrary to prior edicts, to pay taxes of others as if they were mutual sureties, we deem it necessary to reaffirm our previously proclaimed edict on this matter, viz. that no one is to be forced to pay the taxes of another — neither a father for a son, nor a son for a father, nor any one else for any one else — nor substituted for another under claim of any such collection' (*P. Mich.* 529 verso, as revised in *Chronique d'Egypte*, 50 (1975), 202-6).

6. *BGU* 515 = *Select Papyri* 286. For other cases of assault see pp. 77-9.

7. *SB* 9207. See also pp. 181-2.

8. The documents quoted and cited are *P. Oxy.* 2669, *P. Ryl.* 595, *SB* 7462, *PSI* 101, 102. See also above, p. 68 and 108.

9. Josephus, *Jewish War*, Book 2, sect. 386, Aurelius Victor, *The Caesars*, ch. 1.

10. *P. Oxy.* 2670.

11. *P. Oxy.* 2125, and 708 = *W. Chr.* 432.

12. *P. Lond.* 259 = *W. Chr.* 63 (AD 94).

13. See *Scritti . . . Montevecchi*, Bologna, 1981, pp. 196-7.

14. *WO* 1157.

15. The texts quoted are *Select Papyri* 211, *P. Lond.* 1171 verso = *W. Chr.* 439, *Inscr. Lat. Selectae* 214, *SB* 4226, *Revue int. des droits de l'antiquité*, 15 (1968), 137, *PSI* 446 = *Select Papyri* 221, *OGIS* 609, and Dio Cassius, *Roman History*, Book 79[78], ch. 3. See also L-R II, pp. 399-403.

16. *BGU* 1564 = *Select Papyri* 395. The expression 'freedman of Sarapis' is explained on p. 59.

17. *P. Amh.* 107 = *W. Chr.* 417. The four copies were intended, one for the strategos to whom it is addressed, a second for the village elders, a third presumably for the 'nome officials' mentioned at the end (probably the royal secretary), and the fourth to be retained by the issuer of the receipt and eventually filed at his divisional headquarters.

18. *BGU* 266 = *W. Chr.* 245.

19. The calendar of festivals quoted on p. 88 has the following entry under the date of Phamenoth 20 [16 March] : 'Visit of our most

illustrious prefect Septimius Heraclitus: garlanding of all [monuments] in the temple; [payments] for pine cones and other aromatics, to a coppersmith for anointing all the statues, to workmen carrying the cult image of the god to meet the prefect [on his arrival], for garlands for said image, and to a public orator delivering a speech thanking our most illustrious prefect Septimius Heraclitus for adding to the temple treasure a [statue of] Victory and other gifts.'

20. *P. Petaus* 65 (AD 185).
21. *P. Phil.* 1 and *P. Oxy.* 1119 = *W. Chr.* 397.
22. *P. Wisc.* 81. On flight from liturgy see p. 183.
23. *SB* 4284. The edict and inquiry referred to in the preceding paragraph are found in *Hibis* 1 = *OGIS* 665 and *PSI* 1406.
24. *P. Oxy.* 899 = *W. Chr.* 361. The petition of the physician is *P. Fay.* 106 = *W. Chr.* 395 = *Select Papyri* 283 (a translation is available also in L-R II, p. 374).
25. *P. Oxy.* 1405.
26. *BGU* 372 = *W. Chr.* 19: a translation appears in L-R II, pp. 374-5. On the outlaws and brigandage see also pp. 203-4.

CHAPTER 9

1. Tacitus, *Histories*, Book 1, ch. 11, Diodorus, *Historical Library*, Book 1, chs. 93-4. On the development of legal principles and the administration of justice under Egypt's earliest dynasties, one can still read with profit the relevant chapters of J. Pirenne, *Histoire des institutions et du droit privé de l'ancienne Egypte*, 3 vols., Brussels, 1932-5. Procedural material from the Roman period is analysed by R. A. Coles, *Reports of Proceedings in Papyri*, *Papyrologica Bruxellensia* 4, 1966.
2. *P. Teb.* 303 = *Select Papyri* 248.
3. *P. Oxy.* 3130. The Xs at the end, which appear also in several other such orders, were probably placed there to prevent alteration of the order by the addition of modifying or nullifying language.
4. The documents quoted are *SB* 7601 and *P. Oslo* 17. An affidavit charging a strategos with malfeasance appears on p. 24.
5. *PSI* 1100.
6. *SEG* XVIII no. 646 and *P. Oxy.* 2343.
7. The documents cited are *P. Oxy.* 2131 and *P. Yale* 61.
8. *PSI* 1326; *SB* 9050 ii; *P. Oxy.* 237 vii and *P. Ryl.* 75 = *Select Papyri* 258 and 259. On the power of a father to take his daughter away and divorce her from her husband, see above p. 56. On the surrender of property to avoid liturgy see p. 183.
9. The quotations are from *P. Oxy.* 2131 and *P. Wurzb.* 9. These are but two examples of many.

10. *P. Oxy.* 2754.
11. *P. Hamb.* 29 = *Jur. Pap.* 85, *P. Oxy.* 3017, *SB* 7696 (lines 35-6).
12. *P. Oxy.* 899 and 486 = *W. Chr.* 361 and *M. Chr.* 59.
13. *P. Amh.* 77 = *W. Chr.* 277.

CHAPTER 10

1. On Tacitus see pp. vii and esp. 185, for Juvenal pp. 84 and 90, for Dio Chrysostom his *Oration* 32, sect. 31 and *passim*. An example of a modern writer appears in Chapter 4, note 14.
2. See esp. p. 88. The Virgil reference to his *Aeneid*, Book 6, verses 851-3. The theme of the emperor and his virtues has been much discussed, most recently by A. Wallace-Hadrill, *Historia*, 30 (1981), 298-323.
3. Seneca's remark is found in his *Consolation Addressed to Helvia*, ch. 19.
4. C. H. Roberts, *Journal of Roman Studies*, 39 (1949), 79.
5. *W. Chr.* 14 = Musurillo (see note 6) Text IV A.
6. *P. Yale* inv. 1536 (published in *Trans. Amer. Philol. Assn.* 67 (1936), 7) + *P. Oxy.* 33, the whole republished as Text XI in H. Musurillo, *The Acts of the Pagan Martyrs*, Oxford, 1954 and *Acta Alexandrinorum*, Leipzig, 1961.
7. *P. Giss.* 40 ii = *Select Papyri* 215.
8. *SB* 4284.
9. *P. Oxy.* 1408 = *Select Papyri* 244, and *BGU* 372 = *W. Chr.* 19 (the edict cited on p. 183).
10. Philostratos, *Life of Apollonios of Tyana*, Book 5, ch. 24.
11. *P. Oxy.* 2332. Like the Coptic literature of later centuries, *The Oracle of the Potter* is a clear evidence of what A. Momigliano aptly termed 'the vitality of this underground culture' (*Alien Wisdom*, p. 4).
12. *The Decline and Fall of the Roman Empire*, ch. 3.

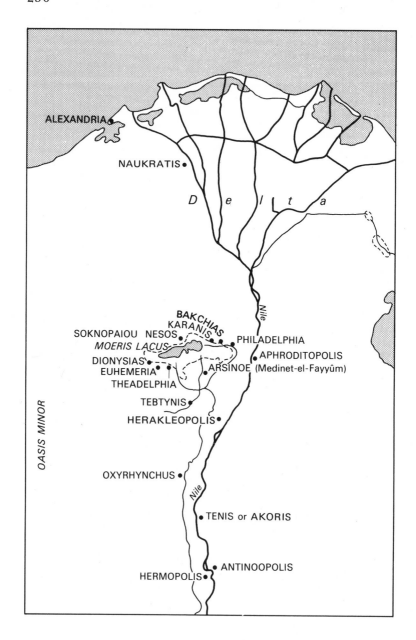

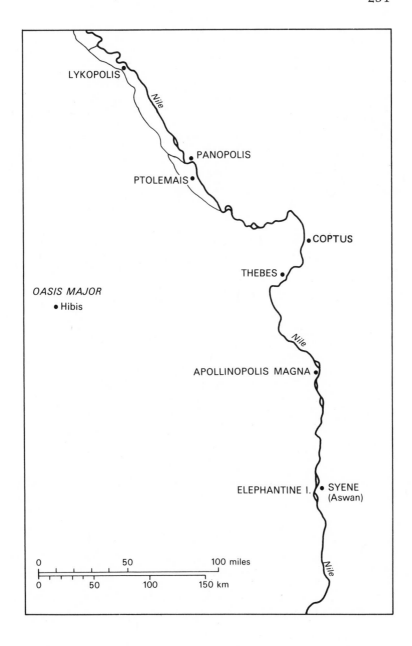

DESCRIPTION OF PLATES

1. The Emperor as Pharaoh. The Roman emperors were depicted on the walls of Egyptian temples in the traditional appearance and role of the Pharaohs. In this typical scene at Latopolis near Thebes the emperor Titus (AD 79-81), left, is conducted by minor divinities for presentation to the great god Khnum, the Creator (not seen here). (Photograph: Brooklyn Museum, Department of Egyptian and Classical Art.)

2. Interior Decoration. A wall in a sizable private house discovered in the 1920s in the excavation of the Arsinoite village of Karanis by the University of Michigan. The decoration, in bright colours, features Harpokrates (one of the names, in Greek, of the Egyptian god Horus, usually identified with Apollo) accompanied by a sphinx and representatives of the flora and fauna of Egypt. (Photograph: Bodleian Library, from A. E. R. Boak and E. E. Petersen, *Karanis 1924-1928*, figure 71.)

3. A Mummy Portrait. In Roman Egypt portraits painted on panels of wood were often placed over the faces of the defunct in their coffins. Several hundred of such mummy portraits have been found, and they may be seen in scores of museums. A relatively few were executed in tempera, most, like this one, in encaustic. The quality of the workmanship runs the gamut from impressive — especially in colour, naturalism and handling of detail — to crude and primitive. This particularly well-preserved example of the early second century is notable for its realism: note particularly the forehead, wrinkles and all. The seven-point star on the forehead signifies that this man was a priest of the sun in the cult of Sarapis. (Photograph: British Museum.)

4. A Religious Celebration. This relief, found at Ariccia near Rome, illustrates the popularity of Egyptian cults in Italy. The upper frieze represents a temple with statues of Egyptian animal gods between a central figure (most of the left side is lost), perhaps Isis, and a Sarapis at the right. The middle, or principal, register shows an almost orgiastic dance ritual: the dancers hold castanets or equivalent devices, whilst the onlookers (right) clap and beat with their hands. The narrow frieze at the bottom depicts the sacred ibis in different poses or actions. (Photograph: Alinari, Rome.)

5. The Nile in Flood. Nilotic subjects, originating in Alexandrian art, enjoyed widespread popularity in the Roman empire, as we see in extant examples ranging from the first-century walls of Pompeii to the sixth-century churches of Cyrenaica. The most dramatic graphic display of the Romans' fascination with exotic Egypt is this mosaic floor, discovered nearly four hundred years ago in the ruins of a Temple of Fortune at Palestrina (ancient Praeneste), near Rome. Measuring almost 7 × 4.5 metres, it is among the largest ancient mosaics ever found. The lavish, exquisitely detailed composition, of which the plate shows the right half, is a half-real, half-fanciful landscape of the Nile flood. 'The mosaic is a large-scale work depicting, in bird's-eye view, a landscape consisting of two distinct halves: an upper rocky terrain inhabited by exotic animals, the majority of which are identified by their names in Greek, and a lower marshy prospect dotted with temple complexes of Egyptian and Graeco–Egyptian form and humbler buildings such as tower-houses, huts, reed shelters and a dovecote. Between the tracts of land the water is alive with boats large and small, from one-man papyrus skiffs to cargo boats, a warship and an elaborate cabined hunting vessel. The mosaic is peopled in the upper part with dark-skinned hunters, in the lower with peasants in working dress, priests in distinctive Egyptian garb, civilians and soldiers, the latter group taking part in a scene which is given some prominence in the foreground' (H. Whitehouse, *The Dal Pozzo Copies of the Palestrina Mosaic* [*British Archaeological Reports*, Supplementary Series, 12, 1976], p. 3). (Photograph: The Mansell Collection.)

6–7. Agriculture: Pumping Water. These Egyptian farmers are using the same kinds of devices as did their predecessors of two thousand years ago for raising water from the Nile and its branch canals to irrigate tilled fields at higher elevations. The operation of the shaduf (6) and the sakkieh (7) is described on p. 114. (Photographs: B.B.C. Hulton Picture Library.)

8. The Prefect as Judge. The town *vs.* country dispute of AD 250 described on pp. 49 and 191 is recorded on this papyrus now in the British Library. The record of the hearing before the Prefect of Egypt spreads over five columns of writing, of which the plate shows the second. As most papyri are found — like this one — dessicated and broken by their long interment in the desert sands, this plate also illustrates the kind of incomplete texts with which the papyrologist and historian have to work much of the time in their efforts to piece together a picture of the life of the times. (Photograph: Ashmolean Museum.)

INDEXES

INDEX OF NAMES
(Roman Emperors are shown in CAPITALS)

INDEX OF SUBJECTS

avoidance of, 181–3
exemption from, 177–8
re prefect's tours, 176
sitologoi, 167–8, 211
tax collection, 178–80
loans, 21, 28, 44–5, 66–7, 71, 118–19

magic, 95–7, 101, 152, 219
'magistrates' in metropoleis, 45–8
marriage,
age at, 55
contract, 55
divorce, 56–7, 71–3
dowry, 55, 73, 155
endogamy, 43–4, 70, 72, 158, 216
intermarriage, 32–3, 62
of soldiers, 20–1, 221
medical profession, 106, 151–4
metropoleis, administration of, 48–51
layout of, 36–9
size of, 36–7
water-supply of Arsinoe, 38–9
metropolites, 39–64
clothing of, 52–3
definition of, 40–1
disdain for Egyptians, 40
education of, 62–4
epikrisis, 41–3, 211
exposure of infants amongst, 54–5
Hellenism amongst, 39–40, 46, 103, 153, 198, 200
houses of, 51–2
as landowners, 44
literacy of, 59–64
marriage and divorce amongst, 43–4, 55–7
as 'magistrates', 45–8
as moneylenders, 44–5
as public benefactors, 45
size of households, 53, 57
slaves of, 57–9
tax privileges of, 41, 170
wealth of, 44–51, 57
milk, 68, 131
mining, 85, 137–8

names, changing of, 32
nomes, 16, 36, 46, 211

oleaginous plants, 127
olives, 126–7, 223
olyra, *see* crops, cereal; grain
oracles, 97–9, 219–20

ostraca,
as evidence, 1, 6, 8
used for receipts, 166–7
oxen, 114, 130–1

papyri,
as evidence, 1–8, and *passim*
collections of, 3–7
dating of, 7–8
preservation of, 2–3, 26
papyrus,
growing of, 128–30
manufacturing of, 134
uses of, 2, 68, 128–9, 143
peasants, 15, 18, 57, 65–83
clothes of, 69
crime amongst, 77–9
as cultivators, 74–7, 116
diet of, 68–9
houses of, 65
Kronion 'archive', 69–73
literacy amongst, 81–2
Sarapion and family, 66–7, 131–2, 217
social harmony amongst, 79–90
village sizes, 67–8
pensions, 150
physicians, *see* medical profession
pigs, 105, 131, 171, 202, 221
police, 77–8, 141, 188, 222
population,
of Alexandria, 26, 29
of Egypt, 158–9
of metropoleis, 36–7
of villages, 67–8
prefect, 15–16, 19, 36, 49–50, 176, 186, 188–93, 211
prices, 208–9
priests, 87, 90–4, 98
Privy Purse, code of regulations of, 32–4, 44, 58, 90, 93, 157
prostitutes, 56, 141, 145–6, 171–2

religion, 84–106, 233
Christianity, 64, 94–7, 99–102, 138, 220
dreams in, 99
festivals, 24, 88–9, 91, 95, 102–6
Jewish, 28–9, 39
magic in, 95–7, 101, 152, 219
oracles, 97–9, 219–20
priests, 87, 90–4, 98
syncretism, 15, 84–6, 88–9, 94

Addenda et Corrigenda

Reviews of *Life in Egypt Under Roman Rule*

American Historical Review 89 (1984) 1058-59 (G. Woloch)
Ancient Society [Australia] 15 (1985) 169-71 (S. Pickering)
Archaeology 37.2 (1984) 67 (R. Bianchi)
Bibliotheca Orientalis 42 (1985) 632-33 (Jean A. Straus)
British Book News Feb. 1984 (Barry Kemp)
Byzantinoslavica 48 (1987) 67-69 (I. Fichman)
Chronique d'Égypte 58 (1983) 271-73 (A. Martin)
Classical Review 35 (1985) 140-41 (J. Rowlandson)
Classical World 78 (1985) 229 (A. Schulman)
Euphrosyne 16 (1988) 476-77 (F. Lourenço)
Gnomon 61 (1989) 176-78 (H. Heinen)
Greece and Rome 31 (1984) 91-92 (J. Paterson)
Gymnasium 95 (1988) 460-61 (H. Heinen)
Hermathena 144 (1984) 114-20 (B. McGing)
IVRA 34 (1983) [1986] 210-12 (L. Migliardi Zingale)
Latomus 44 (1985) 900 (M. Dubuisson)
London Review of Books 1984, 10-11 (Peter Parsons)
New England Classical Newsletter 12 (1985) 32-33 (Edward Phinney)
Orpheus 5 (1984) 242-44 (M. Astarita)
Religious Studies Review 10 (1984) 288 (John H. Sieber)
Revue des Études Anciennes 86 (1984) 345-46 (J. Schwartz)
Revue des Études Latines 62 (1984) 520-22 (G. Husson)
Tijdschrift voor Geschiedenis 98 (1984) 581-82 (P. Sijpesteijn)
Times [London] Education Supplement 83 (1984) 88 (E. Rice)

1. The Emperor as Pharaoh

2. Interior decoration in a private house at Karanis

3. A mummy portrait:
a priest of the sun in the cult of Sarapis

4. A religious celebration

5. The Nile in flood

6. Agriculture: pumping water by a shaduf

7. Agriculture: pumping water by a sakkich

8. The Prefect as judge: part of the record of a hearing before the Prefect of Egypt